MORE PRAISE FOR *1688*

"A totally absorbing book . . . imaginative and erudite."
—Jonathan D. Spence

"A vivid picture of life in 1688 . . . filled with terrifying violence and comfortingly familiar human kindnesses."
—*Publishers Weekly*

"Wills has pulled from the raging silence of history . . . a roiling mass of transnational humanity, and so reminded us that we have been a globalizing planet for more than 300 years."
—Tom Engelhardt, *Washington Post*

"One of the most fascinating and brilliant works of popular history ever written . . . a total triumph."
—Frank McLynn, *The Independent*

"John Wills's book affords eye-opening perspectives on these worlds apart. Equally expert from China to Peru, he paints vibrant vignettes of bustling cities, sumptuous courts and corrupt regimes the world over, the energies of commerce, abuses of power and triumphs of art."
—Roy Porter, *The* [London] *Times*

"Wills examines what particular women and men from all around the world thought, wrote, and did in the span of the same single year. [He] brings all of them alive. No reader will ever forget this book."
—Geoffrey Parker, author of *The Grand Strategy of Phillip II*

1688

A Global History

John E. Wills, Jr.

W. W. Norton & Company   New York London

For information about permission to reproduce selections from this book, write to
Permissions, W. W. Norton & Company, Inc., 500 Fifth Avenue, New York, NY 10110

The text of this book is composed in Berling
with the display set in Wellsbrook initials
Composition by Carole Desnoes
Manufacturing by The Haddon Craftsmen, Inc.
Book design by Chris Welch

Library of Congress Cataloging-in-Publication Data

Wills, John E. (John Elliot), 1936–
1688 : a global history / John E. Wills.
p. cm.
Includes bibliographical references and index.
ISBN 0-393-04744-X
1. History, Modern—17th century. Title.

D246 .W55 2001
909.6—dc21

00-060077

ISBN 0-393-32278-5 pbk.

W. W. Norton & Company, Inc., 500 Fifth Avenue, New York, NY 10110
www.wwnorton.com

W. W. Norton & Company Ltd, Castle House, 75/76 Wells Street, London W1T 3QT

6 7 8 9 0

in memory of
Robert H. Irrmann (1916–1998),
scholar of 1688,
teller of tales,
friend

CONTENTS

LIST OF ILLUSTRATIONS

ACKNOWLEDGMENTS

I stumbled across some of these stories in the course of my conventional research on European relations with China. At first I thought I would collect material on 1687 or 1689, to avoid the complexities of the Glorious Revolution, but Constantine Phaulkon in Siam and Shi Lang's envoys to Madras made 1688 unavoidable. There has been no end of serendipities. I had never heard of the Coronelli globes before I saw one by chance in a museum in Brussels. In July 1995 I followed a historical monument marker to the Slovenian country house of Janez Valvasor, of whom I had never heard. In 1997 I was able to visit Dampier's landfall on the coast of Australia and the fort on Ambon where Rumphius fell under the spell of tropical plant and animal life. In February 1999 I traced Phaulkon's last day in Lopburi. Serendipity, surprise, and letting one thing lead you to another are not attitudes often associated with the methodical world of the professional historian. Not many historians will want to give them as free rein as I have in this book, but many will acknowledge that they are part of what makes their hard work fun. This book has been fun to do. And what a privilege it has been to spend time with William Penn, with Bashô, with William Dampier!

Serendipity produces an amazing and scattered array of debts of gratitude. Many of my colleagues in the Department of History at the University of Southern California have at one time or another responded to my requests for guidance or bibliography for this book. My debts are largest to

Ayse and Hari Rorlich, for indispensable help with Russian and Middle Eastern materials. Others at USC include Marjorie Becker, Gerald Bender, Marguerite Bistis, Michael A. Burnstine, Thomas Cox, Charlotte Furth, Paul Knoll, Philippa Levine, Edwin McCann, Peter Nosco, Edwin Perkins, Carole Shammas, Lisa Silverman, Joseph Styles, and Shaoyi Sun. Connie Wills, Diane Wills, and Jeff Wills were a most helpful focus group in final editing agonies. Widening circles of helpful colleagues, from across the street to around the world, include Kim Akerman, E. M. Beekman, Leonard Blussé, David Ellenson, Lory Friedfertig, Aubrey Graatorex, Richard Hovanissian, Allen F. Isaacman, David Northrup, Demy Ohoilulin, Dhirivat and Pajrapongs na Pombejra, Branko Reisp, and Shalom Sabar. The libraries of USC and their Interlibrary Loan staff have been basic resources. I also have benefited from the riches of the libraries of the University of California at Los Angeles and the Huntington Library. The various funding agencies that made possible my research stays in Beijing and in The Hague and my brief visits to various parts of Europe and ports of maritime Asia, and the local authorities and archivists who facilitated my work, are thanked in detail in my monographs. I owe a special debt to Steven Forman of W. W. Norton & Company, who saw the merit of this eccentric project, waited with amazing patience while it moved forward and backward in my queue of things to be done, and provided a kind of engagement with the intellectual substance of my work I had never encountered in "academic" publishing. Geoffrey Parker's supportive comments and astute criticisms of an early draft were very important.

My wife and our family have been bemused, patient, impatient, as most families are with someone caught in an apparently interminable labor of love. Our daughter, Lucinda, and her husband, Muhammad al-Muwadda, advised me on matters Islamic and gave me a T-shirt inscribed "1688—the best year of my life" that wore out before the book got done. One of the delightful fringe benefits of over forty years with Carolin Connell Wills has been that with her I acquired an uncle, Robert H. Irrmann, for many years professor of history at Beloit College. A scholar of England in the 1680s and a much-admired teacher and teller of stories, he gave much astute advice and always was ready for another 1688 story. This book is dedicated to his memory in affection and gratitude. I am especially pleased that in his last years he knew of the progress of this work and had in his hands a full typescript of it.

1688

A Global History

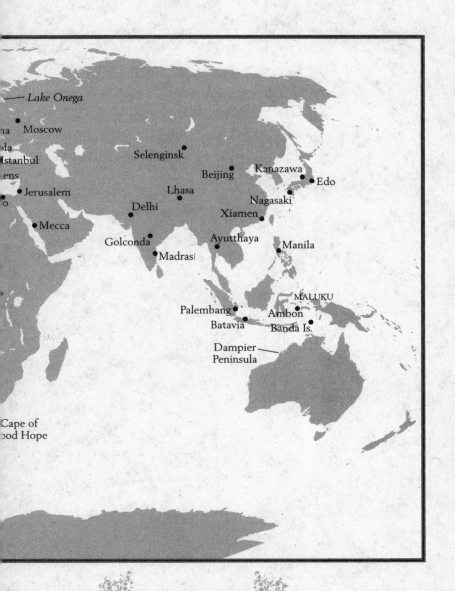

Lake Onega

Moscow

Selenginsk

Istanbul

Jerusalem

Mecca

Beijing

Kanazawa

Edo

Lhasa

Nagasaki

Delhi

Xiamen

Golconda

Ayutthaya

Madras

Manila

MALUKU

Palembang

Ambon

Batavia

Banda Is.

Dampier
Peninsula

Cape of
Good Hope

1688

A Global History

JANUARY 3, 1688

A Baroque Prelude

As the earth turns, the light of the sun moves from the gray and pale blue of the Pacific onto the forests and fields of the coasts of Japan and Luzon. In the seething energy and hard-won order of the streets of Edo, the great capital city of Japan's hereditary military dictators, the heavy wooden gates of residential quarters are swung open. Chanting and gongs are heard faintly from Buddhist temples. Shopkeepers open their shutters and arrange neat displays of fine wares from all over the country. Depleted roisterers slump away from the pleasure quarters and dodge into alleys as samurai horsemen ride past, their swords clattering.

In Manila, on Luzon, the sound of bells echoes from the great churches in the center of the city, south of the swamps along the Pasig River, and from the more modest ones in the Chinese Christian suburbs north of the river. Junks have begun to arrive from the ports of China. There is talk that there may not be as many as last year because of the growing tension between the Chinese and the rest of the population. How will the faraway authorities in Madrid and Mexico City reply to the litany of Chinese violence and treachery in the Manila authorities' letters? Might there even be another descent of Chinese pirates on this farthest outpost of the Spanish Empire of Catholicism and silver?

Far to the south, on a rocky piece of the northwest coast of Australia, William Dampier, gifted naturalist and barber-surgeon to a gang of buccaneers, is up and about, timing carefully the shifts of the daunting tide races, keeping an eye on the native people watching warily from a hilltop. He thinks them pitifully primitive, no danger, but certainly material for a great story if he lives to get home. At high tide the midges swarm and get into his eyes.

As the light reaches the great red walls and yellow tile roofs of the imperial palaces of Beijing, a singular procession heads south through the enormous gates. The banners and guardsmen are present in full array. The emperor himself is walking. He is on his way to the open Altar of Heaven, where he will face the cold winter sky and implore High Heaven to take years from his life and bestow them instead on his dying grandmother.

And as the light comes to the Ox Street Mosque on the west side of Beijing and to the airy, tropical mosques of such southern islands as Mindanao and Ambon, the muezzins call the faithful to morning prayer. Several hours later the muezzins' calls echo across Hyderabad in southern India and the splendid camp on its outskirts of the Mughal emperor Aurangzeb and his huge army. Some of the emperor's generals are Hindu, but he and most of his generals are Muslims, now bowing toward Mecca in their morning prayers before they turn to the exacting tasks of preparing their forces for another campaign. And now the muezzins' calls are everywhere in every dawn, in Isfahan and Samarkand far to the north, in Mecca, Cairo, Istanbul, in embattled Belgrade, Algiers, Timbuktu.

The Christians' morning bells already are ringing. Glikl bas Judah Leib, in Hamburg, knows that they are not summoning her and her people to worship and usually is up and busy by the time they start ringing. Father Vincenzo Coronelli already has been up and at his devotions in the Convent of St. Francis in Venice and now is planning his day's work of global cartography and far-flung correspondence. Isaac Newton hears the bells of the Cambridge churches and college chapels, lying low to avoid aggravating his conflict with the king, waiting for the reviews of his great book the *Principia*. If the sun comes out, he will note that its noon shadow is a bit shorter now that the winter solstice is past.

Beyond another ocean, in the Americas, many peoples are trying to reshape their old ways of life after the devastations of the Europeans and their diseases. A few Europeans have been dreaming new dreams, other than those of wealth and endless leisure, in the New World. In a beautiful upland valley in the remote Sonora Desert, Father Eusebio Kino watches his Pima neophytes gather for teaching and hopes that the dark cloud to the north will bring them life-giving rain. And the light passes on again into the immense ocean.

This portrait of one day in one year is a somewhat artificial construct. It starts in the Pacific, where our modern world-circling days start, only because it was (and is) the widest gap in the density of human settlement and activity. In the chapters that follow we shall learn more about these people and places and much more of the world of the one year 1688. But a focus even on one year is an arbitrary exercise, far easier for us than for the people who were alive in 1688. Many of these people would not have referred to the year as "1688." For the Muslims, it was 1099, then 1100. For the Chinese, it was the twenty-sixth, then the twenty-seventh year of the Kangxi reign. The very concept of the world in a single year is an artificial one, and much more so for the late seventeenth century than for the late twentieth. Now news of major events reaches around the globe in seconds or minutes, and we have access to almost any part of the world via global computer and telecommunications networks. In 1688 communication among the continents depended entirely on people and letters carried on sailing ships, which sailed only at certain seasons when the winds were favorable. Communication from one side of the earth to the other—say, a letter from a Dutchman in the East India Company's trading post in Japan to a cousin in the Hudson River valley—was almost certain to take more than a year.

Even today, with all our opportunities for world travel and our instanta-neous communications, the number of people who have a steady sense of the world as one world or even of the connections among several major parts of it is not as great as we should like to think. In 1688 a full sense of the variety of the world's places and peoples, of their separations and their connections, was confined to a few Europeans such as the philosopher Gottfried Wilhelm von Leibniz, the Jesuit missionaries, the English trav-eler William Dampier, and the literate urban Europeans who read the growing literature of travel and description of other parts of the world. China's Kangxi emperor and some of his ministers certainly were aware of the Europeans as a new element on the far margins of their "All under Heaven," but hardly at all of Africa and the Americas. The world of Islam stretched from Beijing and Mindanao to the Danube and the Niger but reached the New World only when some unfortunate African Muslim survived the middle passage and lived out his or her life in slavery in the Americas. The world of the illiterate farmer of any culture was largely limited to his village and a nearby market town. The world of the Bardi of Western Australia contained a thousand people at most, almost no tools, and a host of spirits and dreams. Thus we find many worlds of human experience within the one geographical world of 1688.

Speed of travel and communication was not the only area of basic difference between our world and that of three hundred years ago. The world of 1688 was much less crowded, with large stretches of forest and grassland where there now are farms and great cities. The courtiers of Versailles could ride out any morning and hunt wolves. It was much quieter, with no electronic amplifiers and no internal-combustion engines. Life expectancies were shorter because no one knew how to prevent the spread of infectious diseases or reduce the hazards of childbirth. Perhaps most fundamentally, no one in the late seventeenth-century world experienced or expected rapid technological change in one lifetime or basic change, even over a longer time span, in the political order or in one's way of life. Almost everyone expected to be and was deeply rooted in and guided by the beliefs and ways of life of his or her ancestors. Where change was sought, it was likely to be in the name of return to the old ways, purification of tradition. Our expectations of change, our sense of the possibility of basic improvement of human life, our fundamental impatience with authority and tradition had just begun to be expressed by a few European intellectuals.

Those few intellectuals were right, however, in sensing the possibilities of fundamental transformation, and in retrospect we can see in the world of 1688 signs of the basic shifts that created our own very different world: the rise of science; the growth of cities and commerce; government policies promoting economic growth; an immense variety of writing and publishing, some of it for broad urban audiences; some very individual and idiosyncratic acceptances and reinterpretations of the great religions; protests against slavery and the subordination of women. All these new developments turn up somewhere, usually more than once, in the chapters that follow. Many readers will be surprised to find somewhat comparable changes taking place in many different parts of the world: commercial and economic growth in Japan as well as Europe; Saikaku as well as Aphra

Behn writing for a vigorous commercial market; highly personal acceptances of great traditions by Wang Fuzhi and by William Penn.

My search for evidence that could be dated to a particular year has contributed to certain omissions and overrepresentations. Illiterate people
appear only as recorded by someone else. We have more rulers than ruled,
more merchants than farmers. Adventurers with tales to tell, most of them
European, make great contributions to our knowledge of the world outside
Europe. I have tried, just as I have done ever since I began reading Dutch
records about events on the China coast more than forty years ago, to read
these records against the grain, not to succumb to the prejudices of the
writers. Above all, I have hoped to convey to my reader some of my aston-
ishment at the voices I have heard. Some of them are in the language of
this book: Dampier retelling his sharp-eyed observation of the Australian
Aborigines; Locke urging us to think sensibly and carefully, especially
about the deepest puzzles of reality, knowledge, and political right. For
some writing in other European languages—Bayle's passionate linking of
free assent and real belief, Vieira's double turn on the Pentecost and speaking in tongues—the language is reasonably transparent. But what about
Aphra Behn, quoting in a fictional voice that is partly hers the operatic
courage of a rebel slave? Do we really grasp Sor Juana's intricate images
and conceits? I have always thought I could catch a bit of the masterful but
ironic voice of the Kangxi emperor, but in addition to knowing that his
pronouncements always were edited for posterity, I can't really be sure if
he was speaking in Chinese or in Manchu. An Indian Sufi's "God damn the
tyrant" seems to ring across gulfs of mentality and translation. We can hear
Saikaku's detached, ironic voice only because some gifted and erudite
translators have struggled with some of the world's most intricately allusive prose.

Of course we don't really hear voices. We're reading, and human speech
comes down to us from 1688 only as converted into written texts. Hearing
voices when we read is a common but still mysterious experience in our
literate cultures. Sometimes if we know the writer or have heard her speak,
we recognize that she has managed to capture something of her voice in
her written style. This uncanny sense of voices can be especially strong in
our texts from 1688. Merchants and people pursuing political, military, or
intellectual careers moved around a great deal. The only way they could
keep in touch with the people they left behind was by writing to them. For

a thousand years literate Chinese had been writing poems when they parted from friends and sending more to them when they were apart, poems that were meant to be chanted and to be shared, as if the writer and his reader were together. The late seventeenth century was the heyday of an easy conversational style in French and English prose that owed much to letter writing. John Locke carried the style he used to talk about farming and finances and to be shyly charming to the ladies all the way into his deepest philosophical inquiries. Much fiction writing was cast as series of letters. Many books began with some kind of preface "To the Reader."

Voices can be impersonal, or claim to be so. The Kongo great man reenacts in word and person the knotting of sacred powers in a charm. The muezzin at dawn, the schoolboys in a Quranic school on the banks of the Senegal, a young Turk captured by Christian pirates on the Danube all repeat the words God's Angel dictated to the Prophet. The great Jesuit Vieira claims that it is the Holy Scripture speaking through him. But voices often clearly are inseparable from singular persons and their lives. Some of the names of these individuals appear in chapter titles: Dampier, Saikaku, Locke, Leibniz, Aphra Behn. Not one speaks simply in his or her own voice, but in every case we hear the voice more clearly when we know a bit of the life that produced it.

There are times when the voices are heard only collectively. We know of the mutter and occasional roar of rage and despair from the holds of slave ships. We can imagine the uncanny harmonies of old Russian hymns among the Old Believers before the flames they had lit reached them. Other voices seem to be drowned out by the winds of the Andes howling around the baroque square corners of Potosí, by the kind of storm on the high seas that could finish the adventures of any sharp-eyed wanderer at any time, or by the roar of one of the great rivers flooding down out of the heart of a continent to the ocean. For Europeans on the coasts of Africa and the Americas, the great rivers spoke of the mysteries of their sources and the promises of riches upstream. For one visionary European, the Amazon was the path to a possible paradise on earth. Even the Yangtze and the Mississippi were better understood than the Senegal, the Gambia, the Niger, and the Congo; the shapes of Africa and the individual voices of Africans (with the terrible exception of the slaves leaving it forever) remain hardest of all for us to hear.

The earth turns, and sunlight and shadow shift. Themes and voices come and go in ways I have not often anticipated, much less controlled, baroque in their intricacy. Quite a few people in different parts of the world in 1688 had a new sense of the ability of rational people to look in the eye the intricacies and ironies of human nature, to give elegant accounts of the orbits of sun, moon, stars, and even the terrifying irregularities of comets. "Baroque" comes to stand for many things, not least the formal interweaving of uncannily individual voices. It is tempting to call Saikaku, with all his layers of irony and allusion, baroque. We begin with the baroque conceits of Sor Juana, and near the end the great passionate voice of the Song of Solomon becomes a sacred line tracing beautiful patterns, and voices join in weaving around the words of the Psalmist harmonies of celebration and longing. We end with a Purcell anthem for the doomed House of Stuart, expressing, but in no way resolving, human hope and risk, from kingdoms to unborn infants.

PART I

A WORLD OF WOODEN SHIPS

In 1688 Father Vincenzo Coronelli of the order of Friars Minor, cosmographer of the Most Serene Republic of Venice, distributed to his subscribers map sheets cut to be fitted together to form the surfaces of globes over a meter in diameter, the largest printed globes yet made and triumphs of the art and science of the seventeenth-century cartographer. The coastlines of the continents were laid out with impressive accuracy, except for the east coast of Australia, both coasts of the Pacific north of Japan and California, parts of the American and Siberian Arctic, and Antarctica; these were either left blank or sketched in to represent some mariner's vague report or guess. The interiors of the continents reflected Jesuit knowledge of the valleys of the Yangtze, the St. Lawrence, and the

Paraguay and recent European explorations up the Senegal and the Zambesi and down the Mississippi. Only in Siberia and Central Asia did the Coronelli globe not display the best European knowledge; for those regions the great Amsterdam merchant-politician Nicolaas Witsen knew more, derived from a century of Dutch trade with Russia, but he had made little of his knowledge public.

Coronelli filled some of the oceanic blanks on his globe with fine small pictures of the European wooden ships that were the global ligaments of 1688. The world of wooden ships included the Spanish galleons that carried silver across the Atlantic and the Pacific and the complex commerce in slaves, gold, cloth, guns, and much more that linked West Africa with Europe and the Americas. Europeans crossing the oceans were building small settler societies in the New World and on the fringes of Asia and Africa and were confronting an undreamed-of variety of peoples, from the great civilizations of Asia to the comfortable agricultural villages of North American Indians to the physically but not psychically meager circumstances of the Aborigines of northwestern Australia.

Father Coronelli himself displayed a confident mixture of faith and empiricism. An influential member of the Franciscan order, one of the intellectual and spiritual glories of the Middle Ages, he was a proud citizen and official of Venice. Venice still was a great Mediterranean power but was watching leadership in European politics, commerce, and culture shift steadily from Italy to France, the Netherlands, and now England. He had gained some of his geographic knowledge on a long stay in France, where he built the largest globe yet seen, over thirteen feet in diameter, for Louis XIV. He stayed in the good graces of his patrons and rulers in Venice by mapping their conquests in the eastern Mediterranean.

In 1684 Father Coronelli founded the world's first geographic society, the Cosmographic Academy of the Argonauts. Among the patrons of the academy were the doge of Venice and Jan III Sobieski, king of Poland and savior of Vienna from the Turks. Branches were established in Milan and Paris. Subscribers included illustrious savants all over Europe; even Father Ferdinand Verbiest, serving as astronomer at the far-off court of Beijing, was enrolled, presumably by a Jesuit colleague visiting Europe. For 3 lire per month subscribers received six plates every month for a great atlas Father Coronelli was producing piece by piece. The triangular globe sheets were also sold by subscription, for 504 lire.

Father Coronelli worked ceaselessly to cultivate his relations with all the princes of Europe, to obtain every new bit of geographic information, and to improve his cartographic and printing workshops in the Franciscan convent in Venice. In one portrait, and in a delightful visual joke in which he peers out around the corner of a cartouche on the 1688 globe, he has a bit of a gleam in his eye and a certain far from ascetic roundness in his face. In the brown robe, rope belt, and sandals of the order founded by Saint Francis of Assisi, he fitted his works of cartography and promotion around the Franciscan schedule of devotions. Many days he must have taken a gondola down a side waterway and out onto the busy Grand Canal, to the gloomy velvet-hung chambers of the Palace of the Doges—still today redolent of the implacably thorough and conscientious government of the Venetian Republic—to consult with the city authorities. Occasionally he must have had to go a bit farther, to the great shipyard called the Arsenal, with its assembly-line stages for the building of war galleys. He was at home in this world of power; indeed, his work depended on the patronage of the powerful. And his maps, which recorded the advance of explorers who were the vanguard of European power, symbolically asserted the power to organize and ultimately to control. Spiritual heir of Saint Francis and anticipator of the geographic societies of the nineteenth and twentieth centuries, rooted in unchanging verities of God and Man but open to every new discovery by Man on God's earth, he and his globes open up to us many facets of the world of 1688, including seas known and unknown, shores surveyed and others not yet reached.

The intensity of commerce connecting Europe, Africa, and America made the South Atlantic one of the best-known and most regularly crossed stretches of open ocean in 1688. It was almost two hundred years since the first projections westward of Spanish and Portuguese power, anti-Muslim, militantly Catholic. No one could have imagined at the outset how those small beginnings would lead to the westward flow of willing and unwilling emigrants and the eastward flow of treasure, the building up in the Americas of new capital cities, new worlds of commerce, power, and plunder. Predators followed as well as settlers. Both predators and settlers had long since found their way across Panama and around South America into the vastness of the Pacific and even across it. On all these new shores they found strange peoples, some of whom, like the miners of Potosí, had their lives transformed by the coming of the Europeans, while others, like the Caddo of modern Texas and the Bardi of Australia, would preserve their ways of life intact for many more years.

CHAPTER 1

THE EMPIRE OF SILVER

On April 28, 1688, a long procession moved out of Mexico City, along the causeways that crossed the nearby lakes, and through the small towns and farms of the plateau, on its way toward the pass between the two volcanoes Iztaccihuatl and Popocatépetl, both more than sixteen thousand feet high, and down to the tropical port of Vera Cruz. The farmers in their villages and fields were used to a good deal of such coming and going, but this time they stopped their work to look and to call out to each other in Nahuatl, the main indigenous language, for this was no ordinary procession. Cavalry outriders and a huge coach were followed by many baggage wagons and a long line of fine coaches. The marquis of Laguna had served as viceroy of New Spain from 1680 to 1686. With their wealth, powerful connections in Madrid, and a taste for elegance and the arts, he and his wife had given the viceregal court a few years of splendor and sophistication comparable, if not to Madrid, certainly to many of the lesser courts of Europe. Now their wealthy Spanish friends were riding in their coaches as far as the Villa de Guadalupe, seeing the marquis and marchioness off on their voyage home to Spain.

A child born of a slave shall be received,
according to our Law, as property
of the owner to whom fealty
is rendered by the mother who conceived.

The harvest from a grateful land retrieved,
the finest fruit, offered obediently,
is for the lord, for its fecundity
is owing to the care it has received.
So too, Lysis divine, these my poor lines:
as children of my soul, born of my heart,
they must in justice be to you returned;
Let not their defects cause them to be spurned,
for of your rightful due they are a part,
as concepts of a soul to yours consigned.

These lines were written sometime later in 1688 and sent off from Mexico to the marchioness of Laguna in Spain. They make use of metaphors and classical conceits to express and conceal the feelings of the author, who had lost, with the marchioness's departure, the object of the nearest thing she had ever known to true love and, with the marquis's departure, her ultimate protection from those who found her opinions and her way of life scandalous. The trouble was not that the author was lesbian—although her feelings toward men and women were unusually complicated and unconventional, anything approaching a physical relation or even passion is most unlikely—but that she was a cloistered Hieronymite nun, who read and studied a wide range of secular books, held long intellectual conversations with many friends, wrote constantly in a variety of religious and secular styles, and betrayed in her writings sympathy for Hermetic and Neoplatonic views that were on the edge of heresy if not beyond it. Her name in religion was Sor Juana Inés de la Cruz. She is recognized today as one of the great poets in the history of the Spanish language.

Mexico in the 1680s was a society of dramatic contradictions. The elegant viceregal court and the opulent ecclesiastical hierarchy looked toward Europe for style and ideas. The vast majority of the population sought to preserve as much as possible of the language, beliefs, and ways of life that had guided them before the coming of the Spaniards; the worship of the Virgin of Guadalupe, for example, owed much to the shrine of an Aztec goddess that had been the setting of the original appearance of the Virgin to a Mexican peasant. In between the "peninsular" elite and the "Indians," the native-born "creoles" of Spanish language and culture managed huge cattle ranches and sought constantly new veins of profitable silver ore and new techniques to exploit old ones. Neither "Spanish" nor "Indian," they experienced the full force of the contradictions of Mexican society and culture.

The literary world in which Sor Juana was such an anomalous eminence thrived on these contradictions of society and culture. This was a baroque culture. The word "baroque," originating as a Portuguese term for the peculiar beauty of a deformed, uneven pearl, suggests a range of artistic styles in which the balance and harmony of the Renaissance styles are abandoned for imbalance, free elaboration of form, playful gesture, and surprising allusion, through which the most intense of emotions and the darkest of realities may be glimpsed, their power enhanced by the glittering surface that partially conceals them. Contradiction and its partial, playful reconciliation are the stuff of the baroque style. So is the layering of illusion on illusion, meaning upon meaning. And what more baroque conceit could be imagined than the literary eminence of a cloistered nun in a rough frontier society, with a church and state of the strongest and narrowest male supremacist prejudices? Look again at the poem quoted earlier: The chaste nun refers to her poem as her child or the harvest from a grateful land. She declares her love once again to the departed marchioness.

Sor Juana was a product of Mexican creole society, born on a ranch on the shoulder of the great volcano Popocatépetl. Her mother was illiterate and very probably had not been married to her father. But some of the family branches lived in the city, with good books and advantageous connections. As soon as she discovered the books in her grandfather's library, she was consumed with a thirst for solitude and reading. Her extraordinary talents for literature and learning were recognized. When she was fifteen, in 1664, she was taken into the household of a newly arrived viceroy, as his wife's favorite and constant companion. She must have enjoyed the attention, the luxury, the admiration of her cleverness. She no doubt participated in the highly stylized exchange of "gallantries" between young men and young women. But she had no dowry. Solitude was her natural habitat. As a wife and mother, what chance would she have to read, to write, to be alone? In 1668 she took her vows in the Hieronymite convent of an order named after Saint Jerome, cloistered and meditative by rule.

This was a big decision, but less drastic than one might think. Certainly she was a believing Catholic. Her new status did not require total devotion to prayer and extinction of self. It did not imply that she was abandoning all the friendships and secular learning that meant so much to her. The nuns had a daily round of collective devotions; but many rules were not fully honored, and the regimen left her much free time for reading and writing. Each of the nuns had comfortable private quarters, with a kitchen, room for a bathtub, and sleeping space for a servant and a dependent or two; Sor Juana usually had one slave and one or two nieces or other junior dependents living in her quarters. The nuns visited back and forth in their quarters to the point that Sor Juana complained of the interruptions to her reading and writing, but outsiders spoke to the nuns only in the locutory especially provided for that purpose. From the beginning she turned the locutory into an elegant salon, as the viceroy and his lady and other fashionable people came to visit her and they passed hours in learned debate, literary improvisation, and gossip.

One of Sor Juana's most constant friends and supporters was Carlos de Sigüenza y Góngora, professor of mathematics at the University of Mexico, an eminently learned creole scholar whose position was almost as anomalous as hers. He had been educated by the Jesuits and had longed to be one of them but had been expelled from their college. He had managed to obtain his position, without a university degree, by demonstrating his superior knowledge of his subject. He had added Góngora to his name to emphasize his distant kinship, through his mother's family, with the most famous of Spain's baroque poets. But he always felt insecure among the European-born professors, churchmen, and high officials. He wrote a great deal, much of it about the history of Mexico. He was in no way Sor Juana's equal as a writer, but he probably was responsible for most of her smattering of knowledge of modern science and recent philosophy.

There was a rule of poverty among the Hieronymites, but it was generally ignored. Sor Juana received many gifts, some of them substantial enough to enable the former dowerless girl to invest money at interest. By gift and purchase she built up a library of about four thousand volumes and a small collection of scientific instruments, probably provided by Sigüenza. Her reading was broad but not very systematic, contributing to the stock of ideas and allusions she drew on constantly in her writings but giving her little sense of the intellectual tensions and transformations that were building up in Europe. She wrote constantly, in a wide variety of complex and exacting forms. Voluntarily or upon commission or request, she wrote occasional poems of all kinds for her friends and patrons. A celebration might call for a *loa*, a brief theatrical piece in praise of a dignitary. In one of hers, for example, a character "clad in sunrays" declares:

I am a reflection
of that blazing sun
who, among shining rays
numbers brilliant sons:
when his illustrious rays
strike a speculum,
on it is portrayed
the likeness of his form.

Sor Juana's standing in society reached a new height with the arrival in 1680 of the marquis and marchioness of Laguna. Even in the public festivities celebrating their arrival, she outdid herself in baroque elaborations of texts and conceits for a temporary triumphal arch erected at the cathedral. It was an allegory on Neptune, in which the deeds of the Greek god were compared to the real or imaginary deeds of the marquis. Much was made of the echoes among the marquis's title of Laguna, meaning "lake," Neptune's reign over the oceans, and the origins of Mexico City as the Aztec city of Tenochtitlán in the middle of its great lake: an elaborate union of sycophancy to a ruler, somewhat strained classical allusion, and a creole quest for a Mexican identity. In parts of the text the author even drew in Isis as an ancestor of Neptune, and in others of her works from this time she showed a great interest in Egyptian antiquity as it was then understood, including the belief that the god Hermes Trismegistus had revealed the most ancient and purest wisdom and anticipated the Mosaic and Christian revelations. These ideas, the accompanying quasi-Platonic separation of soul and body, and her use of them to imply that a female or androgynous condition was closer to the divine wisdom than the male took her to the edge of heresy or beyond and was turned against her in later years.

Sor Juana soon established a close friendship with the marchioness of Laguna. Some of the poems she sent her are among her very finest, and they are unmistakably love poems. Some of them accompanied a portrait of the author. Several portraits in which a very handsome woman gazes boldly at us, her black-and-white habit simply setting off her own strength and elegance, have come down to us.

And if it is that you should rue
the absence of a soul in me [the portrait],

FIEL

Copia de otra que deſi hizo, y deſu mano pinta la R. M. Juana Ynes dela Cruz Fenix dela America, Glorioſo deſempeño deſu Sexo, Honrra dela Nacion deeste Nuevo Mundo, y argumento delas admiraciones, y elogios deel Antiguo. Nacio el dia 12. de Nov. deel año de 1651. años enſe dela noche. Recivio el Sagrado Habito deel Maximo D.S.r Geronimo, enſu Convento de esta Ciudad de Mexico, de edad de 17. años. Ymurio Domingo 17. de Abell deel de 1695. de edad...

Sor Juana Inés de la Cruz

you can confer one, easily,
from the many rendered you:
and as my soul I [Sor Juana] tendered you,
and though my being yours obeyed,
and though you look on me amazed
in this insentient apathy,
you are the soul of this body,
and are the body of this shade.

The marquis of Laguna stepped down as viceroy in 1686 but remained in Mexico until 1688. In that year Sor Juana was very busy. The marchioness was taking texts of her poems back to Spain, where they soon would be published. She added to them a play, *The Divine Narcissus*, interweaving the legend of Narcissus and the life of Jesus, which probably was performed in Madrid in 1689 or 1690. Her niece took her vows in the convent in 1688. Late in the year, after her noble friends had left, she wrote the poem quoted earlier as well as a romantic comedy, *Love Is the Greater Labyrinth*, which was performed in Mexico City early in 1689.

A large collection of her poetry was published in Madrid in 1689. The next year in Mexico she published a letter taking abstruse issue with a sermon preached decades before by the famous Portuguese Jesuit Antonio Vieira. Her casual way with the rules of the religious life, her flirtings with heresy, her many writings in secular forms with intimations of understanding of love inappropriate to her profession had made her many enemies, but they could do nothing while the marquis of Laguna and his lady were on hand to protect her. Now they closed in. In 1694 she was forced formally to renounce all writing and humane studies and to relinquish her library and collection of scientific instruments. In 1695 she devotedly cared for her sisters in the convent during an epidemic, caught the disease, and died.

Mexico City was the seat of one of the Spanish viceroys in the Americas; the other was in Lima. The viceroys, always nobles sent from Spain, ruled in splendor, literally "in place of the king." Reporting to them were the governors of various provinces. University-trained lawyers shaped the decision-making process at every stage; it was very thorough and very slow. It did a respectable job of keeping control of key lines of trade and taxation and of preventing the accumulation by any colonial official of too much independent power. The centralized structure of the Roman Catholic Church and its many orders added more layers of organizational strength. Centers of Spanish settlement and power gained continuity and cohesion by petitioning the king for the legal privileges of citizens and a local city council in the European manner.

The Spanish-speaking population of the Americas in 1688 included many modest people like Sor Juana's rural relatives—people who farmed, traded, mined; people who, though not idle or necessarily rich, did all they could to hire or compel others, often indigenous people on the margins of the Spanish-speaking world, to do the heavy work. The Spanish monarchy often proclaimed that it maintained its American empire in order to save souls, and certainly it gave great support to missionary efforts; but it also worked diligently to tap the wealth of the Americas for its own purposes—most of all its silver.

In commerce and in politics, precious metals mattered enormously to Europeans of the 1600s, for the settling of accounts among merchants and rulers in different countries, for paying troops, including mercenaries, for bribing monarchs and officials—wherever mistrust or secrecy made bills of credit unusable. But their appeal was more than rational. Seventeenth-century Europeans could be driven mad by thoughts of gold and silver. As "noble metals," subject to only very slow oxidation or other chemical change, they were symbols of resistance to decay, even of eternity. Many of the most advanced scientists of the world of 1688 still were interested in alchemy, although they often claimed that their interest was philosophical, not stemming from greed for gold.

So it is not surprising that Europe was fascinated by reports of the "mountain of silver" at Potosí (in modern Bolivia), the main source of the stream of treasure from the New World that made the king of Spain immensely rich and powerful. In the seventeenth and eighteenth centuries Potosí usually produced more silver than the two great Mexican producing districts combined. Silver pesos from the American mints circulated all over Europe and in many ports and coastal districts of Asia. In the dock districts of Amsterdam, in between bouts of drinking, whoring, and telling lies about every port in the world, sailors would join in a chorus in celebration of the greatest of attacks on the Spanish silver fleet, one of the few real successes in the Dutch West India Company's efforts to carry the war against the Spanish-Portuguese monarchy to the Americas, in 1628: "Piet Heyn! Piet Heyn! All praised is his name! . . . For he captured the silver fleet!"

In the early eighteenth century Bartolomé Arzáns de Orsúa y Vela, a native of Potosí, wrote a monumental history of his native city. It is an amalgam of empirical information about its government and society and wonderful stories of passion, violence, divine retribution, miracles, and witchcraft, assembled from other local authors and tales passed down generation to generation. Under the year 1688 he records the adventures of a young woman of good family whom he had known personally. Perhaps he had been in love with her:

> Her face was like white marble, her hair the proper mean, for it was nei-
> ther as dark as night nor as golden as the sun; green eyes, with lashes so
> long that they seemed to serve them as a canopy, and so luxuriant that
> they seemed like a fence protecting her eyes or like an ebony frame and
> embellishment to her face; her brows also luxuriant, broad, and so close
> together that there was no separation between them; her nose so per-
> fect that it was not a whit too small or too large; her cheeks and brow
> adorned with charming ringlets, which, falling over her face, grudgingly
> allowed a little crimson to show in an expanse of snowy whiteness; her
> mouth small and adorned with small, white, and even teeth; her hands,
> bust, and waist all in graceful proportion; a winning charm in her man-
> ner and grace in her walk; her voice (which is often an added embellish-
> ment of beauty) soft, sweet, and resonant; and her intelligence clear,
> keen, and extremely prudent.

She was called Doña Teresa; she was only fifteen.

Who, asks our author, could have failed to fall in love with this wonder-ful creature? Two suitors managed to make their interest known to her, one a married, wealthy mercury refiner, the other an outsider using the apparently bogus title Count of Olmos. But Doña Teresa's parents kept her even more strictly confined than was the norm for young ladies of her class; "On many Sundays and feast days they did not even take her to hear Mass." Thus she was deprived even of that small measure of freedom that "would not have exceeded the bounds of her natural chastity and modesty. . . . Now, freedom is one of the most precious gifts conferred by Heaven on human beings; the treasures enclosed in the earth or hidden in the sea are not to be compared with it; men can and must risk life itself for freedom, as for honor, and, conversely, the greatest misfortune that can befall mankind is captivity."

The mercury refiner persuaded Doña Teresa's parents to let the girl accompany his wife to various festivities but never got the chance he was hoping for to be alone with her and seduce her. The "Count of Olmos" moved into a house across the street from hers and secretly watched her comings and goings; once she learned of his love, they agreed to talk at night, he at his balcony and she at her window, above the narrow street. It seems that once or twice they were able to converse in her room, but their growing love was never consummated. Finally she agreed to climb down knotted sheets and go with him to his house but fell. She somehow managed to get back in her bedroom before her parents found out.

The mercury refiner now realized he had a rival and told Doña Teresa's mother, who beat an Indian maidservant until she told all. The mother then beat Teresa until the blood ran and locked her in a chicken coop in a deserted stable yard, keeping her there from May through July, the coldest months of the year. "If the mother had already ascertained," our author comments, "that her daughter was still a virgin, yet punished her so cruelly because she learned that the girl had let a man into her bedroom, why should she now cast her into despair?" The beating was appropriate, it seems, for letting a man in her bedroom, and the confinement would have been proper if the girl had indeed been "dishonored."

The father had been away on business, and the mother told Doña Teresa, "I wrote to your father to inform him of the evil you have done in discrediting our honor, and I have now received his reply, in which he says that he is coming home only to drink your blood. Take notice, therefore, that you will leave here only to be carried to your tomb."

The "Count of Olmos" finally learned of Teresa's plight by way of her younger brother, who was sent twice a week to clean her chicken coop. The boy carried secret messages back and forth and finally took Teresa a file to cut through the lock on her door. It was agreed that she would climb onto a low roof, where she would affix a strong rope attached at its other end to the count's balcony. Just four days before her father arrived home, they made fast both ends of the rope. But Teresa panicked as she began to pull herself along it, and the count had a servant go across the rope to help her.

As they were moving along the rope two things happened that might have caused serious injury had Teresa fallen from the great height. The first was that as the two of them swung down from the roof, the edge of the balcony (which was of wood and somewhat worm-eaten) gave a great crack and would have split and let them fall had not the count held on to it with both hands. The other was that halfway across the street the girl's arms became so tired that when the servant noticed it he had to hang from the ropes and seize Teresa by her hair and the front of her shift; and although the two hung there motionless for the space of a Credo, at last she recovered her strength and continued until she

reached the balcony, where the count received her with the greatest
affection. They then untied one end of the hempen rope and, pulling on
the other, hastily drew it in, thereby removing the evidence that the
beautiful Teresa had escaped by that route. She spent the rest of the
night in the arms of her lover, who did not behave with as much
restraint as he had on the first, second, and third occasions, especially
because this time Teresa was quite willing.

Doña Teresa stayed in hiding in the home of the count for two months;
nothing more is said about why she didn't marry him. Then she and her little brother slipped away to an aunt's house in another city and stayed away
from Potosí for over two years, during which her mother died repentant
and grieving for her lost children. Doña Teresa found "a noble youth who
wished to wed her. . . . At last Doña Teresa returned to this city with her
husband, where they lived for ten more years in great peace and tranquility, and at the end of that time Teresa departed this life, leaving four sons
and a daughter who bore her name, a girl as beautiful as her dead mother
had been. And she is alive today, her beauty increasing as she grows older."

This little tale of the power of feminine beauty, of passionate whispers
above narrow streets and hairbreadth escapes across them might come
from old Seville, with guitars strumming, fountains splashing in the courtyards, Gypsies conjuring in the shadows. But the setting was about as different from Seville as it could be.

The streams of silver from the mines of Potosí and Mexico gave Spain
its few decades as the first world power and sustained the growth of the
whole net of world trade—in northern Europe, in the Mediterranean, on
the Mecca pilgrimage routes, into India, and both ways around the world
into China. These streams flow all through our stories of the world of
1688. That world knew no more improbable combination of planning and
anarchy, passion and repentance, greed and compassion, church, law, and
silver, Spaniard and Indian than Potosí itself. At an elevation of about thirteen thousand feet in a valley surrounded by barren mountains, bringing all
its food, lumber, and other necessities up from lower elevations, the city
simply would not have been there at all if this location had not been the
site of the largest and richest deposits of silver then known in the world,
discovered in 1545 and coming into production in the 1580s. In the early
1600s Potosí had well over a hundred thousand people, and its core was a
fine Spanish city with well-planned plazas, churches, opulent mansions, a

huge area devoted to fortified refining complexes, and streets deliberately made narrow and crooked to break the howling winds. Every luxury good in the world was for sale—Chinese silks, Italian paintings, Persian carpets, French beaver hats—but Spanish women had learned that they must go down to lower elevations to give birth, for many of their infants would not survive their efforts to get enough oxygen from their first breaths of the thin air. There were not many cities outside Japan whose streets were safe at night in 1688, but few were as wild as those of Potosí. Greed, passion, challenges to honor, long-lasting feuds among Basques, Castilians, American-born creoles, and foreigners led to the endless ambushes, duels, and pitched battles described with such relish by Arzáns. If occasionally one of the wild men repented and ended his life as a Franciscan friar, it gave the tale-tellers of Potosí a treasured chance to describe the most interestingly brutal crimes and provide edification all at once. Black slaves and Indian servants could be counted on to vary their monotonous lives by breaking the heads of their masters' enemies. If greed for silver did not provide enough recruits for the devil, there also was a scattering of Spanish and Indian witches, some of them said to specialize in trances induced by coca, already very much a part of the lives of the people of the Andes.

Potosí and its stream of silver depended on an organized brutality, the mita system of forced Indian labor. From the 1570s on, the Spanish authorities required every Indian village in the viceroyalty of Peru to send one-seventh of its male population every year for a four-month term of paid labor in the mines of Potosí, the mercury mines of Huancavelica (in modern Peru), or other public projects. The wages were far below market levels, the work was hard and dangerous (the worst was amid the poisonous mercury ore at Huancavelica), and disease and bad diet contributed to the high death rates. The mita provided only about one-tenth of the labor supply at Potosí, but these laborers did the heaviest and most dangerous work, which no one would do without compulsion, carrying heavy baskets of ore up rickety ladders out of the mines. The mita also shaped the economy of the rest of the area, as Indians fled villages where they were registered in order to live where they had no mita obligations.

By 1650 the mita was producing only about 60 percent of the numbers of laborers for Potosí it had at the turn of the century, and silver production and royal revenues from it were falling. The mill- and mineowners were demanding restoration of the full labor supply, and the monarchy was supporting them in hopes of reviving production. In 1683, after prolonged discussion and several abortive reform projects, the viceroy, the duke of La Palata, ordered a new census as a basis for full enforcement of the mita. Many local officials repeatedly sought clarification or asked permission to use local variations in reporting categories, and otherwise delayed compliance, while masses of Indians moved away from administrative centers to avoid being registered. The result was a census showing a total population of Upper Peru only half that of a century before. In 1688 the results finally were being pulled together, and a new set of lower mita quotas was laid out. In the eighteenth century the Spanish managed to raise production at Potosí above its late-seventeenth-century level and continued their efforts to revive the mita, but to little effect, as quotas and actual supplies of forced labor continued to decline.

To the first-time viewer, the Sonora Desert is all that the word "desert" connotes: a wasteland, its hard soil broken only by occasional forbidding cacti and dead-looking bushes. Especially in the summer the heat is stunning, the sky cloudless, and as soon as the sun rises, the visitor flinches from its power and seeks what shade he can find. But the visitor who spends some time exploring the region finds surprising variety. Mountains rise to over sixty-five hundred feet above sea level, capped with pine forests. Here and there the saguaro, organ-pipe, ocotillo, and other large cacti grow in such numbers that they form singular gardens and almost groves.

In August rain clouds ride in on the east winds, all the way from the Gulf of Mexico. Thunder rumbles, lightning flashes, and dark clouds pour flash floods into dry watercourses. In the winter the temperatures are milder, and storms out of the North Pacific sometimes reach far enough inland to give the Sonora Desert its second set of life-giving rains. This is the singularity of the Sonora Desert; farther east or west the deserts only have one season per year of possible rains and have nothing like the variety of desert vegetation that the two rains support in the Sonora region.

The people who lived in the Sonora Desert in 1688 called themselves Hohokam, "the people." The Spaniards who were beginning to move into the desert from the south called them Pima and their land the Pimería. They were largely hunter-gatherers, harvesting the variable roots and seeds and hunting the small animals of the desert. Some of them planted corn and beans where there was a reliable water supply. They dug ditches to channel water to their fields and in some places could see traces of the much larger irrigation works of earlier peoples who may have been their ancestors but with whom they felt little kinship.

In 1688 Father Eusebio Francisco Kino of the Society of Jesus was spending his second summer in the Sonora Desert. He never left it again, dying there in 1711 at the age of sixty-six; the site of his burial may be seen in modern Magdalena de Kino, Sonora, Mexico. It seems likely that he spent most of 1688 in one place not far from where he now is buried, the new mission establishment of Our Lady of the Sorrows (Nuestra Señora de las Dolores), on a rocky point overlooking promising alluvial fields and the San Miguel River, an excellent all-year source of irrigation water. Work on this site had begun in March 1687; by 1689 it boasted rich fields, a church, and a house. It may be that in 1688 Kino remained uncharacteristically immobile at Dolores, watching the farming and construction work and ministering to the Pima who came to settle nearby.

Eusebio Chini or Chino was born in 1645 at Segno in the Val di Non near Trent. Martino Martini, S.J., a famous cartographer, geographer, and historian of China in the seventeenth century, was a relative. Chino was educated at Jesuit colleges in his home area and in German-speaking lands, including Ingolstadt. Much later in his life he wrote that he was not sure if he should call himself an Italian or a German. During a serious illness he took a vow that if he recovered, he would seek to become a Jesuit and a missionary. From 1670 on he repeatedly petitioned his superiors for assignment to the missions in China. Despite his deep longing—he even preferred to have a room facing east, so that he could gaze off in that direction—he was of course an obedient Jesuit, ready to go where God and his superiors sent him. When his superiors dispatched him and a colleague to Seville for assignment to missions, one in Mexico and one in the Philippines, the two drew slips of paper to let God choose between them, and Eusebio drew Mexico.

While they waited at Seville, Chino and his colleagues spent many evenings watching an extraordinarily bright comet that appeared in November and December 1680. Comets, coming so mysteriously and unpredictably, were taken in many cultures as portents of heavenly wrath and disaster. They also were very hard to fit into the late scholastic cosmology of unchanging crystalline spheres that was increasingly rejected by up-to-date European scientists but was still the orthodox Christian view. The 1680 comet prompted apocalyptic fears in Puritan Massachusetts and among the hard-pressed French Calvinists, but among the latter it also

evoked a memorable counterblast against portent-mongering and apocalyptic preaching from the French Protestant writer Pierre Bayle, whom we
shall meet in a later chapter. It also attracted the interest of advanced scientific minds, one of whom, Edmond Halley of London, would be ready
for observations of unprecedented accuracy and sophistication when
another comet appeared just two years later.

Arriving in Mexico in 1681, Chino still hoped that a China assignment
might turn up, but it was not to be. In his brief stay in Mexico City he met
briefly Sor Juana de la Cruz and tangled memorably with Carlos de
Sigüenza y Góngora on the subject of comets, specifically the bright one
that had just been observed with so much dread. Sigüenza had published a
short work that cautiously deprecated the ominousness of comets and
developed some of the more modern theories of their nature and their
orbits; he already had been furiously attacked by several more conservative
authors. Chino apparently wished to demonstrate his own astronomical
learning by publishing a short book that asserted that everyone took seriously the ominousness of the comet, "unless there be some dull wits who
cannot perceive it." It is not likely Chino intended a direct reference to
Sigüenza, but the latter, ever the prickly and insecure creole, wrote a furious reply, which was not published until 1690; by that time Father Chino
was well settled in his mission field, and there is no evidence that he ever
knew how he had inadvertently offended.

Father Chino's first missionary assignment was an unsuccessful effort to
plant a mission on the forbidding coast of Baja California. Then in 1686
and 1687 he set out for a new assignment on the far northwest frontier of
the Spanish domains, in the Sonora Desert. The Italian spelling *Chino*, pronounced "kino" in Italian, was pronounced in Spanish as it would be in
English and meant "Chinese," sometimes an ethnic slur in Mexico and a too
painful reminder of his lost dream of the China missions. He began to spell
his name Kino.

In most of his many years in the Pimería, Kino made at least one long
trip on horse- or muleback through the deserts, seeking new sites for missions and Indians to convert. He often rode thirty miles a day, almost never
with any soldiers to escort him. Sometimes he found welcome when one
chief or group saw advantage in gaining the support of the Spanish against
another. But the more usual reasons for welcoming the black robe and his
little train of livestock and Indian helpers were healing and hunger. In the
desert year there were times when food was scarce and others when the

mesquite beans ripened and people got sick gorging on them. Agriculture and the storing of grain at the missions produced a more stable food supply, some of which Kino carried with him in his expeditions into the desert. The Pima also seem to have accepted Kino as a healer, staying by him if someone he treated and prayed over got well, following the ceremonies he taught them as they might have one of their own healer-shamans. Now little by little they themselves traveled to Dolores to see the strange healer, accept his little gifts, rest in the cool interior of the church, and stay at least for a time to dig some ditches, plant some crops, and eat regularly. They came on their own; by no means were there enough Spanish soldiers on this far frontier to force them to come.

In later years Kino worked indefatigably to plant more mission stations, always with provision for cattle ranching and a bit of irrigated agriculture. In addition to the native corn and beans, he encouraged the planting of wheat, onions, garlic, and a variety of European fruits and vegetables, including wine grapes so that the fathers could make their own wine for communion and for a very occasional drop with a distinguished visitor. When one adds the pioneering of desert cattle ranching, it is clear that Kino had brought a large number of new food resources to the relatively well-watered upland valleys of Sonora. Despite Kino's constant lobbying with his superiors in Mexico and Europe for more missionaries, there never were enough fathers to staff all the missions he started. Sometimes when the Pima heard of an influential visitor to Dolores, they would come many miles to plead for more fathers to bring the planting, medicine, and prayers to their areas once more.

Eusebio Kino made the mission at Dolores his base until his death in 1711. He pushed the frontier of his little mission empire north as far as San Xavier del Bac, about 130 miles north of Dolores, where a fine old church still stands on the outskirts of Tucson, Arizona. During his long journeys he gathered geographical knowledge as well as souls. It was generally believed that the long peninsula we call Baja California was an island and that the Gulf of California continued north to some kind of connection with the Pacific. A land route to Baja California would greatly facilitate efforts to establish missions and other settlements in those forbidding deserts, where the failed effort in which Kino had participated had been followed by others that were just barely hanging on. Several times Kino had crossed the daunting lava desert just south of the modern Arizona-Sonora border to the gulf. His observations suggested it was unlikely that the gulf continued to the north. In 1706, aged sixty-one, he led a party on a rugged muleback trip up Pinacate Mountain in the heart of the lava desert. The view of continuous coastline to the south and the curve into the Baja California coast to the southwest convinced all of them that California was not an island.

If Eusebio Kino had gotten his wish, he would have boarded another Spanish ship at Acapulco and crossed the Pacific to Manila. He might have joined a mission in the Philippines or perhaps, despite the jurisdictional claims of the Portuguese crown, made his way to his heart's desire in the China missions. Either one would have been very different from Sonora.

In May 1688 the city of Manila was agitated by rumors that the Chinese bakers were putting ground glass in the bread, which had been circulating for many months. The independent crown judge in his reports seemed to believe these rumors, but the governor found many things to doubt and imposed some fines but no more severe punishments. The crown judge, apparently fearing a further escalation of the quarrel, took refuge with the Jesuits. It is likely that the bakers had been adulterating the bread, but not lethally, and the crown judge had been too ready to listen to rumors amplified by the fear and hatred of the Chinese, a constant feature of life in Manila.

Manila in 1688 was a little more than a hundred years old, a small, fortified Spanish city with a few crowded neighborhoods outside its walls, situated at sea level on the waterlogged plain separating the inland Laguna de Bay from the excellent harbor of Manila Bay. Its Spanish governor claimed jurisdiction over the rest of the Philippine Islands but commanded only a few small garrisons and very little settlement or commerce elsewhere. The most important Spanish presence outside Manila was that of the great missionary orders—Jesuit, Franciscan, Dominican, and Augustinian—already well embarked on their singular achievement of making the Filipinos the only predominantly Christian people in Asia. Politically the Spanish authorities were an improbable appendage of the viceroyalty of New Spain, with its capital in Mexico. Economically Manila was the passive meeting point for two great phenomena of the seventeenth century: the stream of silver from the mines of Spanish America and the sophisticated manufactures and energetic commercial enterprise of the Chinese. Every year a galleon or two crossed the Pacific from Acapulco to Manila, bringing a cargo of New World silver to be used in buying Chinese silks, Chinese and Indian cottons, and other fine consumer goods that were in great demand in the New World. In Lima, it was said, even the slaves of the great households were dressed in Chinese silk. The goods were brought to Manila by a few ships from India or Java, but mostly by Chinese junks, largely from Xiamen and other ports of Fujian Province in South China. Spanish customs records list seventeen junks from China in 1685, twenty-seven in 1686, fifteen in 1687, but only seven in 1688. There may have been some falling off from 1685, but as so often in the decayed empire of Carlos II, massive collusion in customs evasion probably also contributed to the low total.

Manila depended on the Chinese for more than the trade with China. A few Chinese had traded and perhaps settled there before the Spanish conquered it in 1571. The infant Spanish settlement had almost been extinguished by a Chinese pirate. But thereafter thousands of Chinese had settled in the Manila area, and they provided almost all the craft production of the city—blacksmithing, leatherwork, tailoring, and of course baking—a singular occupation for South Chinese rice eaters living in a rice-growing country. Resident Chinese became key middlemen in the trade with the Chinese junks. They also contracted with the Spanish authorities for the monopolies of various retail trades and the collection of commercial taxes from the Filipinos. Some of them became Roman Catholic converts of every degree of purity and syncretism, fervor and opportunism. Most of them were typically low-profile, cautious mediators, although there also was a pirate/gangster element among the seagoing Chinese. There were violent streaks among the Filipinos as well, and to the usual Spanish hand-on-the-sword attitude was added the special flavor of a place where the American authorities could exile some of their worst problems; to Manila, said one eminent Dominican of the late 1600s, "are transported all the feces of New Spain."

Manila had been born in conflict with Chinese pirates and had been threatened by a dissident Chinese regime on Taiwan in the 1660s. Moreover, the Spanish had dreamed of a pure Christian commonwealth at this far end of the earth but had found themselves irremediably dependent on the heathen Chinese for its maintenance. Various blends of Spanish and Filipino fears and hatreds had been ignited in massacres of the Manila Chinese in 1603, 1639, and 1662. In 1683 there was some danger that the collapsing regime on Taiwan might try to save itself by attacking Manila. This may have contributed to fresh worries about the Chinese and new letters about them sent on their slow way around the world; all we know is that in September 1686 a royal order was issued in Madrid that all non-Christian Chinese were to be expelled from Manila. While that order was making its way back across the Atlantic and the Pacific, more trouble was brewing. The large numbers of Chinese ships arriving in 1686 brought quite a few immigrants, and the Spanish began to talk about new measures to keep them confined to the previously assigned Parian, or Chinatown. Rumors of these discussions may have set off a small outburst of violence, beginning when a band of Chinese assassinated the Spanish collector of the Chinese head tax in his own house in May 1686, and three other Spanish officials were seriously wounded in attacks on the same night. It was at this time that rumors of ground glass in the bread began to circulate. Several days of sporadic violence followed, while many Chinese fled their homes in fear of Spanish and Filipino retaliation. Seven suspects in the assassination were brought to trial, and order gradually was restored.

All this and the alleged plot of the bakers left the Spanish primed for action when the royal order of expulsion of non-Christian Chinese, sent from Madrid in September 1686, finally reached Manila in October 1688. The Chinese of course were at least the equals of the Spanish in delay and the manipulation of paper work. When the expulsion order was announced, some said they wanted to become Christians and requested prebaptismal instruction. Some asked to be allowed to stay until the Acapulco galleons came in because many Spaniards owed them money that they could not repay until they received the returns on their investments in the trade with Mexico. The Spanish authorities thought this reasonable and asked for a list of debtors and creditors but, when it came in, found that *all* the Chinese threatened with expulsion claimed to be creditors of the crown because of loans (probably forced) to help pay the Spanish garrison. Despite all this, it seems that about a thousand non-Christian Chinese were deported on the junks that came in 1690; but many more were not sent for lack of shipping, and the Spanish dependence on the Chinese and unwilling toleration of the non-Christians among them remained unbroken. Even today there are important Chinese elements in the Manila business elite, although their relations with the Filipino elite and government sometimes are uneasy. The Chinese cemetery of Manila, whose central chapel displays both Christian and Buddhist images, is one of the world's finer exhibits of a tolerant syncretism that now is more conspicuous than the bigotry of the seventeenth century.

CHAPTER 2

MANY AFRICAS

On February 22, 1688, an African local ruler who signed himself "Dom João Manoel Grilho, who treads on the lion in his mother's belly" wrote a letter in Portuguese from the town of Lemba on the lower reaches of the Congo River to an Italian Capuchin priest who was somewhere in the vicinity: "Praised be the Most Holy Sacrament. . . . Christ preserve you. I received with great pleasure your loving letter. . . . For my part as your spiritual son I remain most ready to receive your commands, and the same is true of your [spiritual] daughter, my mother Dona Potenciana. . . . I do not know when by God's mercy I will see the benign face of Your Paternity, or when you will come to save the souls of my sons." This letter, he explains, is being carried by a trusted slave who has orders to find the father, give him gifts, and discuss other important matters with him.

This phenomenon of a Kongo prince writing a letter in Portuguese (even if it was written for him by, say, a literate Portuguese in his employ) was the product of two hundred years of Kongolese adaptation to the Portuguese and to Christianity. In the decades after the arrival of the first Portuguese ships at the mouth of the Congo River in 1485, the Portuguese had been amazed to find a Kongolese king and much of his court converting to Christianity, learning Portuguese, writing letters to the pope and the king of Portugal, and sending embassies to Europe. Formal adherence to Christianity and kings with Portuguese names had continued in the kingdom of the Kongo down to a disastrous battle with the Portuguese in 1665 and the nearly complete collapse of the old kingdom.

Reading the records of this long connection in the light of modern knowledge of the cultures and religions of this region, we can understand a bit more of the complexity of the relation. For the Kongo people, the worlds of life and death were separated by an expanse and depth of water. The soul of the dead person went off into the water and there took on another body, colored white, and stayed in the tranquil realm of death. Those left behind paid homage to and sought to communicate with the dead at regular intervals. It is probable that the white-skinned Portuguese coming from across the water were greeted as if they had come from the kingdom of the dead. When Kongolese envoys took ship to Europe with them and came back telling of the wonders they had seen, it was clear that the newcomers had some compelling kinds of spiritual power. A Kongolese prince who converted and then had to fight to win the throne, becoming the first Christian king of the Kongo, tapped those sources of power. Much of the Kongo elite converted, and a dense web of Portuguese trade and influence developed. But the Kongolese soon discovered that they could pay for European goods only by exporting slaves, and the slave trade became the overwhelming reality of the relation. The kings did manage to keep the delivery of slaves within their kingdom orderly, passing through slaves taken in wars beyond their borders, condemning criminals to slavery, and extorting gifts of slaves from the rich and noble.

For the Kongolese elite in the big towns, Christianity and the Portuguese connection provided new forms of display through access to foreign goods and new ways to harness supernatural power, but they changed little of fundamental importance in Kongolese culture and politics. Out in the villages the occasional visiting missionary priest with his prayers, his ceremonies, his crosses to set up or give away usually was seen as a holy man of a somewhat novel type in contest with the indigenous ones but not radically different. Threats and intrigues from a new Portuguese center at Luanda, farther south on the coast, menaced the Kongo kingdom, but the most basic source of its instability in the seventeenth century was the arrival of dozens of Capuchin missionaries, sent by the Vatican Congregation for the Propagation of the Faith and not under Portuguese control. The Capuchins were much more intrusive and less willing to compromise with Kongolese custom than earlier Portuguese priests had been. Carrying their attacks on the traditional culture into many areas of the kingdom, the Capuchins united the Kongolese against the Europeans. In the resulting war with the Portuguese in 1665, the Kongolese king was killed, his capital was devastated, and the kingdom of the Kongo disintegrated.

In the mid-seventeenth century the Portuguese commanders at Luanda used ferocious African auxiliaries to spread violent slave raiding far inland. In 1656 one queen of a slave-raiding people made a treaty with the Portuguese admitting their traders and missionaries to her realm and obtaining a reliable outlet through Luanda for the slaves her armies captured. The raiding spread into the southern edge of the Kongo kingdom, accelerating its disintegration. The Portuguese had been convinced without much evidence that the raider queen's armies were cannibals; now the captives staggering out to the beach at Luanda looked at the great food cauldrons on the ships and were convinced that the white men were going to eat them.

Farther north, at the mouth of the Congo River, a major center of African-Portuguese interaction became nearly independent of Kongo, with its own set of connections to the north and inland, where Lemba, seat of power of "Dom João Manoel Grilho, who treads on the lion in his mother's belly," was a major riverside crossroads and trade center.

But what are we to make of this opaque little text? Can we hear the voice of Dom João Manoel Grilho? Not much can be made of the body of this little letter. His reference to his mother, Dona Potenciana, is important in a society where descent and rank were matrilineal. Perhaps he hoped the Father would come to "save the souls of his sons" because they had not yet been baptized. It is not likely, however, that he thought of baptism as completely different from other forms of divine cleansing and protection provided by the ancestors and local gods or as requiring the baptized to shun the local powers in the future. We come closer to a real African voice, though still with great difficulty, if we look again at the way the author of the message refers to himself: "Dom João Manoel Grilho, who treads on the lion in his mother's belly." In Kongo culture, down to our own times, praise names are sources of power, conferred after long and exacting ceremonies. We cannot find in these names, or in this culture in general, anything like our apparently sharp distinctions among wealth, political power, and supernatural efficacy. A man who had accumulated wealth, as our Dom João Manoel probably had through trade, could use some of it to pay for ceremonies that legitimated his local political dominance and gave him supernatural powers. In a way he *became* a charm, a powerful bundle of objects, what Europeans called a fetish. From modern times we have a record of one such ceremony that made a great man a new embodiment of powers that had originated when a woman gave birth to four things: a human being, a leopard, a snake, and a lump of chalk. These powers then also could be embodied in a charm object of leopard skin, snake skin, and chalk. The "lion" of the Portuguese text must be a mistake or broad usage for "leopard," as feared and revered in the forests as lions were on the savannas. The man who wears or sits on a leopard skin taps its power. Treading on, in these ceremonies and Kongolese explanations of them, implies violation, desecration, appropriation of powers. Is Dom João Manoel then claiming the power of one who already annihilated the leopard and stole his powers when they both were in the mother's womb? It is hard to imagine a knot of symbols more expressive of the Oedipal roots of will to power or more at odds with European Christian convention.

Were the sons ever baptized? Did Dom João Manoel Grilho live on, sitting on his leopard skin, in ambivalent communion with the Church of Rome, watching the boats, the long lines of porters? And what of the great river, already in his time sometimes called Congo and sometimes Zaire? Crossings of it, like the one at Lemba, were obvious centers of transshipment and extortion from trade. And not much farther up the river one could hear the roar of miles and miles of impassable rapids.

African storytellers performed prodigies of memory and transmission of ruling lineages and important events, but their accounts cannot be linked precisely enough to our dating system to focus on events in 1688. Where Islam already was influential, Arabic sources provide some dates. But still we are disproportionately dependent on Europeans feeling their way along the coast of Africa. We are interested in their experiences, their bafflements, frustrations, and very occasional successes. We also need to read against the grain of their records, to try with the help of modern historians, quite a few of them African, to understand a bit more of the African realities than the seventeenth-century Europeans did. The long connection with the Portuguese and the many writings of the Capuchins make the Kongo story one of the better-documented and richer cases for such reading. It is of great importance not only for the history of that area of Africa but also for Brazil, the destination of most of the slaves exported from Luanda. Europeans had many trading posts along the Gold Coast, roughly modern Ghana, but its history is much less clearly known; the Europeans rarely ventured far from their coastal forts and had only the most patchy understanding of what was going on inland.

For the Europeans in the 1680s a stretch of coast running east from the Gold Coast, roughly matching the coasts of the modern republics of Benin and Togo, between Ghana and Nigeria, was a zone of fresh promise and more than usual bafflement. In 1688 Jean-Baptiste Ducasse, an important agent of the French Company of Guinea, which held a very insecure royal monopoly of French trade on this coast, was visiting the coastal kingdom of Whydah in this region, attempting to establish good relations with the African rulers so that the French could regularly export slaves. The principal deity to whom the kings of Whydah paid homage was the python god Dangbe, resident in a shrine under a magnificent high tree about two miles from the capital town. Sometime in 1688, when the time came for King Agbangla of Whydah to make his annual ceremonial visit to the shrine of Dangbe, other European residents professed themselves scandalized to see Ducasse marching along in the procession, dressed in leopard skins "and other sorts of trifles."

The indignation was disingenuous. All Europeans were in Whydah on the sufferance of the king, participating in a trade controlled by his officials. Every European nation or company had a shrine to local gods somewhere in its compound. Europeans in this period had some interest in making sense of the African society and culture around them but little imaginative or emotional sympathy for it; even a mention of the "very beautiful lofty tree" under which the shrine of Dangbe was built stands out as a rare betrayal of feeling.

The scattered trees of this coastal region stood out impressively in the open landscape, so unlike the forests that came down to the shore farther east and west. This was the Dahomey gap in the forest belt, which made movement of goods and people much easier than in the dense forests, so that the gap became a natural focus of trade from inland. The python deities represented not only the power and danger of big snakes but also phallic power; one European observer tells us that during the crop-growing season people feared that pythons out at night would seize young women and drive them mad, so they kept the young women shut up in a special sanctuary in that season. Nor were female power and fertility neglected; kings and great men accumulated and displayed their wealth largely in the form of households full of dozens or even hundreds of wives and female dependents and slaves. Only a few served the king or shared his bed; most of them worked on his farms. Occasionally it was said that a jealous senior wife would force the king to sell a favored female slave to the Europeans. That was not the only way in which the power of female sexuality was present in the trade of the Europeans. Their most important import was cowrie shells, most of them from the Indian Ocean, especially from the seas around the Maldive Islands off southern India. Cowries had been used as money for thousands of years in places as far apart as China and West Africa. They were valued for their uniformity, durability, and the resemblance of their oval shape with a long cleft down the center to female external genitals.

The Europeans were glad to be able to sell cowries, metals, cloth, liquor, and increasing amounts of guns and gunpowder. They bought some ivory for the European market and other goods to be sold in other African ports. But by far the most important reason why they continued to swelter in the coastal heat, die of mosquito-borne diseases, make their baffled ways through volatile local politics, and occasionally even dress up in leopard skins was the ever-growing demand for slaves in the towns, mines, and plantations of the Americas.

There were very few places on the African coast, and Whydah was not one of them, where Europeans ventured more than a few miles from the coast. If they considered doing their own capturing and enslaving of Africans, cutting out the cost markups of the African middlemen, they simply didn't have many chances to take slaves in this way. At Whydah about one slave in twenty was of local origin, enslaved by actions of powerful Africans: judicial sentence, sale as surplus (or object of a senior wife's jealousy) out of some great man's household, or bondage through bad debts. Nineteen of twenty were brought down from the interior by merchants who had bought them in the towns of other kings and chiefs. Most of these slaves had been taken by violence—wars, raids on neighboring towns, ambushes as they went to their fields or to market. The growing European-American demand for slaves was increasing the incentives for the violence that fed the dreadful trade.

Few African participants in the trade had a full understanding of the horrors to which they were condemning the slaves they brought to the coast and sold: the fetid, crowded, pitching ships, the exhausting labor and brutal discipline of sugar plantations, the system of law and government that made the slave property a "chattel," not a person. In Africa—to make some very broad generalizations about hundreds of diverse societies and cultures—everyone fitted somewhere in a hierarchy of superiors and inferiors, which often was expressed in terms of a big family of senior and junior relatives. The positions we would call slave were inferior ones, but never void of human identity and connection, and often with chances to improve one's position by hard work, by sharing the senior man's bed and producing a child or by marrying another dependent of slightly higher status. Male slaves of warrior age, more dangerous and more likely to make common cause with the people from whose midst they had been captured, were more likely to be sold to traders who would resell them in some distant place. This fitted nicely with the coastal trade, where strong young men sold at a premium. But they still were human beings, while in a household or on their way to be sold.

That is not to say that King Agbangla of Whydah and his merchants and officials were not aware that selling slaves to the Europeans was different from selling them to other Africans. There was nothing in Africa like the ships rocking out in the surf. Many believed that the Europeans were buying the slaves and taking them away in order to eat them. But an insidious shift in the long-followed practices of slavery and the slave trade within Africa was under way. Kings and chiefs were increasingly eager to buy the goods brought by the Europeans, and now it was increasingly hard for them to defend themselves against their enemies without imported guns and gunpowder.

All slaves brought to Whydah were delivered to stoutly built stockades, where they were kept under the supervision of officials appointed by the king. The Europeans worked through African middlemen, also appointed by the king. Payment to the king for permission to trade was negotiated in advance. The king had the right to sell some of his slaves before the trade was open to others; often they were high in price, weak, and sickly. As trading then began with other sellers, the body of each slave was examined carefully without any respect for the modesty of men or women, and defective individuals were refused. Once slaves were selected, and their prices agreed on, they were branded with the mark of the European purchaser so that they could not be switched thereafter for less desirable slaves. All possible care was taken, our informant tells us, not to burn them too hard, especially the women, "who are more tender than the men." They were kept in the stockades, not at the offices of the buyers, until they were taken out to the ships.

Whydah and nearby ports probably exported six to seven thousand slaves in 1688. Early in the year shipments were very large; if they had continued at that level for the whole year, the total might have been more than twelve thousand. But then supplies from inland dropped off sharply, some traders paid higher prices for their slaves, and others accepted a higher proportion of women in their cargoes. Ducasse recorded that the interruption was the result of "some differences with the King of Fon in the interior, who prevents their passage."

This is characteristic of the vagueness of most European information about African politics, especially about areas which Europeans rarely saw. Fon was an early name for the kingdom later called Dahomey. It had begun its rise as an independent kingdom sometime earlier in the 1600s. By the 1680s it was a major supplier of slaves to the coast and was becoming more and more warlike, alternating slave-taking raids with mercenary service of its soldiers under other rulers. In the 1720s it broke out to the coast, conquering Whydah and nearby ports. Europeans who had to visit its capital brought back fearsome stories of its well-drilled soldiers adept in the use of firearms and its palace festooned with the skulls of enemies killed in its battles. A few such skulls could be seen even at the palace of the kings of Whydah in the 1680s, but the complete reshaping of Dahomean society by constant war, already beginning in 1688, was a result of the ever-growing need for war captives to be taken to the coast, branded, and put on the waiting ships.

At the farthest western bulge of Africa was one of the few regions where Europeans were managing by 1688 to gain any direct knowledge of the interior. There two great rivers flow down to the ocean, the Senegal and the Gambia. By 1688 Europeans had been trading in the region defined by the lower courses of the two rivers, which modern scholars call Senegambia, for more than two hundred years and had speculated about the possibility of access to the riches of the interior that the rivers might provide. But they had not managed to do more than maintain a fort or two at the mouth of each river, the French on the Senegal and the English on the Gambia, and occasionally send a small expedition upriver for some trading. They were entirely marginal to the complex political and economic life of the region.

The African peoples of Senegambia shared broad characteristics of language and society. Crops were at the mercy of highly variable rainfall. Heavy rains higher up the rivers produced unpredictable floods, which might wipe out a crop and at the same time leave a layer of fertile silt for the next year's planting. North of the Senegal there rarely was enough rain for a crop, but one of the area's important commercial resources was the gum, like gum arabic, that was collected from wild trees. The edge of the desert near the Senegal also was a cultural frontier; the people who came in out of the desert on their horses and camels had lighter skins, spoke Arabic or Berber, and were culturally and socially oriented to the world of Islam.

The Senegal frontier experienced episodes of militant Muslim intrusion; a new series of Moroccan raids south of the Sahara was already under way in the 1680s and was to become more threatening in the early 1700s. But the really effective carrier of the message of Muhammad here, as in many parts of the world, was peaceful trade. Arab and Berber merchants might affect the beliefs of Senegambian merchants, or they might settle down, marry local women, and raise their children as Muslims. Local rulers might employ Muslims for their literacy and be influenced by their beliefs. Thus, although traditional worship of ancestors and many other gods and spirits remained strong in the countryside everywhere, there were many in the towns who were more or less good Muslims. A teacher or a local resident who had acquired a stronger conception of orthodox Islam at school or on a pilgrimage to Mecca might lead a movement for Islamic purification of a whole court or city; by 1688 a first wave of such movements had reached its peak and subsided. More peaceful adjustments were possible; a Muslim teacher and his followers might be allowed a good deal of autonomy in a ward of a town or a separate town. In the 1680s a group of people of varied origin had followed their teacher into a sparsely populated area between the upper courses of the Senegal and the Gambia and were setting up their own state, which would be an important factor in the politics of the region and would be ruled by several dynasties of imams, or Muslim prayer leaders. Elsewhere networks of long-distance traders called *juula* were more observant of Islam than the rest of the population and frequently lived in their own quarters of towns.

In these societies everyone had a place, but that place might change. Rules of kinship determined who was eligible to become a local ruler or one of his officials. Blacksmiths, dealing in the dangers of molten metal and the making of weapons and therefore thought to have special spiritual powers, kept somewhat apart from society and married only among themselves. There also was a considerable population of slaves. Only those who had been bought from elsewhere could be sold. Many had secure status as subordinate members of their masters' households. Some were royal slaves, who might become very powerful if employed as soldiers or administrators.

Both the Arab and Berber traders from the desert and the Europeans on the coast bought slaves in Senegambia, but the supply was highly variable; only in a period of major internal warfare late in the 1500s did the region supply a large percentage of the slaves crossing the Atlantic. In the 1680s slaves counted for slightly over half of the value of European exports from the region. Other trade goods, for the Europeans and the North African Muslims, were the products of a varied and commercialized regional economy. Iron was widely smelted and worked, and the best products were of very good quality. Cotton was grown, and cotton textiles were woven for local use and trade within the region. Other goods that moved in interregional trade and also appealed to outsiders were the gum arabic mentioned above, cattle hides, beeswax, ivory, and gold. Gold was produced in small quantities by methods that involved digging and sorting large quantities of soil and gravel. This work was done by peasants during the season when no farm work was done and was a modest source of supplementary income, probably not enough to pay for the workers' food while they were engaged in it.

But any appearance of gold in trade was enough to drive Europeans mad. Sweltering in their forts at the mouths of the two great rivers, watching six out of every ten new arrivals die during the first year, they hatched project after project to explore up the great rivers, open direct trade there for slaves and other exports, and find the sources of those trickles of gold. In July 1688 one sieur de Chambonneau was in Paris, reporting to the authorities of the Royal Company of Senegal, one of a succession of French companies that sought without much success to expand and monopolize French trade on the African coast, on his remarkable explorations up the Senegal River in 1686 and 1687. In 1687 his men, on two small barks, had made it all the way to the Felu Falls, the head of navigation on the Senegal, more than five hundred miles from the mouth of the river. The local ruler had received them hospitably and had told them they were not far from the great inland trading city of Timbuktu or from one of the upper branches of the Gambia. The French explorers also thought the Senegal would be navigable above the Felu Falls; it was not. The local ruler promised them a quantity of gold within eight days, but they could stay there only one day, "everyone on the barks being ill, because they had been eating only millet, and because of the great heat of June, July, and August and the continual rains."

Chambonneau's proposed solution to these difficulties, in his 1688 report, was radical. France should send an expedition of twelve hundred men and women, including four hundred soldiers, to take possession of some of the rich lands along the lower Senegal and establish a real European settler colony. The natives would resist for a few months but then would acquiesce, since there was no private property in land in their societies and there was plenty of uncultivated land in any case. The French, farming their own land and having few or no slaves, could grow wheat, so that all Frenchmen in the area could eat bread instead of millet, which they thought unhealthy; tobacco, of which excellent quality already was being grown; sugar; indigo; cotton; and even silk. The settlers would not compete with the Royal Company of Senegal for slaves and other exports but rather would provide it with fresh food for its trading posts and new exports, in the tobacco and other cash crops of their farms. Drawing much on failed ideas for European settler colonies in the West Indies, ignoring the real obstacles of climate, disease, and local people quite able to defend their own lands, this was an amazingly unrealistic proposal, and we have no evidence that it ever was given serious consideration.

From their bases on the Gambia River the English were well aware of the French advances along the Senegal and were doing what they could to explore the potentialities of trade up their river, though as far as we can tell without any fevered dreams of European housewives spinning cotton and tending silkworms on the banks of an African river. The report of one Cornelius Hodges on his explorations up the Gambia in 1689 and 1690 adds much to our understanding of the obstacles the Europeans faced and the uncertainties of the commercial rewards upriver. The river was hard to navigate at low water; but once the rains started, it ran "like a sluice," and sometimes there was nothing the English could do except head back downstream with the flood. At various points along the river people seemed to have good stocks of ivory that they were eager to sell. In one area there had been a gold boom, begun in 1683, when an old woman noticed flecks of gold on the roots of a tuber, but recent years of drought and famine had brought production to a halt. Advancing across the Senegal and out into the desert fringe, Hodges also noted reports of the menacing Moroccan raids not far off.

In the eighteenth century the trade of the Europeans on the Senegal and the Gambia expanded, primarily in slaves (but still only a small percentage of the massive eighteenth-century stream across the Atlantic). The Moroccan raids and the trans-Sahara connections also continued to shape Senegambia. The closing down after 1800 of the slave trade across the Atlantic was followed by a remarkable growth in the gum arabic trade and by the intrusion of French imperial power, but never by anything like the sieur de Chambonneau's colony of cash-cropping French farmers.

In the centuries before 1688 the major routes of trade in West Africa led out from the northern edges of the forest belt and across the savannas to the jumping-off points for caravans across the Sahara. The centers of empire building were at or near those jumping-off points. By about 1800 the dynamics of trade had shifted decisively toward the coast, and the most important centers of state building were those, like Dahomey, that were not on the coast but largely oriented toward dominating it. Dependent on European sources and better informed about coastal ports and maritime trade than about anything else in African history, we are likely to see the growth of maritime trade as the main cause of the shift. It was important, but there were other changes inland.

Not until the late eighteenth century did Europeans explore above the Felu Falls. But many Africans knew the routes to the east, farther up the branches of the Senegal and then overland to the upper reaches of the great river Europeans were to call the Niger. A long run down the Niger, almost as far as from the mouth of the Senegal to the Felu Falls, would take the traveler to Timbuktu, which became an English metaphor for impossible remoteness but in African perspective was an important and well-known crossroads and center of culture. Another two hundred miles down the river was another great crossroads, Gao. From there it still was more than twelve hundred miles to the forests and mangrove swamps where the Niger met the Atlantic.

In 1688 Timbuktu and Gao were shadows of their flourishing days. For centuries the focuses of power and trade in West Africa had been along the Niger, where the trade routes took off across the Sahara to the Mediterranean coast. Islam had come along those trade routes and put down deep roots; Timbuktu had many mosques and schools, with scholars who wrote in Arabic about African history and Islamic topics. The disruption of trans-Sahara connections and prosperity after 1500 had many sources. The Ottoman Empire advanced along the southern shore of the Mediterranean, disrupting trans-Sahara trade temporarily. The Portuguese mounted a long, nasty, disruptive, and pointless invasion of Morocco. Partly as a result of that disruption, Moroccan forces crossed the desert in 1591, devastated Timbuktu, and maintained a loose presence along the Niger for decades. Nomads invaded from the desert; in 1688 they held Gao and threatened Timbuktu. One people had built a wide structure of power upriver from Timbuktu, but it was falling apart after the death of their most capable leader about 1680. Moreover, on the Senegambia frontier, as we have seen, Moroccan raids were again becoming more frequent. The really massive changes in trade and state building in the forest belt were just beginning in 1688, but on the Niger, far from European eyes, Timbuktu and the other splendid old crossroads cities were in long declines, which the rise of the coast would simply accelerate and make irreversible.

CHAPTER 3

SLAVES, SHIPS, AND FRONTIERS

Two young Frenchmen, Jean l'Archevêque and Jacques Groslet, spent much of 1688 living among the Caddo Indians of what is now East Texas. Sometime around the end of the year they took a precious relic of their European origins, a parchment with a painting of a ship on it, wrote two messages on it, tied a fine lace neckcloth around it, making a kind of fetish of its European origin that would be instantly recognized by any European, and sent if off in the hands of a friendly Indian. One of the messages can be read in full:

Sir:
I do not know what sort of people you are. We are Frenchmen. We are among the savages. We would like very much to be among the Christians, such as we are. We know well that you are Spaniards. We do not know if you will attack us. We are very vexed to be among beasts like these who believe neither in God or in anything. Sirs, if you are willing to take us away you have only to send something in writing. Since we have little or nothing to do, as soon as we see the note we will come to you.

Sir, I am your very humble and obedient servant,
Jean l'Archevêque of Bayonne.

Much less of Jacques Groslet's note on the same parchment can be read; he says they are young men and have given the parchment to someone to bring to the Spaniards.

When the two young men finally met a Spanish party in May 1689, their skins were painted like Indians' and they wore nothing but deer skins. They had been on their own among the Indians of Texas for about two years. The Spanish sent them on to Mexico City, and they were able to continue on to Spain before the end of 1689.

These two young men were among the last-known survivors of the effort of Robert Cavelier, sieur de La Salle, to extend French power and trade down from the middle of North America and to plant an outpost on the coast of the Gulf of Mexico. La Salle had the keen sense of strategic geography and commercial opportunity that is characteristic of all great founders of empires; he saw that the French, starting from their bases on the St. Lawrence, could create a real empire in the middle of North America before the Spanish or the English could stop them, by building on the beginnings they already had made in the fur trade, using large cargo vessels and permanent posts on the Great Lakes and the Mississippi River system. His vision did not even stop there: In 1684 he obtained royal approval and led almost three hundred settlers to found an outpost on Matagorda Bay, near the modern site of Corpus Christi, Texas. Very much on his mind were the silver mines of northern Mexico and the possibility of access to those areas via the river we now call the Rio Grande; he sent several small expeditions to probe up the river and make friends with the Indians there.

But La Salle's choice of a location for a first settlement was disastrous. The area was low-lying and swampy, and it meagerly supported a sparse Indian population. Malnutrition and disease soon began to reduce the little colony. Its last two ships were driven aground and destroyed on coastal sandbars. It now seemed vital to open a route to the northeast and to get help from the French settlements in the Mississippi River valley. In January 1687 La Salle set out to the northeast at the head of a small party. The rivers were flooded, the Texas plains were almost impassable, his men became mutinous, and some were deserting. Finally, on March 19, La Salle was shot by his own men. Jean l'Archevêque apparently was among the mutineers, but not the actual assassin; Jacques Groslet already had deserted to try life among the Indians but later rejoined the French party. When the party set out northeast toward the Mississippi in May, the two young men turned back.

However homesick they may have been for Christian society, the young Frenchmen were far better off among the Caddo than they would have been among the Karankawa around La Salle's fort on the coast. The Karankawa had killed most Frenchmen who fell into their hands and eked out a miserable existence scavenging whatever washed up on the beach. The Caddo had an ordered way of life, with regular cooperation in farming and house building, grave deliberation in governing, good order and lack of crime in their towns, that few parts of France could have matched in 1688. Growing corn, beans, pumpkins, squash, berries, and fruit in the good soil and mild climate of what is now East Texas, fishing and hunting deer and bear, they were less likely to go to bed hungry than peasants in many parts of France. Acknowledging a god in heaven, lighting all their fires from a perpetual sacred fire in a special temple, sending off their dead with moving ceremony, they followed a cycle of rites tied to the agricultural year. They made beautiful baskets and reed mats, sturdy leather clothing, and some of the finest pottery of aboriginal North America. Already in the 1680s they were getting trade goods from French settlements to the east and horses—descendants of those brought by the Spanish—from the tribes of the plains to the west. They were confident of their ability to welcome French or Spanish visitors without losing control of the situation. Later they won the respect even of the early missionaries who wanted to change their way of life at its roots.

Perhaps the young Frenchmen could not get over the sight of enemy scalps hanging in the houses. Perhaps they had seen a prisoner of war tortured to death. Perhaps they could not overcome their revulsion at the elaborate tattoos with which the Caddo covered their heads and chests, which Europeans usually described as "disfiguring." Both the Frenchmen were tattooed, or perhaps just painted, on their faces and arms when the Spanish found them.

L'Archevêque and Groslet could not return to France because France and Spain were at war from 1690 to 1698. They were taken to Spain, then back to Mexico, and, their names Hispanicized as Archibeque and Gurule, joined in the reconquest of the upper Rio Grande Valley from the Pueblo Indians who had expelled the Spanish in 1680. L'Archevêque/Archibeque became a prosperous trader and interpreter and a respected adviser on Indian affairs at Santa Fe. In 1720 he accompanied an expedition out onto the high plains to the east against some Pawnee who apparently had a Frenchman advising them and was killed by the Pawnee. Today large numbers of Archibeques and Gurules, proud of their distinctive origins, may be found in New Mexico and in southern California.

In 1688 Europeans found themselves on American frontiers, along Atlantic coasts and islands from the Río de la Plata to the St. Lawrence, along inland rivers, and in a few places far inland like Potosí. Sometimes they were as completely on their own and dependent on the goodwill of the native people as l'Archevêque and Groslet. Sometimes they conquered and transformed a region as completely as the Spanish had at Mexico City and at Potosí. A few saw in a frontier of European settlement and power an opportunity for a new beginning for humankind. Sometimes European violence destroyed and built nothing. But some settlers worked patiently to make the land their own, even in the small space of Jamaica.

In 1688 Major Francis Price, his wife, and their three children were living in a substantial wooden house—three rooms on the ground floor, three on the second, kitchen, washhouse, buttery, and coach house in separate buildings—on his estate of Worthy Park in the beautiful Lluidas Vale in central Jamaica. Ringed with wooded mountains, its climate cooler than the coast, with good soil and ample but not excessive rain, the vale was one of the most promising agricultural areas in the entire island and one of the most comfortable places for a European to live. Originally forested, by 1688 it was supporting substantial herds of cattle. Dr. Hans Sloane, visiting Jamaica in 1688, noted that Lluidas Vale was especially famous for its excellent but expensive veal and that such backcountry farms also raised pigs, to be slaughtered, smoked, and sold as "jerked pork," and turkeys to sell in Spanish Town, the largest coastal town, west of modern Kingston.

Major Price, so called from his rank in the colonial militia, twice served as a member of the assembly. In 1688 he and his fellow settlers frequently shared the small stage of island politics with an unusual royal governor, the duke of Albemarle, whom we shall encounter later in this book, and with an extraordinary representative of a kind of frontiersman very different from the peaceful and hardworking frontier farmers. Henry Morgan, lieutenant governor of the little colony, was a not very thoroughly reformed buccaneer, given official rank and powers and ordered to turn his considerable talents for war and intrigue to the suppression of other buccaneers. The buccaneers had had their origins as deserters and escapees who lived on their own on the islands. They hunted the large numbers of feral pigs and cattle, curing the meat on big wooden frames—*boucans*—over smoky fires for sale to colonies and ships. As the rulers of the islands, especially the Spanish on Hispaniola, sought to push them out, the buccaneers turned more and more to pillage of ships and towns. The English, the French, and the Dutch all commissioned them to attack the Spanish or other enemies at one time or another. Year after year the buccaneers brought the treasure of looted Spanish ports to Port Royal, on the coast of Jamaica near modern Kingston, to spend in orgies of drink, sex, and fighting that shocked even those accustomed to the dock areas of London and Amsterdam. In 1670 Henry Morgan led a march across the Isthmus of Panama to sack Panama City. From that year on, however, all the European rulers wanted to move toward peaceful development of their island colonies. They sought to promote trade, including trade in Spanish ports, and to suppress the buccaneers. Morgan did his part sometimes in campaigns against his former comrades. He died in August 1688. The gradual suppression of the buccaneers continued. In 1692 there was a great earthquake, and much of Port Royal sank beneath the ocean. One did not have to be a Puritan preacher to talk of divine punishment.

In 1688 the interior of Jamaica harbored yet another kind of frontier, the settlements of the escaped slaves, or Maroons. They were especially prevalent in the cockpit country, full of limestone cliffs and sinkholes, where a single armed watchman might be able to protect the narrow access to a cliff-bound sinkhole where hundreds of people planted their gardens and lived in peace and freedom. The Maroons also had their origins in the days of Francis Price; slaves of the Spanish had been left to run more or less free and to herd cattle in the interior. Some of them had had small farms in Lluidas Vale, had been pushed out by the English, and had retreated toward the less accessible mountains to the west. There were reports of slave escapes in 1684 and 1686 and of a bigger outbreak in 1690; soon these people were to form the nucleus of growing settlements of fugitives from the growing numbers of slaves on the sugar plantations.

There was a persistent conflict of interests in the Caribbean between settlers like Francis Price and merchant groups, especially the Royal African Company, that wanted to sell slaves not just to English settlers but to the highest bidders, who often were the Spanish. The Spanish took no direct part in the African end of the trade at this period, but their American possessions were the ultimate destination of perhaps one-fifth of all slaves that reached the New World in the late seventeenth century. Fearing Protestant pollution of their Catholic realm and breach of their monopolies of gold and silver, the Spanish forbade almost all trade between their settlers in America and other Europeans. Spanish settlers got their slaves by welcoming foreign ships to their ports in violation of royal commands, by going to Jamaica, Curaçao, and so on to trade, and by taking advantage of a major legal concession called the asiento, in which a Spanish or foreign merchant combine received, in return for a large advance on the duties it would owe and other contributions to the Spanish crown, a near monopoly of the legal delivery of slaves to Spanish American ports. In 1688 this practice had led to the baroque tangle of the Coymans asiento.

A baroque style can be seen in more facets of this period than literature and the arts, for Sor Juana and Purcell and Vivaldi. In politics and trade there also were many cases of elaborate structure and formal argument from which the underlying realities emerged only occasionally but dramatically. In the early 1680s the asiento was held by a Spanish merchant house headed by Juan Porcio. It is clear that he in fact obtained many of his slaves from the Dutch and that the residents of Cartagena and other mainland Spanish ports also were delighted to trade with any Dutch or English ship that came along, no matter what was said in Madrid. Porcio encountered financial difficulties in 1684 and was unable to make his payments to the crown, alleging that the local authorities in Cartagena were working against his interests.

In 1685 the authorities in Madrid began negotiations with Balthasar Coymans, a Dutch resident in Cádiz, who clearly was working for the interests of the important Amsterdam merchant house of Johan Coymans, which was less openly fronting for the Dutch West India Company and the interests of its slave trade emporium at Curaçao. An agreement soon was reached under which Balthasar Coymans was to administer the asiento originally granted to Porcio, making an immediate payment toward some frigates for the Spanish navy being built in Holland and an advance on the dues he would be liable for on goods imported to Spanish America.

Porcio of course had wanted the Spanish court to give him new concessions and financial assistance, not take his asiento away from him, and now he sought allies in his attacks on the new arrangement. He found them especially in ecclesiastical quarters, where it was feared that heretic ships in Spanish American ports would lead to contamination of the Catholic faith, especially among recent converts whose faith still was inadequately nurtured and disciplined. The discussions now wound on with the complexity and slowness for which the Spanish court was famous. The objections of the churchmen made a good deal of sense to the dimly conscientious and devout Carlos II, and late in 1686 he appointed a special commission to study the question. But in 1687 the Dutch government and the West India Company showed their hands, alleging that the contract with the heirs of Balthasar Coymans, who had died in 1686, was a firm royal commitment and could not be reconsidered by a commission of dubious authority. In June 1688 the commission delivered an opinion that the Dutch must recognize its authority before discussions could proceed. The Dutch, in any case, had continued to ship slaves and goods to Curaçao to be sold in Spanish American ports, asiento or no; in 1688 they had about five thousand slaves ready for sale in Curaçao. Of course the local Spanish authorities were happy to tolerate the trade with them. In 1689 the Spanish court canceled the Coymanses' asiento and returned the contract to Porcio. The Coymanses continued to protest, and Madrid continued to form committees to study the matter, but the Coymanses' objections were ignored, and the Spanish apparently never returned the first payments Balthasar Coymans had made back in 1685. But the Spanish in America remained dependent on supplies of slaves and goods from the Dutch and from the growing trades of the English and the French.

The ultimate baroque concealment of the asiento was that it legalized, commercialized, and quantified the involuntary transportation of many thousands of terrified and miserable Africans and made possible their sale and continued enslavement in the Americas. Modern works on the slave trade often include maps showing a tangle of black lines of varying widths from various African ports, coalescing in mid-Atlantic and then diverging to destinations from the Caribbean to the Río de la Plata. Slaves from Angola mostly stayed within the Portuguese sphere and were sold in Brazil. Those from the many ports and kingdoms between the Senegal and the Niger usually passed through the West Indies and either stayed there or were sold in Spanish mainland ports.

The black ship rocked out beyond the surf, sometimes scarcely visible in the hot, damp air. On the shore the slaves were sold to the Europeans, branded, and taken out in longboats to the ship. By the time the ship completed its cargo and set sail, many of the captives had already spent several weeks on board, locked up belowdecks at night, brought out on deck during the day for meals and for regular enforced dancing and other exercise. Many of them were convinced that when the ship arrived on the far side of the water, the white men would eat them. Some were watching for a chance to overpower the watchful crew and escape to the shore before it was too late. Others were refusing to eat, believing that if they starved to death, their souls would return to the African shore.

Desperation was especially acute as the ship hoisted sail and left the shore behind. Sailors stood on the fore and aft decks with lighted fuses, ready to discharge small cannons toward the crowd of slaves at any sign of disorder. The lucky ship caught a good wind and made a quick voyage. But if it was unlucky or too late in the season, it might spend days or weeks becalmed before it got away from coastal waters. The captain of course was concerned to keep his cargo alive; a dead slave thrown to the waiting sharks was a loss on his account books. The best captains paid careful attention to the feeding of their slaves—primarily cornmeal mush, seasoned with peppers that were thought to prevent or moderate intestinal disorders. On a well-managed ship, overcrowding was avoided, the holds were regularly cleaned out with vinegar and hot water, and the routine of regular exercise was kept up. But much depended on luck, not only with the winds but in the avoidance of contagious diseases that despite all precautions might sweep through the holds, killing half the slaves, or even all, and in a few cases all the crew as well.

Modern historians may not agree with seventeenth-century (or twentieth-century) ideas on the importance of the bullion trade, but they are far more likely than contemporaries were to recognize the vast changes on both sides of the Atlantic resulting from the African slave trade. In 1688 European condemnation of the enslavement of Africans, a vital element in European political debate a hundred years later, had scarcely begun. (Later in this book we look at one of the first pieces of antislavery literature, *Oroonoko*, published in 1688, and at its author, Aphra Behn.) When participants in the slave trade in the 1680s wrote about it, their views and even their language betrayed not the consistent defensiveness of men reacting against moral and political attacks on their livelihoods but inconsistency and ambivalence. On one page they might exclaim that there was no difference between the Africans and themselves except skin color and call them "poor wretches," then turn to self-pity on the next page and call themselves "slaves" to the dreadful business.

Doing our best with patchy figures, we might hypothesize for 1688 a total English purchase of slaves on the coasts of Africa of five thousand. The Portuguese trade from Angola to Brazil was larger, perhaps shipping seven thousand, while the Dutch West India Company, with fine bases on the African coast and a thriving slave depot at Curaçao, may have shipped another three thousand, and the Danes, Prussians, and French still another two thousand, for a speculative total of seventeen thousand. The English Royal African Company records trade in 1688 at the mouth of the Gambia, on the Gold Coast, at Whydah, and at Benin and Calabar, all areas where it had permanent forts of its own or well-established places of business in coastal towns under African administration. But *one-third* of the company's total investment was in goods for voyages to the Windward Coast, a stretch roughly equivalent to the modern coasts of Liberia and Côte d'Ivoire. There were no forts, no settled European presence on these coasts. Ships seeking trade kept close to shore, and Africans with slaves or other goods to sell signaled their presence by smoke signals. Some thought it a slow and uncertain trade, but the traders and the companies liked the lack of the fixed expenses and local entanglements of fort or settlement, and down to 1690 the Windward Coast trade was an important contributor to Africa's total trade with the European ships. Thereafter the Windward Coast could not offer either the security the Europeans needed when they were at war with each other or the reliable and increasing supplies of slaves needed as the trade grew in the eighteenth century. Still, it remained important for some traders some of the time. Since there were no permanent European observers onshore, even less than usual is known about the organization of trade on the African side of the Windward Coast. But somehow it was efficient enough, and African resistance to selling other Africans was low enough, that this zone without permanent ports or European stations provided as many as a thousand slaves to company and other British merchants in the one year 1688.

On the eve of Pentecost in 1688 Father Antonio Vieira of the Society of Jesus preached a sermon in the chapel of the Jesuit College in Bahia in Brazil. He began with the double image of the tongues of fire that appeared above the apostles on that day of dread and grandeur and of God's destruction of the Tower of Babel by the multiplication of tongues: "Such was the transgression, and such the chastisement in ancient times, but today we are on the eve of a day on which, turning from justice to mercy, and wanting to build a tower of his own, God took the trace of the transgression, and from the chastisement his instruments. . . . This tower is the Catholic Church. . . . What were the instruments with which God struck down and chastised the Tower of Babel? They were the new and various tongues into which the universal tongue which all spoke was divided and multiplied. Thus for this the Holy Spirit descended on the Apostles, in the form of tongues, many, and divided."

Father Vieira's sermons were masterpieces of baroque rhetoric. In this one we see a brilliant use of reversal, as language becomes first an instrument of God's wrath and then of His church and of the work of the Holy Spirit. There was a growing fascination with the multiplicity of tongues and with the lost Adamic language as ocean-crossing Europeans discovered the full variety of human speech. But Father Vieira had more in mind than the elaborate recalling of a key moment in the work of the Holy Spirit in the church. He was speaking to fellow Jesuits of all ages, including novices, and he did not like the trend of language learning and language use among his confreres of the Jesuit Province of Brazil.

Vieira, a vigorous preacher, was arguing for major changes in mission policy. Already eighty years old, he had just begun a three-year term in the important office of Visitor of the Jesuit Province of Brazil. He had grown up in Bahia and run away from his parents to the Jesuit College, where he now was preaching. As a novice he had served in an inland mission and learned to speak the Tupi-Guarani language used to communicate with most Brazilian Indians. Everywhere in the world the Jesuits took seriously the need to learn the languages of the people to whom they wished to preach, becoming the European world's first masters of the languages of the Huron, the Iroquois, the Chinese, the Japanese, and the Tamils of southern India. In the Brazilian Jesuit colleges and missions of Vieira's youth it was said that Tupi-Guarani was used as much as Latin.

It probably was talent as a preacher that led to his selection in 1641 as one of the bearers of assurances of Brazilian loyalty to João IV of Portugal, who had just broken away from Spanish rule and reestablished an independent Portuguese monarchy. João was generally sympathetic to the Jesuits, and Vieira became influential at court. On a visit to Amsterdam he had long conversations with Rabbi Menasseh ben Israel, who was writing a prophetic work titled *The Hope of Israel*. Those conversations, recurring apocalyptic prophecies about the coming triumphs of the Portuguese monarchy as God's instrument, and Vieira's deep identification with the missions to the Indians began to interact in his fertile mind.

In 1653 Vieira returned to Brazil as superior of the Jesuit missions in the Amazon basin. For him and his colleagues this was the greatest frontier. Every journey up the enormous river seemed to lead to an exploration up a different tributary and the discovery of more Indian peoples, strange and frequently alarming in their body paint and their dress or lack of dress, sometimes dangerous with their poison darts shot from blowguns but more often just wary and responsive to patience and kindness. Along the rivers where traders came and went the missionaries usually could find someone who spoke Tupi-Guarani, but beyond those first contacts they had to deal with an ever-growing Babel of languages that taxed even their zeal and commitment to language learning. Many of their first-stage conversions no doubt represented quite limited understanding and commitment, largely responses to the kindness, gifts, and medicines of the Jesuits and efforts to tap the new sources of supernatural power they seemed to represent. But the conversions were counted in the tens of thousands in Vieira's first two years. That meant trouble between the Portuguese settlers and the Jesuits, who tried to protect their converts from the labor levies of the settlers and the dissipations of the frontier towns. Vieira tried to be conciliatory, hoping to draw the settlers into his vision of a glorious multiracial Christian destiny for the Amazon. Since there was no printing press in the region and many of the settlers couldn't read anyway, his skills as a preacher were especially vital. But there was no end of conflict.

In 1655 Vieira was back in Lisbon, lobbying effectively for new regulations protecting Indian converts and for the appointment of a governor who would enforce them. In Lenten sermons in Lisbon he dwelled on the sinfulness of old Europe and the image of the Jews following the pillar of fire in their Exodus to the Promised Land. The Portuguese already had opened up new promised lands in their world-girdling voyages, and now they must follow God's will into their empire, especially Brazil, where the sins of the Old World would be redeemed and history would open out toward the universal victory of Christ. Vieira returned to the Amazon. A long journey to the Ibiapaba Mountains in 1659 led to many conversions. He began filling out his millennial expectations for the Amazon in a work he titled *The Hopes of Portugal*, much of it written in dugout canoes. He continued his dual strategy of conciliating the settlers and protecting the Indians—to no avail. In 1661 the settlers rebelled and expelled the Jesuits from the Amazon.

Vieira again took the Jesuit case to Lisbon. He preached that prophecies in the Bible, especially the prophecy of a fifth empire in the Book of Daniel, referred to the coming Christian realm in the New World. It was not he commenting on Scripture, he said, but Scripture commenting on him and his experiences. The fact that these prophecies had not yet been fulfilled confirmed that they were indeed prophetic. The Book of Daniel's mysterious phrase translated as either "bells with wings" or "ships with wings" was a prophetic anticipation of the war canoes of the Indians of the Amazon with big drums on their bows.

The death of João IV in 1656 had given new openings for anti-Jesuit forces. From 1663 to 1668 Vieira was held in house arrest and in prison by the Inquisition and pressed to recant his more extreme prophetic views. His conviction of his own prophetic rightness deepened by his stay in prison, he denied the jurisdiction of the Inquisition but submitted to royal authority and went into self-imposed exile in Rome, where he was forbidden to preach but had many admirers. In 1681 he returned to Brazil. There he abandoned his efforts to draw the settlers into his visions of Christian empire, worked to expand missionary efforts in areas remote from Portuguese settlement, and turned the Jesuit novitiate at São Luis de Maranhão into a seminary for the Amazon missions. Thus it was that in 1688, the newly appointed Visitor, he was haranguing several generations of younger colleagues about the decline of Jesuit learning of Amerindian languages and even arguing that they ought to learn some of the languages spoken by the African slaves in the coastal areas.

Later in 1688 Vieira preached a sermon in celebration of the birth of a royal prince and heir in Lisbon. (Another royal infant of destiny, like the one in London in the same year, whose birth was to seal the fate of the House of Stuart!) This news rekindled his hopes that the Portuguese monarchy would fulfill its worldwide destiny and become the prophesied fifth empire. He did not know that the infant prince had lived for only eighteen days. Vieira largely retreated from public life in 1691 and died in 1697 at the age of eighty-nine.

In the eighteenth century the Jesuits made some advances in conversion and protection of their converts in the Amazon, against continued furious settler opposition, until they were expelled from the Spanish and Portuguese empires and their society was suppressed in the 1750s and 1760s. The real transformation of the Brazilian frontiers began soon after 1688, as word filtered out to the coastal cities of gold strikes in the inland area that soon was called Minas Gerais, the "general mines." Gold rushes, a diamond rush, armed struggles between *bandeirantes* and other settlers, and savage government efforts to get the revenue created a brutal frontier world. Brazil and Portugal entered an age of opulent church and palace building that could not entirely conceal a frontier world with little room for Father Vieira's dreams of the final frontier of the human spirit.

The conditions of the Portuguese Empire in America that provoked Father Vieira's dreams were at least as violent and sordid as those of the West Indies, and on a much larger scale. The bases of the Portuguese were along the Atlantic coast of what is now Brazil. The first important source of wealth for the settlers and the home government, beginning in the 1530s, had been the sugar plantations of the northeast, in decline in 1688, as West Indian production began to grow. Sugar production in the New World was inseparable from the exploitation of African slave labor. Far to the south the Portuguese had a small colony at Sacramento on the Río de la Plata that was above all a center for the smuggling of silver out the back door of Spanish America, from the mines of Potosí. A bigger center at São Paulo was the opening into a complex system of inland river valleys that were incessantly explored by Brazil's most famous frontiersmen, the *bandeirantes*. The business of the *bandeirantes* was enslaving Indians. Themselves often of Indian or mixed parentage, usually speaking Indian languages among themselves, they became prodigious horsemen and fighters, and in their hunt for more captives they developed an unparalleled knowledge of much of what is now Brazil. As Spanish Jesuits developed large colonies of Indian converts in Paraguay, the *bandeirantes* found it much more profitable to raid those settlements, seizing at one stroke large numbers of Indians who already had learned how to till the white man's crops and herd his cattle and avoiding the hard, dangerous work of chasing Indians dispersed over their native territories. In the middle and late seventeenth century the Portuguese authorities were encouraging the *bandeirantes* to employ their knowledge of the backcountry and talent for survival in it to prospect for gold and other minerals.

In addition to wary native peoples, marauding *bandeirantes*, and struggling plantation owners, the frontiers of Portuguese settlement in Brazil
were dotted with settlements of escaped slaves called *quilombos*. The most
famous of these settlements, the *quilombo* of Palmares, in 1688 probably
had endured in more or less the same location for more than a hundred
years. In broken country southwest of Recife covered by palm forests—*palmares* in Portuguese—the settlement sometimes had as many as twenty
thousand residents, grew all its own food, and was defended by more than
three miles of wooden palisades and by armed men posted in various directions. The *quilombo* had its own smiths and managed to obtain fresh supplies of tools and weapons from the coastal towns. Slaves fled to it
regularly, and some Portuguese, to the great indignation of their neighbors,
made payments to the *quilombo* and traded with it in order to be left in
peaceful possession of frontier farms.

From the early 1600s on, improvised armies of Portuguese settlers
launched one expedition after another into the difficult country to
attempt to destroy this and other *quilombos*; there were twelve such expeditions between 1666 and 1687. Usually the Palmares warriors put up
some resistance but then fled into the woods when the attackers set their
palisades on fire, only to return and settle down again once the Portuguese
had withdrawn. In 1677 and 1678 the Portuguese made more serious
efforts under more competent leadership but, still unable to wipe out Palmares, offered its leaders peace and some autonomy within the framework
of the Portuguese colony. Most of the leaders were ready to accept, but
some of the more militant younger ones, led by one Zumbi, melted into
the woods to continue the struggle, and the agreement unraveled. Zumbi,
who was said to have a Portuguese wife, acquired in the following years a
formidable reputation as a military commander, and an aura of lost-cause
heroism clings to him in Brazilian popular lore down to our own time.

In the 1680s the Portuguese leaders of the coastal towns complained
frequently about Palmares raids in their rural districts. Decisive action
must be taken to get rid of the problem once and for all, they wrote; the
higher authorities ought to send in regular troops. But in the same documents they also complained constantly of their general impoverishment
and the inability of the towns to meet even their current fiscal obligations.
Then, in 1687–88, the area faced major Indian attacks and a yellow fever
epidemic. But already in 1687 the negotiations that were to change the
terms of the conflict had begun. *Bandeirante* groups had started to wrest

land from the Indians and settle inland. In 1687 the towns and the *ban-deirantes* already were moving toward an agreement, finally approved in 1691, by which the *bandeirantes* would contribute their forces and be rewarded after the extinction of the *quilombo* of Palmares by grants of title to much of its land. The *bandeirantes* were defeated in a first campaign in 1692; but when they returned in 1694, both sides seem to have understood that it was war to the death, and after a twenty-two-day siege Palmares fell, and its remaining people were killed or enslaved.

We have noticed that many slaves in Brazil had been brought from Angola, mostly sold in the violent trade from Luanda that had so thoroughly undermined the kingdom of the Kongo. In that trade slaves who managed to escape before they reached Luanda sometimes were able to form improvised settlements under war chiefs in remote mountain areas. They were called *quilombos*. The name and the practice had come to Brazil from Angola, on the ships of misery and terror.

CHAPTER 4

DAMPIER AND THE ABORIGINES

In January and February 1688 two small English buccaneer ships were anchored in a rocky inlet on the desert northwest coast of Australia. There they waited out a dangerous season of storms and contrary winds in the tropical seas to the north. While they cleaned the ships' bottoms and repaired their sails, an officer of one of the ships, William Dampier, had plenty of time to observe the Aborigines. When the English first arrived, the Aborigines threatened them with their wooden weapons. "At last the captain ordered the drum to be beaten, which was done of a sudden with much vigor, purposely to scare the poor creatures. They hearing the noise, ran away as fast as they could drive, and when they ran away in haste, they would cry 'Gurry, gurry,' speaking deep in the throat."

After the Aborigines had become more accustomed to them, the English tried to induce some of them to help carry barrels of water to the ships, by giving them some old clothes.

> We put them on them, thinking that this finery would have brought them to work heartily for us . . . but all the signs we could make were to no purpose, for they stood like statues, without motion, but grinned like so many monkeys, staring one upon another; for these poor creatures seem not accustomed to carry burdens, and I believe that one of our ship boys of ten years old would carry as much as one of them. So we were forced to carry our water ourselves, and they very fairly put off the

clothes again, and laid them down, as if clothes were only to work in. I did not perceive that they had any great liking to them at first, neither did they seem to admire any thing that we had.

The inhabitants of this country are the miserablest people in the world. The Hodmadods [Hottentots] of Monomatapa, though a nasty people, yet for wealth are gentlemen to these; who have no houses, and skin garments, sheep, poultry, and fruits of the earth, ostrich eggs, etc., as the Hottentots have; and setting aside their human shape, they differ but little from brutes. They are tall, straight-bodied, and thin, with small long limbs. They have great heads, round foreheads, and great brows. Their eyelids are always half closed, to keep the flies out of their eyes; they being so troublesome here, that no fanning will keep them from coming to one's face; and without the assistance of both hands to keep them off, they will creep into one's nostrils, and mouth too, if the lips are not shut very close; so that from their infancy being thus annoyed with these insects, they do never open their eyes as other people; and therefore they cannot see far, unless they hold up their heads, as if they were looking at somewhat over them.

They have great bottle-noses, pretty full lips, and wide mouths. The two fore-teeth of their upper jaw are wanting in all of them, men and women, old and young; whether they draw them out, I know not. Neither have they any beards. They are long-visaged, and of a very unpleasing aspect, having no one graceful feature in their faces. Their hair is black, short and curled, like that of the Negroes, and not long and lank, like the common Indians. The color of their skins, both of their faces and the rest of their body, is coal-black, like that of the Negroes of Guinea.

They have no sort of clothes, but a piece of the rind of a tree tied like a girdle about their waists, and a handful of long grass, or three or four small green boughs full of leaves, thrust under their girdle, to cover their nakedness.

They have no houses, but lie in the open air without any covering, the earth being their bed, and the heaven their canopy. Whether they cohabit one man to one woman or promiscuously I know not; but they do live in companies, 20 or 30 men, women, and children together. Their only food is a small sort of fish, which they get by making weirs of stone across little coves or branches of the sea; every tide bringing in the small fish and there leaving them for a prey to these people, who constantly attend there to search for them at low water. This small fry I take to be the top of their fishery. They have no instruments to catch any great fish, should they come; and such seldom stay to be left behind at low water; nor could we catch any fish with our hooks and lines all the while we lay there. In other places at low water they seek for cockles, mussels, and periwinkles. Of these shellfish there are fewer still, so that their chiefest dependence is upon what the sea leaves in their weirs, which be it much or little they gather up and march to the place of their abode. There the old people that are not able to stir abroad by reason of their age and the tender infants wait their return, and what Providence has bestowed on them they presently broil on the coals and eat it in common. Sometimes they get as many fish as makes them a plentiful banquet, and at other times they scarce get every one a taste, but be it little or much that they get, every one has his part, as well the young and tender, the old and feeble, who are not able to go abroad, as the strong and lusty. When they have eaten they lie down till the next low water, and then all that are able march out, be it night or day, rain or shine, 'tis all one; they must attend the weirs, or else they must fast, for the earth affords them no food at all. There is neither herb, root, pulse, nor any sort of grain for them to eat, that we saw; nor any sort of bird or beast that they can catch, having no instruments wherewithal to do so.

I did not perceive that they did worship any thing. These poor creatures have a sort of weapon to defend their weir, or fight with their enemies, if they have any that will interfere with their poor fishery. They did at first endeavor with their weapons to frighten us, who lying ashore deterred them from one of their fishing places. Some of them had wooden swords, others had a sort of lances. The sword is a long straight pole sharp at one end, and hardened afterwards by heat. I saw no iron, nor any other sort of metal. . . .

At last we went over to the islands, and there we found a great many of the natives; I do believe there were 40 on one island, men, women, and children.

They found more Aborigines on another nearby island; some of the women and children fled as the strangers approached their camp, while others "lay still by a fire, making a doleful noise, as if we had been coming to devour them; but when they saw we did not intend to harm them, they were pretty quiet, and the rest that fled from us at our first coming returned again."

The Aborigines seemed to have no boats of any kind; once the English spotted some swimming from one island to another, brought four of them aboard, and gave them some rice and boiled meat. "They did greedily devour what we gave them, but took no notice of the ship, or any thing in it, and when they were set on land again they ran away again as fast as they could."

William Dampier was a gifted observer and stylist. Although he had little formal education, later in his life he was quite welcome in literary London and among the scientific correspondents of the Royal Society. His great passion had been to see distant corners of the earth. In the 1680s the days of the great first reconnaissances of the maritime world (Columbus, Magellan, Barents, Hudson) were long past, and the age of systematic scientific exploration (Bougainville, Cook, and on to our own times) was still far in the future. The most frequent European voyagers in uncharted waters in the 1680s were buccaneers. Dampier was not happy about the company he kept, but in his writings he neither concealed the pillaging of his companions nor apologized for it. Frequently we find him observing plants, animals, and natives, keeping up his notes day by day, recording the many times when his good advice was rejected, amid the brawls, the splittings up of squadrons, the constant craziness of people who seem to have been more like a motorcycle gang than a Mafia.

In 1688 Dampier, thirty-six years old, was nearing the end of his first voyage around the world, a series of improvisations and misadventures that took him twelve years. After finding little worth pillaging on the Pacific coast of South and Central America and waiting in vain for the rich prize of the annual galleon from Manila to Acapulco, he and his captain, both eager to quit buccaneering and take up honest trade, had persuaded their crew to set out across the Pacific. They were lucky to make it to Guam before their food supplies were exhausted; later the crew told them that if the food had run out, they had resolved to eat first the captain, then Dampier and others who had promoted the venture. Europeans confronting unknown and warlike peoples often feared that they would be eaten, as did the Africans who were loaded on the slave ships. In Dampier's experience it was not the shy and weak Bardi who were the potential cannibals but his fellow Englishmen.

After an effort to trade at Mindanao in the southern Philippines and the stop on the Australian coast, Dampier and a few others jumped ship and made a risky voyage in a small native boat to Aceh on the north end of

Sumatra. After more wanderings in Asian waters, including a voyage to what is now northern Vietnam and a spell as chief gunner of the dismal little English outpost at Bengkulu on the west coast of Sumatra, Dampier finally made his way home in 1691. He was made much of in London as a source of excellent, clear information about previously unknown parts of the world and as a teller of wonderful stories. In 1693, in what may have been the finest meeting of diary stylists in the history of the English language, he dined with John Evelyn and Samuel Pepys. They convened at Evelyn's house, which was soon to be let to—and trashed by—Tsar Peter the Great and his suite. Dampier's book about his voyage, published in 1697, was a great success. Some think his description of the Australian Aborigines influenced Swift's picture of the Yahoos in *Gulliver's Travels*. In 1699 Dampier was off again, this time as captain of a royal ship on a formal and legal voyage of exploration. He did some important exploring around Australia and even returned to the same barren stretch of coast he had seen in 1688. But there were many difficulties with his ships and crews, and he ended his homebound voyage ignominiously when his rotten ship sank at Ascension Island in the South Atlantic and his crew had to wait to be picked off the island by a passing ship. He made more voyages and published more books about them but never had another voyage as carefree and as full of delight in new sights as his first.

Dampier's habit of careful observation of non-European peoples had begun early in his travels, when he encountered the Miskito Indians of the Central American coast, excellent fishermen often hired by the buccaneers for that skill. He was not interested in languages or kinship, key problems for the modern anthropologist, but he always noted food and ways of getting it, boatbuilding skills, and a bit about any festivals he saw. It is not surprising that this fine observer could not see much more than material deprivation in the Aboriginal peoples of Australia; modern anthropologists have needed all their resources of hard work and imaginative sympathy to begin to understand these remote people. Well into the twentieth century, anthropologists found the Bardi people still clinging to their ancient way of life on the Dampier Peninsula, still fishing in their coastal weirs. They have a beautiful language with twenty-two different affixes to modify the use and meaning of a verb. People lived in small exogamous bands, with complex rules about who was and was not marriageable in nearby bands. Elaborate rituals took place, especially for the initiation of young men into adulthood, at special grounds not to be approached for ordinary purposes.

Tiny childlike spirits, born as spirit guides of particular children, were said to live in special places, accompany men on journeys, warn them of danger. They made themselves known in dreams. Everything important came to a man in a dream. Poor in objects, building nothing more elaborate than their fish weirs, the Bardi found their riches in the elaboration of human basics—language, story, ritual, kinship, dreams. Today they live in houses in a nearby settlement, their old ways increasingly in disarray.

Dampier's account of his sojourn on that remote coast, with its distinctive ironic voice, had been shaped by repeated tellings and by some forgetting. He was a wary pilot and a meticulous observer of the tides; his expertise may have been responsible for the decision to repair the ships in an outer bay, where they would not have to risk the strong tidal currents of some of the channels. He noted that the native people were aware of the tides and came down at low tide to check their weirs. He recorded seeing some of them swimming from island to island. But there is no trace of amazement at the level of understanding of the tides that such swimming must have required; a swimmer could have survived only if he or she had known how to wait for slack water at low or high tide or exactly how to swim with a current.

It is highly probable that the ships on which Dampier arrived were the first the Bardi had ever seen. They built no structures, saw no different people, wore almost no clothes. How could they even begin to describe the wooden sides of the ship, its masts and flapping sails, its pale-skinned humans wearing clothes? Dampier says they ran away, shouting, "Gurry, gurry." Probably, says a modern student of the Bardi language, they were calling the strangers *ngaarri*, the most feared, most tricky and malevolent of all the kinds of spirits.

PART II

THE WORLD OF THE GREAT COMPANY

In the seventeenth century the wooden ships of the Dutch sailed almost every European trading route except the Spanish routes on the west coast of the Americas and across the great ocean to Manila. From the Cape of Good Hope to Japan almost all the Dutch ships flew the flag of the state-chartered Dutch East India Company, a centralized, statist creation of the least centralized and statist of the European great powers. In the Netherlands the company's ultimate authority lay in the hands of a governing board called the Gentlemen Seventeen, on which Amsterdam had eight seats, the province of Zeeland four, and other smaller trading towns a total of five. Amsterdam usually was able to call the tune, but not in the face of unified opposition of the other members. The building of ships and investment in outbound cargoes from the homeland also were in the hands of the "chambers" of the company in Zeeland and the various cities. But Batavia (today Jakarta) was the capital of a systematically centralized empire in which the governor-general and council, meeting in Batavia Castle, appointed the officials who directed all the company's voyages and trading stations from the Cape of Good Hope to Nagasaki. Batavia received regular reports from the far-flung officials and sent them detailed instructions concerning their purchases, sales, and relations with local powers. No Dutchman resident in Asia was permitted to compete with the company anywhere in its massive web of intra-Asian trade, much less in the shipping of goods to the homeland. In a century when birth and class counted for a great deal everywhere in Europe and in Asia, the company was an island of openness to talent; men who had first signed on as common soldiers, some of them hounded out of the Netherlands by debts, had ended their lives as governors-general, councillors, or commanders of major posts and island realms. In Batavia Castle rows of young clerks sweated and nodded over the reports that came in from outlying posts and expeditions, making copies of everything to be sent home to the Gentlemen Seventeen. In the 1680s fifteen to twenty-five big folio volumes of such copies were sent home every year. They are beautifully preserved in the General State Archives in The Hague, have made my career and those of quite a few other historians who somehow found their way to them, and still have many untapped treasures. These sources, and the web of connections that produced them, make the world of the great company one of the most diverse and accessible facets of the world of 1688.

CHAPTER 5

THE CAPE OF GOOD HOPE

Here is a resolution of the commander and council of the Dutch East India Company at the Cape of Good Hope dated January 14, 1688:

> The Honorable Commander having noted that some of the free residents by carelessness give their slaves opportunities to obtain their masters' firearms and to assemble and hide the same for nefarious escapades, by which this colony easily could be brought to a great and irremediable misfortune, it was decided after mature consideration of the matter, in order to take prompt measures against this highly threatening danger, for the securing of the public good and the peace of the inhabitants, to have it proclaimed by public handbills that all free residents who have slaves are seriously ordered to take their firearms, be they muskets, blunderbusses, carbines, or pistols, whether hung on a rack or kept elsewhere, and at once screw off the upper lip that holds the flint, and keep it in a secure place, on penalty of a fine of 25 Rijksdaalders to be forfeited to the person who made the complaint or who notifies an officer of this gross negligence and disobedience.

On January 20 the soldiers of the garrison were permitted to go hunting twice a week to maintain their skills; on September 27 this was supplemented by a set of rules in thirty-two articles for competition among the soldiers in target shooting on foot and on horseback.

By then the Dutch had experienced a bit of what they feared and sought to prepare against. On March 10, 1688, the council considered a report that a party of ten slaves, under the leadership of a free African and a slave, both from the Cape Verde Islands off West Africa, had armed themselves and escaped inland. Nighttime raids on isolated farms, murders, and house burnings were feared. "In order to strangle in the cradle" the threat of the spread of slave rebellion, a reward was offered for the capture alive of the leaders, and if any other escaped slaves offered any resistance to recapture, they were to be shot through the head or otherwise dealt with as the pursuers wished. By March 31 it was reported that six of the slaves already had been recaptured, and the feared slave rebellion did not materialize.

The slaves whose revolt the Dutch feared were not drawn from the native people of the Cape area, whom modern scholars call the Khoikhoi. The slave whose revolt was feared was likely to be larger and stronger than the Khoikhoi and thoroughly accustomed to warfare with iron weapons. More than half the slaves at the Cape were bought on Madagascar, which was a great stew of conflicts among peoples of Indonesian and African heritages, with incessant warfare and slave taking. The slave, wherever he came from, was an unwilling resident at the Cape who could not freely depart— after all, he or she was property, an investment—taking orders day after day from the master.

But what of the people who had inhabited the Cape area before the coming of the Europeans? They were not the ancestors of the present African majority population of South Africa but a smaller, lighter-skinned people who appear in the Dutch records and in Dampier's writings as "Hottentots"; "Khoikhoi" is one of the ways they referred to themselves. They had emerged from a hunter-gatherer culture and begun herding cattle and sheep just a few hundred years before. In 1688 the Khoikhoi chief who had closest relations with the Dutch was one whom they called Klaas, who by then had spent almost fifteen years demonstrating his loyalty to the Dutch in many visits to the Cape fort. He bought up large numbers of cattle and sheep from other Khoikhoi for sale to the Dutch, returned their runaway slaves, offered refuge to shipwrecked Dutchmen, and attacked Khoikhoi who were hostile to the company. In return he received company recognition as its agent in the purchase of livestock, gifts of brandy and tobacco, a

Dutch suit, a wig, and perhaps even the ultimate sign of trust of a native ally, four guns.

On February 16, 1688, Klaas appeared before the council at the Dutch fort to complain of attacks on him and his people by another Khoikhoi chief—the Dutch called him Koopman (merchant)—with whom he had a long-standing feud. The council gave Klaas some liquor, tobacco, and other goods and agreed to summon Koopman and order him "with sharp threats" to keep the peace and to treat Klaas as his overlord, giving him back the cattle he had stolen. In 1693, however, the Dutch governor abruptly switched to support of Koopman and imprisoned Klaas on the bleak Robben Island, about six miles out in the Atlantic; he eventually was released, spent his last years in drunken decline, and was killed in a fight at Koopman's camp.

Klaas's decline was a small piece of the longer and even sadder story of the decline of his people in the Cape region. Khoikhoi groups amassed large herds of cattle and sheep as they prospered, but in time of drought, war, poor leadership, or other misfortunes they might lose all their herds, become dependent servants of other Khoikhoi, or disperse into smaller bands that survived by hunting, gathering, and stealing livestock. The Dutch responded to the little they knew of the Khoikhoi in ways that made the "Hottentots" one of the best known to eighteenth-century Europeans of all examples of bestial, subhuman savagery; Dampier had referred to them in this way in his description of the Australian Aborigines. But the Dutch had little to fear from them, found them useful as stock traders, and did not set out to exterminate them. However, the trade drained cattle and sheep from Khoikhoi society as a whole, and when a group was down on its luck, it drifted not into hunting and gathering but out of organized Khoikhoi society, into hired labor for the Dutch or prostitution and begging in Cape Town. A smallpox epidemic in 1713 marked the disappearance of independent Khoikhoi society from the Cape area.

The Afrikaners have been called the white tribe of Africa. To them, South Africa is home. Their language is spoken nowhere else. Their culture is no more similar to that of the Netherlands than that of Americans of northern European ancestry is to that of England. For the Afrikaners, as for the Americans, one important reason for this is that people from several European nations contributed to the making of this new people.

There are old French surnames among the Afrikaners: De Villiers, Joubert, Du Toit, Le Roux, Fouché, Malan, Marais. Many of them can be traced back to early Huguenot (Protestant) settlers, refugees from persecution in the France of Louis XIV, the first of whom reached the Cape of Good Hope in 1688. It is not at all out of place to see their arrival as a milestone in the emergence of the Afrikaner people and at the same time to be reminded of other Huguenots we shall meet in this book, all living in exile in 1688: Pierre Bayle and many others in Rotterdam; Elihu Yale's bankers in London.

The Dutch outpost at the Cape of Good Hope had been founded in 1652 by the Dutch East India Company, not as a foothold for expansion into the great continent to the north but as a way station providing fresh water, meat, and food for the ships of the company on their long voyages between the Netherlands and India and Indonesia. For the company's purposes the Cape might as well have been on an island, as long as there was enough room to raise cattle, sheep, and fruit and vegetables to supply the ships. The company had its own herds and gardens, tended by slaves, and tried to encourage the settlement of free burghers—Dutchmen not in company service—to farm on their own and sell their produce to the company for provisioning of the passing ships. But the company did not pay them very well for their produce, many of them preferred tavern keeping to farming, and most Dutchmen who left their prosperous homeland did so in the expectation of a softer or more adventurous life than that of a small cattle farmer. In 1688 there still were only about three hundred company servants, four hundred free burghers, and eight hundred slaves in the little colony, and its farms were just beginning to reach beyond the narrow confines of the Cape Peninsula. The Cape authorities had found the climate excellent for vineyards but had not been able to find settlers who understood the making of wine, vinegar, and brandy.

A few French experts in those fields already had been sent out when, late in 1687, the ruling council of the company decided to offer free passage, as much land as he could farm, and loans of cattle and implements to any Huguenot who would take an oath of loyalty to the Netherlands and emigrate to the Cape. A Huguenot clergyman would be supported by the company to minister to them. Between December 1687 and July 1688 about 180 to 190 Huguenots had responded to this offer and sailed for the Cape. They included a wealthy merchant, a hatmaker, a wagon maker, a vintner, and about 30 women and 50 children. Even if a few of them had

been on a ship before, in the Mediterranean or along the Atlantic coast of
Europe, none of them had experienced anything like this voyage, in
wooden ships less than three hundred feet long, for periods of two months
at the best of times, four or six at the worst. Most of them sailed out of a
northern European winter, through the stifling doldrums and anxieties of
the tropical waters off West Africa, and arrived in April through August, in
the Southern Hemisphere winter. Losses to sickness and accident en route
were moderate by the standards of the time; by the end of January 1689 I
estimate that about 150 Huguenots had reached the Cape alive. Since
there were only about 400 free burghers before that, the European population not on the company payroll now was about one-fourth Huguenot.
The Huguenots were given farms in the magnificent Drakenstein Valley
about twenty miles east of the Cape fort and settlement. The land was fertile but never had been touched by a plow, and clearing it took years of
backbreaking work. The settlers needed a good deal of support from the
company authorities in their first years and were viewed with suspicion,
especially when France and the Netherlands were at war. But eventually
they put down roots and prospered, contributing greatly to the Cape wine
industry, and they added to the mix of Afrikaner culture a Calvinism
steeled by persecution and a sense that Africa now was the only home they
had.

South Africa was transformed almost beyond recognition by the great
treks inland of the Afrikaners, beginning in the eighteenth century, and the
subjugation of large African populations. But the fear remained into our
own time, and Robben Island, where Klaas spent his years of captivity,
became the harsh prison where the enemies of apartheid were confined.
Nelson Mandela spent eighteen years there; study groups flourished, and
the African leaders came to call it Mandela University. In March 1998 President Bill Clinton accompanied the frail but still fiery President Mandela
on a visit to his old cell on Robben Island.

CHAPTER 6

THE ISLAND WORLD

In the cool room the blind man remembers and dictates. His helpers struggle to keep up with the torrent of vivid detail. On the seas there might be schools of jellyfish with crests reaching like sails above the water, shining like blue and purple crystals. The vines, the luscious fruit, the palm trees on the horizon as a ship approached a low-lying island: All are still clear to him. Driven on by his direction, his helpers are nearing completion of the new set of drawings, replacing those lost in a fire the year before. Is the plate of the durian done? Yes, and it's fine, good images of the big spiny fruit and the big leaves. The blind man smiles as he remembers the first time he tried one, how terrible it smelled and how wonderful the taste was. Do we have one? A boy is sent running to the market. The stench fills the cool room, and then he tastes the rich, creamy fruit.

Thanks to one brilliant and obsessed German in the service of the Dutch company, we can get a sense of the Spice Islands in 1688 not only as scenes of baffling and violent human encounters but also as a world of amazing natural beauty, of exuberant plant and animal life on the islands and in the seas. The great folio volumes of the *Ambonese Herbal* and the *Ambonese Curiosity Cabinet* by Georg Everard Rumpf or Rumphius are monuments to the curious, classifying, detail-noting eyes and intricately designing pens of late-seventeenth-century Europeans in their encounters with the natural world.

Rumpf grew up in Hanau near Frankfurt, the son of a successful architect and supervisor of building projects. He got a respectable education, including good Latin. Around the end of the Thirty Years' War in 1648 many restless young men from devastated and depressed Germany made their way to Amsterdam and eventually to Dutch outposts and trading networks around the globe. In 1646 Rumpf, at the age of eighteen, responded to an announcement by a German prince of an opportunity to join a force that would serve under the Venetian flag in the Mediterranean. The call actually was intended for service with the Dutch West India Company in the last fraction of northeastern Brazil it was defending against Portuguese reconquest. Rumpf's ship never made it to Brazil, and as a result of either shipwreck or capture at sea, he spent several years in Portugal. There he may have heard of the wonders of the Asian tropics, perhaps specifically of Ambon, far out in the "Spice Islands" of what is now eastern Indonesia. After a short visit back in Hanau he went to Amsterdam and signed on as a soldier with the Dutch East India Company. By the end of 1653 he had passed through Batavia and on to Ambon; he was never to leave the eastern islands again and died in Ambon forty-nine years later.

Rumpf arrived in the late stages of a thorough and nearly definitive suppression of local resistance to Dutch domination and monopoly of the export of cloves. He showed some competence as a military engineer, but he did not like the soldier's life and in 1657 was able to become a civil official, in charge of an outlying fort on the north side of Ambon Island. Here he had to maintain order among the local people, be on the alert for any anti-Dutch activity by local people or strangers, and prevent the smuggling of cloves. But that scarcely took up all his time. Like other such outpost commanders, he had some of the privileges of a local ruler, receiving supplies of fish, game, and fruits every day. The climate was among the healthiest in the islands for Europeans. He had married a local woman, probably of mixed ancestry and cultural heritage. He began to study the immense abundance of plant life around him, starting with the coconut and areca palms and the fruit trees, going on to the trees and vines of the jungle tangle that pressed close to the coast and clearing. He could step out on the dock of his little fort and watch the fish and crabs in the clear shallows. Making rapid progress in Malay and Ambonese, he began to learn from the people about the medicinal properties of plants. He made occasional voyages in the region; coming back from Banda in 1662, his ship sailed for a whole day through those shoals of jellyfish he remembered and described.

Soon Rumpf conceived an ambitious project to write a book in Latin about the plant life of Ambon. In keeping with his new ambition and hopes for eventual recognition in European learned circles he began to latinize his surname as Rumphius. By 1668 he was so far along that he asked for a year's leave from his official duties to go to Batavia and finish his book but was turned down. Then disaster struck: By 1670 he was almost completely blind, seeing only a glimmer of light in one eye and nothing at all in the other, suffering intense pain if he went out in the tropical sunlight. Glaucoma or a parasitic infection are the most likely explanations.

The Dutch company was at best erratic in its promotion of learning and disinterested curiosity; but Rumphius was a valued official, and his work, if brought to completion, was likely to be useful. He was brought to the main town and castle of Ambon and kept in his honored positions as a member of the governor's council, where his knowledge of local peoples and languages was exceptionally useful, and as head of a subordinate Council on Marriage Affairs, a sort of domestic court. His son soon was drawing plants better than he ever had. The company furnished a clerk to whom he could dictate. His wife was deeply involved in his work; he gave a particularly fine orchid her name. Then, in February 1674, his wife and youngest daughter went to see the splendid lanterns and processions in the Chinese quarter on the fifteenth day of the first month of the Chinese year; his wife may have been of Chinese ancestry. There was an earthquake, and the wife and daughter were killed by a toppling wall.

Rumphius's blindness and the loss of his loved ones seem to have increased his focus on his studies. Since it would be very difficult to dictate his work in Latin, it now would be written in Dutch. He prepared a series of less ambitious works: a report on the earthquake, another on agriculture on Ambon, and books on the geography and history of the island, all immediately useful to his company colleagues. The company appointed a second clerk to his staff, then an artist, and by 1688 his son, who had been moving about in company service, also was back in Ambon to help him. He even received some academic recognition from Europe; in 1680, on the recommendation of two Germans who had served the Dutch company as doctors, he was named a member of the Academia Naturae Curiosum in Vienna, and some extracts from his letters were published in its journal.

By 1687 most of the text of his most important work, the *Herbal*, was done, and the time-consuming work of preparing the drawings was moving along nicely. Then, on January 11 of that year, a fire swept through the town of Ambon. Rumphius's staff managed to save the text of the book, but the drawings were destroyed. Still, neither he nor the company gave up. He estimated that the drawings could be redone in a year and a half or two years. The company appointed a new artist and transferred Rumphius's son back to Ambon. In fact by 1690 Rumphius had sent off to Batavia manuscript and illustrations for the first six books of twelve planned. He had also picked out the site where he wished to be buried on Ambon. So we have every reason to picture him in 1688 pushing his staff

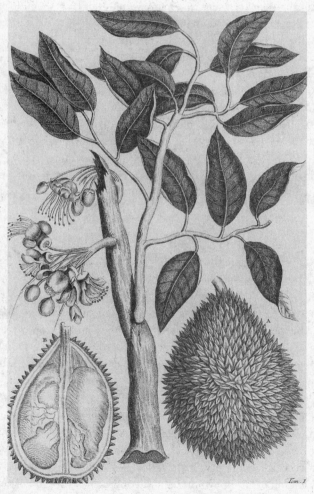

The leaves and fruit of the durian, from Rumphius's *Ambonese Herbal*

along on the copying and drawings, listening as they read chapters to him, and trying to think of what he had left out. He recalled to his mind's eye the coconut palms rising out of the sea as a ship approached a low-lying island (the word picture with which he begins the *Herbal*), the appearance of the wonderful fruits whose smells, tastes, and textures still were so vivid to him, the spectacular tropical sunrises and sunsets year after year on Ambon. The last books of the *Herbal* were done and sent off to Batavia in 1697. He already was at work on the *Curiosity Cabinet*, describing the beautiful shells and sea stars, the many varieties of crab, including the formidable nut-cracking land crab of Ambon (these pages are particular triumphs of exact description of structure and behavior), and all the rest of the incredible riches of the tropical seas.

Over seventy, blind, frail, with more than forty years in the service of the company, Rumphius still took part in council deliberations at Ambon and plunged on into the study of the minerals of the area. He died on June 15, 1702. The *Curiosity Cabinet* was published in 1705, but the manuscript of the great *Herbal* suffered many misadventures. When it finally was received by the Gentlemen Seventeen in the home country, they had great difficulty finding the funds for such a massive project; it was published only in 1741.

Batavia, headquarters in Asia of the Dutch East India Company, was built on the site of a Javanese town the name of which the Dutch heard as "Jakatra"; the modern Indonesian capital of Jakarta is in the same location. The voyager arriving by sea for the first time was amazed to find, on the low-lying north coast of Java, facing shallow waters at six degrees south latitude, a bustle of Indian, Indonesian, Chinese, and European ships; an orderly realm of islands used as recreation grounds for the Dutch rulers and shipyards for the company; a formidable fortress, Batavia Castle, commanding the entrance to the inner harbor; streets of Dutch-style houses along canals; a thriving and well-organized Chinese community; and abundant facilities for drink and other pleasures of the flesh. In the fine houses of prominent Dutchmen one would find scores of slaves, baroque furniture made of dark tropical hardwoods, Dutch blue and white tiles, and elaborately carved openwork panels above the doors between rooms to allow for the circulation of any stray breeze in the oppressive tropical heat.

Batavia and its island world presented a baroque spectacle of complexity. The surface appearance of order concealed layers of private interest and arrangement often very much at odds with the unity of power and purpose embodied in Batavia Castle. There was a large population of Portuguese-speaking people of mixed ancestry and an influential Chinese community with its own headmen and its own hospital. In the 1680s the Chinese were prospering greatly from regional trade and from the revival of the trade of Chinese merchants coming from their home ports to Batavia. In 1688, for example, the Chinese coming to Batavia to trade bought from the company eight thousand guilders' worth of pepper. But there was another side to this growing traffic that was less to the liking of the Batavia Chinese. The 1688 junks from China also brought in more than seven hundred people, most of whom planned to stay and start new lives in Java. Already in 1687 the Dutch authorities were complaining of the large numbers of "bankrupts and vagabonds" arriving on the junks from China. New arrivals from China were blamed for a rash of burglaries. The established Chinese suffered from much of this crime, and their hard-won toleration by the Dutch and the Javanese was threatened by reactions against the newcomers. In 1690 the Dutch authorities adopted an expanded set of controls on Chinese immigration and immigrants. In the rural plains around Batavia many established Chinese started sugar-refining mills, and impoverished recent immigrants did most of the hard work in the growing sugar industry. When the rural Chinese exploded in rebellion against the Dutch in 1740, the Batavia Chinese elite sided with the rulers, not with their fellow countrymen.

As the governor-general and council in Batavia reviewed the figures on trade, they could not help noticing the rising importance of the commerce with India, especially in Indian cotton and silk fabrics. Still, the spice trades held a special place in their world. Nowhere in the company's sphere had a monopoly been more ruthlessly pursued than in the Banda Islands, a tiny archipelago that was the world's exclusive producer of nutmeg and mace. In the 1620s the Bandanese had been accused of violating monopoly contracts, which they did not fully understand and had not all agreed to, and had been deliberately exterminated, driven away from the cultivated areas to the slopes of a volcano, where they died of starvation and disease during the rainy season. In 1688 there were almost no Bandanese left. The nutmeg groves were in the hands of Dutch entrepreneurs who bought slaves to do the work. The slaves came from Bali, Papua, and India, in a thriving and little-studied slave trade throughout maritime Southeast Asia. In their 1688 letters to the home country the Batavia authorities reported that on the Banda Islands there were 160,000 fully grown nutmeg trees, 185,000 half grown, and 315,000 young. The population of 6,642 included 1,070 Dutch, 3,716 slaves, and just 3 free Bandanese and 25 Bandanese slaves. The letters commented on the horrible cruelty with which the plantation entrepreneurs treated the slaves and other Asians but gave no details.

By 1688 the Dutch had a grip on the centers of clove cultivation almost as firm as for nutmeg and mace. Their seat of power and administration was on the island of Ambon, where we already have met Rumphius. The trouble with the cloves business was that they were too easy to grow and faced an inelastic demand in Europe and Asia. If the Dutch were to continue to buy cheap and sell dear, they had not only to exclude all competitors but also to limit strictly the quantities available in Dutch-controlled ports; if they didn't, their own servants would succumb to the temptation to divert cloves into private channels and ship them to ports that the Dutch didn't control. Since the 1650s the Dutch, more or less with the consent of local rulers, had engaged in ruthless campaigns to chop down clove trees in areas where they didn't have tight enough control or simply when the abundance of tropical nature outran the demand in foreign markets. At the end of 1688 the Batavia authorities noted in their letter to their superiors in the Netherlands that they still faced a chronic overproduction problem; only a small part of the area now planted to cloves was needed to meet the demand of all ports, European and Asian, served by the Dutch company. In the past, when they cut down trees or forced the local people to do so, they had made regular payments to the people to compensate them for the loss of income. But they were not willing to increase the amount paid out in this way, and they feared that if they cut down trees on a few islands, the people would just move to other islands where they were out of reach of the Dutch and plant more clove trees. So they were not cutting down any more trees and were having vague thoughts of trying to induce the local people to switch to agriculture, but they thought that those people would not respond very well, preferring to continue their "lazy" fruit-eating ways rather than switch to growing rice, which was not feasible on Ambon in any case. They were also making final plans to build another substantial fort on an island near Ambon.

North of the Ambon area, the region called Maluku or the Moluccas, around the twin volcanic islands of Ternate and Tidore, had been a center of clove production and European rivalry since the arrival of the Portuguese in the early 1500s. The people of Maluku conceived their political world as having two complementary focal points in Ternate and Tidore; the ideal state was one of balance and manageable rivalry, not the victory of one over the other. The influence of Islam had strengthened the idea of hereditary monarchy, but there still was a strong feeling that a would-be king had to prove his abilities and spiritual powers to the elders of the various settlements. There were many legends of men arriving from across the ocean, proving themselves to the "lords of the land," and becoming king.

The dualism of Ternate and Tidore had worked pretty well for the people of Maluku as long as they could align with rival European powers. But the Dutch expelled the Portuguese, and the Spanish withdrew their last remnants in the early 1660s. Thereafter the brotherhood of the rulers of Ternate and Tidore became a sibling rivalry for the favor of Father Company. The Dutch got along well with collective and nonmonarchical forms of government in the home country, but in Asia they were more comfortable dealing with monarchies, which made it easier to know whom to support and whom they should pressure to live up to a treaty. Some of them were inclined to see danger for themselves in any growing Islamic influence, and they were not entirely wrong. From the 1660s on they kept steady pressure on the rulers of Maluku to adopt European customs, dress, and a more centralized form of monarchy. The sultan of Ternate named his sons Amsterdam and Rotterdam. When Sultan Amsterdam came to the throne in 1675, he went along with the Dutch program of cultural assimilation and sought to strengthen his control in outlying areas by force, provoking a great deal of resistance and even some opposition from the Dutch. On Tidore, on the other hand, Sultan Saifuddin refused to go along with the Dutch program and relied on traditional consensus-building forms of politics, so that he was much more popular among his own people but on much worse terms with the Dutch. After Saifuddin died on October 2, 1687, the company intervened to place his son on the throne despite the strong claims of Saifuddin's brother. The Batavia authorities hoped they might now have better relations with Tidore, but by the end of 1688 they were writing that the new sultan was as troublesome as his father. In the harbor at Ternate, Tidore marauders had attacked some fishermen very close to the company ships lying at anchor and beheaded six of them: When the Dutch complained to the new sultan of Tidore, he sent six of his people to the Dutch, saying they could kill these and then they would be even; the Dutch refused, "it being contrary to all Christian laws."

Across the Sunda Strait from Java was the great island of Sumatra, extending about nine hundred miles to the northwest, forming the west side of the Strait of Melaka, much of its mountainous, densely forested interior little known to the people who frequented its coasts and harbors. On the north end of the island the port kingdom of Aceh maintained its independence and Islamic orientation, welcoming all kinds of European and Asian traders as long as they did not seek monopoly privileges or political hegemony. The central interior produced considerable gold; the Dutch company had gotten its hands on some of the gold-producing areas, which it worked with slave labor, not very productively. Closest to Batavia and of constant concern to the governor-general and council were twin ports and kingdoms on Sumatra's southeast coast, Jambi and Palembang. Their rulers frequently described themselves as brothers, but fraternal rivalry was a permanent possibility that had been exacerbated by the actions of the Dutch. In 1688 the situation at Jambi was especially baffling and dangerous in the eyes of the Dutch.

The physical settings of the two kingdoms were similar. The capital was a port town, several days' sail up a twisting river, in a broad coastal zone of mangrove and swamp forest, large parts of which frequently were inundated by high tides or high water in the rivers. Most houses were built on pilings and had water beneath them at least part of the year. The landscape was so flat that any small hill drew attention; one such hill near Palembang had become the center of many legends of the origins and burials of local kings. Europeans and other outsiders found these hot, damp, mosquito-plagued places unhealthy. There was not much population or production near these cities; they were simply nodes for transfer of wealth, and sometimes power, between the more populous areas upriver and larger centers of wealth and power across the seas.

Access to the upriver areas depended on networks of rivers and tributaries. When the water was too low, they were impassable. When they were running fullest in March and April after the rainy season, the trip downstream was rapid and more than a little dangerous, the return voyage against the flood impossible. In between, trips upstream might take weeks of rowing. The lure upstream was fertile land in the river valleys that could be cleared and planted with pepper vines. In the sixteenth and seventeenth centuries traders from China and Europe came to Jambi, Palembang, Banten, and other ports in quest of the large quantities of pepper they could sell in the expanding commercial economies of their homelands. Clearing tropical forests with mediocre tools was slow work. The pepper vines began to bear only in the fifth year after they were planted. By 1688 it had been clear for decades that too many vines had been planted, too much production stimulated. Warehouses in Amsterdam and Batavia were overflowing with pepper.

That was only one side of the troubles Jambi and Palembang were encountering in the wake of their commercial expansion and especially of the Dutch involvement in their affairs. Relations between rulers and ruled, between the lords of the downstream port cities and their numerous and distant upstream subjects, were expressed and worked out in terms of kinship. All systems of hereditary power do this to a greater or lesser degree, but here the implications were more pervasive than for China's vast bureaucracy or Europe's structures of law, privilege, and commerce. Rulers were supposed to be like clan elders, having great prestige but not absolute power, keeping people's respect by settling disputes and giving generous gifts. Their people's recognition of them would be expressed in deference, obedience, and gifts. The looseness of such a ruler-subject relation was enhanced by the physical distance and difficulty of movement between the upriver areas and the ruler in his city in the swamps. Many local power holders upriver were royal relatives who had chosen to carve out semi-independent spheres for themselves but might intervene in capital politics if they did not like what was going on there.

This kind of political give-and-take came under drastic pressure once the Dutch had a contract for the delivery of pepper and the exclusion of competitors from trade. They would support the ruler as sovereign if he would keep firm control and increase deliveries of pepper, but it was just such firm control and pressure to maximize production and delivery that would disrupt the delicate balances of the traditional political order, including its ceremonial and reciprocal ways of collecting goods to send downstream. Despite the tensions this brought about, in 1688 the sultan of Palembang, Abdul Rahman, seemed wealthy and secure on his throne, his reign marred only by a fitful rivalry between his two sons. But in Jambi Sultan Ingalaga was a weak ruler, the trade of his kingdom was in decline, and he had been challenged by an upriver leader with an explicitly Islamic and anti-Dutch agenda. In 1687 the Dutch had sent a small force to Jambi and had been astonished to find many Jambi nobles deserting their sovereign and supporting his son, who now was installed on the throne. Ingalaga fled upstream. In March 1688 he came back to his capital, threatening to attack, but then lost his nerve in the face of wide support for his son and sought protection from the Dutch commanders, who sent him off to a lonely and uncomfortable exile in Batavia. Abdul Rahman of Palembang supported the new sultan of Jambi. The Islamic, anti-Dutch threat had been shunted aside, at least for the moment. Palembang continued to prosper, and Jambi continued to decline.

Cornelia van Nijenroode arrived in the Netherlands on August 10, 1688. She never had set foot there before in her fifty-eight years of life. She was pursuing her legal case against the efforts of her estranged husband, Johan Bitter, to make off with all of the fortune she had inherited from her first husband. She must have had the dress, manners, and language of a wealthy Dutch lady returning from the Indies, but her features betrayed a still more exotic origin: She had been born in Hirado, Japan, in 1630, the daughter of a Dutch merchant and a Japanese lady. After her parents died, she was raised in the orphanage in Batavia and does not seem to have ever traveled far from there until she boarded ship for Holland at the end of 1687. The short days and damp chill of the end of the year, so unlike Batavia's equatorial even days and moist heat, and the absence of the many servants chattering in Portuguese in her big Batavia house must have added to her unease as she conferred with her attorney and prepared the suit that she filed with the High Court of Holland in November 1688. Her story builds a bridge back from Batavia to the home country and shines a narrow, bright beam into the murk of high-level Batavia society.

Cornelia's upbringing in the Batavia orphanage, probably eased by an inheritance from her father, does not seem to have been especially unpleasant. She had some social connections with a small community of Japanese exiles in Batavia and appears to have written regularly to her family in Hirado. In 1652 she married Pieter Cnoll. Between 1653 and 1670 she gave birth to ten children, only one of whom lived to adulthood. A fine portrait has come down to us of Pieter, Cornelia, and two of their daughters; the artist has caught Cornelia's elegant Dutch dress and her Japanese features.

Pieter Cnoll rose to responsible and lucrative positions in the company hierarchy and died in 1672. His will designated his widow as his major heir and the guardian of his children. There was ample wealth; she would have a big carriage and a household with forty slaves. In 1675 the lawyer Johan

Bitter arrived in Batavia from Holland. His wife had died on the voyage out. He had four children to support. His salary as a member of the Court of Justice was not adequate to support his family in the lavish style of the Batavia elite. He was attracted by Cornelia's wealth, she perhaps by his legal expertise and high connections, which might help her preserve her wealth and status. She insisted on a prenuptial agreement by which she remained in exclusive possession of all the money and property she brought to the marriage. They were married just over six months after Bitter's arrival in Batavia.

Things went bad quickly. When Cornelia proposed to make a small investment in her own name, Bitter informed her that although it was clear that he did not share *ownership* of her property, nothing was said in the agreement about its *management*. She could not do anything without his participation and approval. There were ferocious quarrels. Friends intervened and persuaded Cornelia to try to buy peace by giving Bitter the sum he had been promised if she died before him. But the quarrels continued. Bitter beat her, dislocating her shoulder. She moved out but came back. Bitter offered to divorce her for a cash payment of f125,000;* she refused. Cornelia sued for divorce, and Bitter filed a countersuit, claiming that the prenuptial agreement was invalid and he was entitled to half her assets. When the Batavia Church Council, more interested in Christian harmony than in anyone's rights, tried to effect a reconciliation, Bitter slandered the motives of its members, refused to apologize, and made endless procedural delays.

Cornelia was trying to get some of her money safely deposited under the names of friends. Bitter got his hands on some of her money and sent some diamonds and a bill of exchange to Holland. The diamonds were discovered; he was accused of smuggling diamonds in violation of the company's monopoly, dismissed from its service, and sent home in 1680. In Holland he filed a new suit, asking that Cornelia be ordered to reconcile with him and that half her assets deposited with the company be sequestered as his by right. The court ordered only a reconciliation, ignoring what was for Bitter the key question of Cornelia's fortune. But now he began to win a few rounds. The diamond-smuggling charge was dropped, he was reinstated in the company's service, and he returned to Batavia in 1683. Compelled by the court order, man and wife now shared a house and

---

*The standard abbreviation for the Dutch guilder is "f."

seem to have settled into an uneasy peace. But then he transferred f50,000 of her money to his own account and sent most of it to Holland. On January 5, 1686, three sailors saw a man beating a middle-aged lady until she bled from her mouth, while he shouted, "You whore, beast, bitch, come here and I'll trample you under my feet until the blood spills from your throat." The authorities arrived; but after all, Bitter was a member of the Court of Justice, and after a night in jail the three witnesses decided not to testify against him. Now Cornelia appealed for permission to live apart from Bitter and safeguard her assets but was turned down. The authorities still were seeking a Christian reconciliation, but they finally gave up and in 1687 sent both parties to the Netherlands.

Arriving some time in the summer of 1688, Cornelia retained a good attorney and filed a suit in November 1688 before the High Court of Holland requesting legal separation from Bitter, the restitution of f45,500 he had taken of her assets, and the proceeds of the sale of her house, coach, and other assets in Batavia. Bitter countersued, asking that she be named a "malicious desertrix" and that he be granted one-fourth of her assets outright and the administration of the rest. The High Court did not pass sentence until July 4, 1691. It then ordered Cornelia to live in peace with her husband and declared him entitled to half the income from her assets. There was to be a further consultation after the August recess; it never took place, and it is likely that Cornelia died that summer. Bitter lived on in Holland in very comfortable circumstances and died in 1714.

For many years Cornelia had been a good Japanese daughter, writing regularly from Batavia to her mother's relatives in Hirado. Now, so far from Batavia, did she remember the little town on the island side of the narrow strait, the daimyo's castle looming above it, and the Chinese junks and high-walled European ships in the bays around the island? Surely she remembered Batavia, its lonely little Japanese community, the prosperity and intelligence of the Chinese, the earnestness and hypocrisy of the Church Council, the sailors and taverns, the fresh fish and wonderful tropical fruit, the stink of the canals, the giggling slave girls doing her bidding, the endless pregnancies when her first husband was alive, the fun of being on her own and making investments that paid off, the nightmare of Johan Bitter dodging truth and right. The canals weren't too clean in Holland, and the drunken workmen and sailors sounded familiar; but the streets were narrow, the breeze sometimes was chilly even in midsummer, and the long days were getting shorter at an amazing rate as the summer wore on.

CHAPTER 7

PHAULKON

The Dutch East India Company traded in many Asian ports where it had no fort and few or no special treaty rights. Sometimes it did not even have a warehouse ashore and conducted its trade on board its anchored ships. But wherever they were, servants of the company kept careful records of their own trade. In the late seventeenth century they were especially likely to keep careful records on local political situations and on the trade of their competitors. The company was somewhat overextended in trade at ports where competition was brisk and profits were doubtful and was trying to decide where to go on struggling and where to give up. The rising commercial and political power of the English East India Company, the less consistent but occasionally daunting efforts of the French, and even a Danish presence in South India all required careful monitoring. The excellent records they kept are crucial for our accounts of Ayutthaya, capital of the kingdom of Siam, which the Dutch heard as "Yudia" and often spelled "Judea."

In 1688 Ayutthaya was the scene of one of the strangest of all baroque political crises. An adventurer of Greek origin who called himself Constantine Phaulkon had risen to great power as director of the kingdom's finances and foreign trade. He had many enemies, but King Narai had great faith in him. Prompted by Narai's interest in the French as a counterweight to the commercial dominance and occasional bullying of the Dutch, Phaulkon had used his own back channels to pursue some high-risk relations with the French. The French, whose power in the Indian Ocean lagged far behind that of the Dutch and the English, had responded with alacrity. A splendid Siamese embassy to France in 1686 had led to the dispatch of a return embassy, accompanied by six hundred troops. Some entertained the hope that the king might become Catholic. But by the end of 1688 both King Narai and Phaulkon were dead and the French and their forces were gone.

In fact, although the events of 1688 led to a great deal of anger and a bit of bloodshed, the fundamental stability of the Siamese kingdom had never been in doubt, and the French hopes for either military domination or royal conversion had been very much overblown. The Siamese polity was open to participation of individual foreigners in the management of foreign trade and finance; Chinese residents had played such roles for centuries, especially as managers of Siam's tribute embassies to the Chinese court, which were accompanied by substantial amounts of duty-free trade. But the activities of foreign merchants supported royal power and did not threaten at all an impressively solid and prosperous state with a rich mix of divine kingship, large and splendid temples and monasteries, and pervasive Buddhist practice and faith.

The most basic sources of strength of the great kingdom of Siam were the wide, rich rice lands that surrounded Ayutthaya, about forty miles up the Chao Phraya River from modern Bangkok. The annual inundation fertilized the soil, and there were no crop failures. Land, much of it uncultivated, was abundant. Freemen might be called on to serve the king for six months or more of a year, a burden that was bearable only because their family members and slaves could harvest enough to support them. This royal control of manpower could produce, as it did in 1688, large fighting forces to control and wear down a foreign intruder. However, the levies of manpower were easily diverted into the control of regional governors or high officials. In the seventeenth century the kings attempted to counteract this centrifugal tendency by increasingly direct control and promotion of foreign trade. It was common in early modern Southeast Asia to find rulers actively involved in the foreign trade of their kingdoms, but we know of no other royal involvement as active and well organized as that of Siam. Dutch records contain examples of Siamese "king's ships" as far afield as Java and Japan.

Ayutthaya was full of temples of all sizes, the larger capped with great pagoda spires that the Buddhist faithful covered with gold leaf. Some had

long rows of statues of Buddhist deities, one a huge reclining Buddha figure. Saffron-robed monks were everywhere; progress toward breaking
earthly emotional ties and eventually achieving Nirvana could not proceed
far except in the monastic life. Monks were deeply respected, and many
boys spent a few early years in a monastery and were educated there before
they resumed lay status and married. The royal court was splendid and ceremonious; in Buddhist belief the king was a chakravartin, a turner of the
wheel of the Buddhist Law. In and around Ayutthaya were large settlements of Chinese and of Portuguese (many of the latter of mixed Asian and
European heritage), a substantial trading post of the Dutch East India
Company, a church of the Society of Jesus, and the central seminary for all
Asian missions of the French Society of Foreign Missions. Some of the royal
bodyguard were descendants of Catholic Japanese who had settled there
early in the century. Muslims from Persia and India were a substantial presence but less influential than they had been a few years before. The very
capable King Narai (reigned 1656–88) spent much of the year at Lopburi,
about forty miles farther north, where a royal hunting lodge had gradually
expanded into a modest palace and attached monastery.

For the Dutch and the other European traders Siam was not a great
source of riches. Large quantities of deer hides could be bought, largely for
the Japanese market, as well as some important dye woods. But these were
not high-profit items, and the competition of other traders, especially the
Chinese, was vigorous. In the 1660s the Dutch had used military threats to
get a rather leaky monopoly of deer hide exports. Still, the post was just
barely justifying its existence. King Narai resented Dutch bullying and had
been looking for a counterweight to them. The English had proved incompetent. Narai had been interested in a possible French connection as early
as 1674 and had sent an embassy to Louis XIV, which was lost at sea, in
1681.

The man who called himself Constantine Phaulkon was a Greek from
Cephalonia, which in the 1680s was ruled by Venice. He had come to Siam
in the service of the English East India Company, and his way into the service of King Narai had been paved by the payments and recommendations
of the English, who hoped to use his influence to smooth the way for their
own trade. He had turned out industrious and extremely intelligent. Working in the royal trade management hierarchy, he favored independent English merchants, who were trading in violation of the English company's
monopoly, over the fractious and incompetent servants of the company.

He expanded the fleet of ships owned by the royal court, hiring independent Englishmen and other Europeans to officer them. He spoke good Malay and good Portuguese, and he learned Siamese quickly. He came to King Narai's notice when he interpreted at a missionary's royal audience in 1682 and soon was having long and regular interviews with the king. He converted or reconverted to Catholicism, partly so that he could ask a missionary returning to Europe to seek favor for his family from the Venetian rulers of Cephalonia. He now became the key intermediary in Narai's efforts to gain support from France. In 1684 he arranged for a diplomatic feeler to France. In response Louis XIV sent in 1685 a curious ambassadorial team of the abbot of Choisy, something of a cynical *boudoir abbé*, and the chevalier de Chaumont, a recent convert from Protestantism with a convert's zeal and narrowness. They were to seek concessions for French trade in Siam and make a first effort to persuade the king to convert to Catholicism. The French Jesuit astronomers going to China whom we shall meet later sailed on the same ships. Lopburi became the center of the drama; a special residence for the ambassadors was erected there, and the king donated land to the Jesuits for a residence and then came there to observe a lunar eclipse.

From this time on Phaulkon was walking whole networks of tightropes. Catholic zealots like Chaumont, who knew nothing of Siam, dreamed of the conversion of the king and thereby of the kingdom. Phaulkon knew that the monarchy was so deeply linked to the Buddhist faith of the people that the chances of that were nil, but he could not refute too bluntly an important element in French interest in Siam. If King Narai got his French connection, Phaulkon would get much of the credit for it, and a modest French presence in Siam might make it easier for Phaulkon to save himself if his king died or if he otherwise lost power. But if the presence was too large, too obtrusive, it would increase Siamese hostility more than it would enhance his own safety. His immediate problem was that Chaumont included in many of his addresses to King Narai little lectures on the saving truths of Christianity. Phaulkon simply left them out of his translations. Then he convinced Chaumont that more could be done if he would offer Narai an alliance with the Sun King. This was done, and the very pleased king of Siam sent three high-ranking envoys off on the long and dangerous voyage to France. There they were much gawked at and written about, and Louis XIV, determined to project his majesty even more emphatically at that great distance than in Europe, received them on a throne glittering with jewels on a raised dais at one end of the great Hall of Mirrors. The real business of this exchange was in the hands of the Jesuit Guy Tachard, who carried a secret proposal from Phaulkon that France send a substantial body of troops to garrison Singora, a Siamese port partway down the Malay Peninsula.

When the Siamese ambassadors went home in 1687, they were accompanied by two new French envoys, one of whom, Simon de la Loubère, made use of his few months in Siam to compile materials for one of the most intelligent and observant European books written about any part of Asia before 1700; Father Tachard, who was to carry out the real instructions of Versailles by back channels, dealing only with Phaulkon; and six hundred troops on six warships. Even after about two hundred died on the voyage out, this was a substantial force, certainly more than Phaulkon had had in mind. Moreover, Phaulkon was appalled to find that Tachard's instructions were to seek the installation of this force in Bangkok, downriver from Ayutthaya, which would give the French a stranglehold on the kingdom.

If Phaulkon agreed to these terms, many Siamese would accuse him of betraying the country to the foreigners, but it might be easier for him to run for cover at Bangkok. If he refused, the French might stay as a hostile invading force, and he, widely recognized as the man who brought them there, would be very lucky indeed to get away with his head on his shoulders. He made sure that he would be the sole spokesman for King Narai in these negotiations and then accepted the presence of the French at Bangkok on the condition that the soldiers swear allegiance to the king of Siam. The troops took the oath and settled down to improve the fortifications amid the diseases and insects of that near swamp. Their general, the elderly Desfarges, went along with Phaulkon's plans. The ambassadors both set sail for France around the end of 1687.

Then Phaulkon's tightropes started to fray. King Narai was in Lopburi, and Phaulkon was just a five-minute walk from the palace, in the residence that had been built for the French ambassadors. The king was in poor health, and the question of succession became critical. Phaulkon supported Narai's choice, an adopted son named Pra Pi. The king also had two brothers who had no use for Phaulkon, clearly were playing their own game, and were beginning to give audiences in quasi-royal style. But the most capable candidate, the one best placed to exploit widespread feeling against Phaulkon and the French, was a high official named Phetracha, who had both a sister and a daughter among Narai's wives. Armed men, drawn by the succession crisis and the need to defend the country against the French menace, began to swarm toward Ayutthaya from all directions. Phaulkon asked Desfarges to send more of his troops up to Lopburi, north of Ayut-thaya, to defend him, Narai, and Pra Pi. But by now Desfarges was turning against Phaulkon, as a result of long conversations with a disaffected agent of the French East India Company and a priest of the Society of Foreign Missions, who thoroughly understood how much resentment Phaulkon had aroused and who had no use for Phaulkon's Jesuit connections. Des-farges refused to take his troops any farther than Ayutthaya.

Some friends told Phaulkon that he was in great danger and should flee, but he refused. According to stories recorded by the Dutch, he stayed away from the palace for a few days but then went again on May 19. His silver palanquin came home empty. He was tortured to extract a confession and details of his treasures, which would be confiscated, but there were not many treasures because he had invested most of his money in shares of the French East India Company. He was beheaded on June 4, and his body was cut in half and put in a shallow grave from which dogs soon dug it up. By that time Pra Pi already had been killed, and his head thrown before the horrified Narai: "There's your king." On July 9 Narai's brothers were beaten to death with sandalwood staves; it was the custom that no royal blood was ever spilled. Narai died on July 11, and Phetracha assumed the throne with a minimum of opposition. The Dutch went a few miles upriver to greet him when he came downriver to Ayutthaya on August 1 in a splendid procession of barges that also bore the body of King Narai.

The French troops still were in their fortifications at Bangkok. Another ship had arrived in August with two hundred fresh soldiers. Still other ships had come in from outposts and patrols against piracy to reinforce Bangkok. A Siamese flag flew over the Bangkok fortifications. But no one wanted the French there, and although the Siamese soldiers were less well trained and well armed than the French, they were much more numerous. The new king was willing to let the French go quietly. They started down-river on November 2. The new king signed a commercial treaty with the Dutch on November 14. On December 26 some of the French stopped at Melaka. Siam was a swamp, the commanders said. The people were brutal. They very much hoped that their king would not want to have anything more to do with them. And he didn't.

PART III

THREE WORLDS APART

RUSSIA, CHINA, JAPAN

I n the 1550s Europeans had begun to make regular trading voyages to the ports of three great empires of which they knew very little. In 1688 all three remained in European eyes worlds apart. To Europeans, Japan and China were more thoroughly "other" than Russia, their civilizations built on foundations that owed nothing to the Mediterranean and Europe. In 1688 there was no permanent foreign presence in Edo, capital of Japan's military rulers, and in Beijing the only Europeans were a few hundred Russian war captives and a handful of Jesuits. Japan's extremely tight control of its foreign relations had grown out of responses to threats of subversion by Catholic missionaries and converts. Apart from that, the politics and cultures of these two peoples had been little altered by their contacts with the Europeans.

Europeans had been more changed by distant reports of China than the Chinese had been by European ships in their harbors. The picture of China built up by the Jesuits was widely published in the 1680s and soon provided leverage for new trends of thought idealizing the rationality of the rulers of China. For some European intellectuals, China was about to become the Great Other, showing possibilities of ways of thinking and organizing society radically different from their own. China, Japan, Russia—and India—all have been Great Others for European and American social thought at various times down to our own. The availability of knowledge of them and the use of them as examples and objects for comparison are an intellectual transformation that was just beginning in 1688. It continues today to open up to us one frontier after another of the possibilities of the human condition.

CHAPTER 8

TSAR PETER'S RUSSIA

General Patrick Ivanovich Gordon spent all of 1688 in the vicinity of Moscow, talking to people in high places, sometimes learning things he did not dare write even in his private diary. A great success, a senior commander in the armies of the two tsars, he still cringed at the viciousness and instability at the center of the Russian state. Gordon was a Scottish Catholic who had left home at the age of sixteen to seek his fortune and had fought successively in the armies of Sweden, Poland, and the Holy Roman Empire, usually under Scottish officers. As soon as he entered Russia to seek further service there, he regretted his decision, finding the towns dirty and the people "morose." But he was informed that since he was a Catholic and had come from countries with which Russia was often at war, he would be taken for a spy and sent to Siberia if he tried to leave the country. He rose in the service of the tsars, distinguished himself in a campaign against the Ottomans, commanded the garrison of Kiev, served as the quartermaster of a bungled 1687 expedition against the Tatars, and in 1688 became colonel of a regiment. There were quite a few Scottish and German Catholic officers in Moscow. Occasionally they, or their sons, were allowed to leave the country. They kept in touch with relatives in their home countries and were reasonably well informed about events elsewhere in Europe; Gordon's diary for 1688 mentions the arrest of the seven bishops in London, the invasion of England by William of Orange, the

French conquest of Philippsburg on the Rhine, and the Hapsburg victories at Belgrade and in Bosnia.

Most seventeenth-century cities were dirty, disorderly, and dangerous. Moscow was one of the worst. With endless forests in all directions to supply logs, it is not surprising that most building was of wood; when painted and decorated with carvings, houses might occasionally remind the visitor of the larger and more comfortable wooden structures of a greater city far to the south, Istanbul. Tall, narrow Orthodox churches with their onion domes were everywhere. The summer days were very long, but then came winters of short days and deep cold, and springs when mud made the streets impassable.

Moscow's politics were as messy as its streets, and here too the observer might be reminded of Istanbul. The Ottoman sultans depended for their large expeditionary forces on troops recruited by provincial commanders who drew revenue from lands that they did not own but that were assigned to them according to the numbers of soldiers they would provide. So did the Muscovite tsars. That was all very well for an annual campaign, but not for the year-round task of protecting the ruler and his court from their many internal enemies and maintaining a bit of order in the capital. For this, full-time professional soldiers were needed: Janissaries in Istanbul, the *streltsy* in Moscow. The soldiers around the court found that they had power over it, and they came to take part in every struggle for succession or control of the court. They passed their positions on to their sons and made use of their privileged status in the capital to open shops and make money in many unsoldierly ways.

But Moscow was much less open to foreigners than cosmopolitan Istanbul. The Russian city experienced nothing comparable to the new talent and new genes, slave bureaucrats and palace women, that constantly infused the Ottoman power structure. Moscow was not a crossroads of world trade and cultural exchange. Such foreigners as made their way there were confined to a ghettolike foreign settlement on the outskirts of the city. Foreigners who came to Russia in search of wealth or employment found that it was hard to get permission to leave again. In the middle of the city stood the imposing Kremlin palace-fortress, with its magnificent old churches. The tsars left the Kremlin only in rare and ceremonious procession.

In 1688 Russia had two tsars. Ivan, who lived in the Kremlin, was twenty-two years old, sickly, dim, scarcely able to stand on his own. Tsar

Peter, Ivan's half brother, just sixteen, lived most of the time at a country estate. He was lively, curious, outgoing, and big for his age; when he was eleven, the members of a Swedish embassy thought he was sixteen. He appeared at the Kremlin only for the necessary ceremonial functions. When Tsar Fedor died in 1682, the ambitious relatives of Peter's mother had persuaded a council of dignitaries to bypass Ivan and place the obviously more promising Peter on the throne. Then Ivan's maternal relatives had instigated a revolt of the *streltsy*, two of Peter's maternal relatives had been cut to bits and trampled into the mud outside the Kremlin, and Ivan and Peter had been named cotsars. But the real power in the Kremlin was Ivan's sister, Princess Sophia; Peter and his mother had no power and were lucky to be allowed to live quietly on a country estate.

Very lucky. In the Kremlin the tsar and his court spent their days in rigidly prescribed ceremonies. Ivan could not have learned or accomplished much even if he had been less constrained. But Peter made good use of his freedom. The foreign quarter was not far from his estate, and he used it to learn about foreign countries, their goods, their knowledge, even their crafts; he learned some carpentry and blacksmithing himself. Above all, he was fascinated by the arts of war. He led his group of young noble companions in drill and maneuvers. Being tsar, he could requisition weapons, even cannons if he wished, and direct his troops in building small-scale fortifications. His "forces" swelled and took in some nonnobles. Some of the foreign military officers helped with their training. Peter did not make himself colonel, but started out as an enthusiastic drummer boy and worked his way up—quite rapidly, to be sure. Soon he had three hundred young men under his command and then another three hundred at another estate—no match for the *streltsy*, but a most impressive indication of the young tsar's drive to learn and improve, especially in military matters. The two regiments of three hundred each were the nuclei of the most famous of the Imperial Guard regiments down to 1917.

While Tsar Peter and his widowed mother were kept out of the way, Princess Sophia and her favorite, Prince Vasily Golitsyn, gave the country an effective government. A major military expedition against the Tatars of the Crimea in 1687, commanded by Golitsyn, accomplished nothing; Golitsyn was not a gifted commander, and the Russians had no idea how to deal with the mobile Tatar cavalry. In 1688 the Moscow rulers kept their armies at home. They were wary that French pressure in Germany might lead the Holy Roman Empire to make a separate peace with the

Ottomans, freeing Ottoman and Tatar forces for use against Russia. Above all, the failure in 1687 had been embarrassing to a regime that had come to power in a bloody coup, that kept one anointed tsar in a marginal role, and in which Princess Sophia was coming closer and closer to claiming autocratic power for herself.

Early in 1688 General Gordon had some hope that there would be another expedition against the Tatars that year. He was especially frustrated by constant disorders among the Cossacks, Russians who had fled poverty and serfdom and lived under their own commanders on the vast open plains. The turmoil was aggravated at this time by the flight of many Cossacks to settlements along the Volga of Old Believers, dissenters from recent ceremonial reforms in the Russian Orthodox Church. He also noted that Moscow tended to encourage the independence of many Cossack leaders, not wanting to place too much trust in any supreme leader, and that probably worsened the turmoil. Moscow suffered no serious political disorders in 1688, but there were several major fires, one of which was said to have burned ten thousand houses. The government lent so much money to people who had to rebuild their houses that it could not pay Gordon and other officers. He must have known a great deal about the explosive political tensions at the center of the court, but he hardly ever confided this knowledge to his diary; there is one cryptic reference to "secret conjunctions." Tsar Peter was demanding more and more pipers and drummers from Gordon's and other regiments.

Gordon does not tell us about some remarkable advances in the young tsar's education in 1688. Peter requested a sextant from a diplomat returning from France and found a Dutch merchant, Frans Timmerman, who could show him how to use it. Then in June he and Timmerman happened to look in a storehouse at an imperial estate and found the keeled hull of a small Western-style ship. Peter was amazed to hear that such a ship could be sailed across and almost against the wind. Another Dutchman was found who managed to repair the hull, rig it, and demonstrate what it could do on a nearby river. Peter was even more entranced than he had been by drill and artillery. Soon he had established a little shipyard where several small ships were under construction, and he was working alongside the shipwrights to learn their craft. None of the ships was done before winter; but the work continued the next year, and Peter never lost his new fascination with ships and the sea. The boat he and Timmerman found has been preserved to our own day as the first seed of the Russian Navy.

In 1689 Golitsyn led another expedition against the Tatars, this time all the way to the Crimea, but turned back without a fight. On his return to Moscow he was received as a victor, but knowledge of the truth spread quickly. Princess Sophia seemed ready to take full power for herself. Some of Peter's supporters forced his hand by waking him in the middle of the night and telling him that the *streltsy* were coming to seize him. He fled in a panic to a fortified monastery, where nobles and commanders began to join him. He summoned the foreign officers. Gordon went to consult with Golitsyn. Seeing Golitsyn hesitant and frightened, Gordon made up his mind for Peter, and the other foreign officers followed him. Golitsyn was exiled to the Arctic, Princess Sophia to a nearby monastery, and Tsar Ivan renounced all governing powers. Peter was fully in control. He spent the 1690s laying the groundwork for the great changes that were to follow. He went to Archangel on the Arctic and saw a real ocean for the first time. He led an amazing embassy to France, Holland, and England, where he worked in a Dutch shipyard, he met the Amsterdam statesman-savant Nicolaas Witsen, and his party wrecked John Evelyn's country house. He also ruthlessly crushed a revolt of the *streltsy*. Neither Russia nor Europe was ever the same.

Tsar Peter's empire confronted him with astonishingly varied challenges, at the greatest distances, sometimes in the most fearsome rigors of the Russian winter. Our one year provides examples, from its beginning and its end.

From January 25 to March 25, 1688, Fedor Alexseevich Golovin, ambassador of Tsars Peter and Ivan sent to negotiate a peace with the Qing (pronounced "ching") Empire, was besieged by Mongols in the Russian outpost at Selenginsk, just south and east of Lake Baikal. Eventually Cossack reinforcements arrived, and the Mongols were forced to withdraw, and none too soon; food had been running low, and the animals had been weakening. If conditions had been bad inside the log fort, they cannot have been comfortable inside the felt yurts of the besiegers. Their mounting of a siege in the dead of a Siberian winter suggests that the Mongols understood how much was at stake in Golovin's embassy.

The greatest geopolitical transformation of the world of the seventeenth century was the explosive expansion of Russian trade and settlement across Siberia. Beginning with the raids of the Cossack adventurer

Yermak in the 1580s, Russian parties using the great river systems reached the Pacific in 1639. A series of outpost forts became centers for buying furs from the local people or simply demanding them as *yasak*, tribute traditionally owed to the dominant local power. Small numbers of settlers, many of them outlaws and few of them literate, began to settle and farm near some of the forts. Especially promising areas for grain production were discovered in the 1640s, in the valley of the Amur River, on the present northeastern border of the People's Republic of China and on the northern approaches to the homeland of the Manchu people, rulers of the Qing Empire. The Russians were pushed back from the Amur basin in the 1650s; but then the Qing relaxed their vigilance, and they came back. Not until 1683, after their conquest of Taiwan, did the Qing resume efforts to get them out, by diplomacy if possible, by war if necessary. The Russian outpost at Albazin was besieged in 1685; the Russians withdrew but soon returned, and after another siege in 1686 the Qing withdrew when they were informed that a Russian ambassador was coming to arrange a peaceful settlement.

Four hundred years earlier the Mongols had ruled Beijing and Nanjing, Kiev and Moscow, Isfahan and Baghdad. Pushed back to their homeland after the breakup of their vast empire, the Mongols still were feared because of the extraordinary mobility and fighting power of their cavalry. But the firearms of the sedentary empires were beginning to shift the military balance against them, and the Russian advance worked against them in a subtler way. It was not that the Russians were so strong or that the territories they occupied were so important to the Mongols. Rather, the Russian expansion put the Mongols in a difficult geopolitical position. Since the Qing and the Russians each feared an alliance of the Mongols with the other, both were predisposed to seek a peaceful settlement of their differences, despite their almost total ignorance of each other and the sensitive issues that divided them, especially the delineation of an Amur frontier. As long as the Russians and the Qing were at peace, neither had to fear a combination of the other's wealth and firearms with the Mongol cavalry. Both could develop their edges of the Mongolian steppe in relative peace. The Mongols would be isolated, caught in a great vise between Russia and China.

At the end of 1687 both Golovin and the Kangxi emperor sent envoys to Urga, the most important political and religious center of the Mongols. The Qing envoy may have helped encourage the siege of Selenginsk, but it was in any case a particularly advanced and exposed Russian position much resented by the Mongols. The siege left Golovin even more ready to talk peace with the Qing, and an envoy arrived from Beijing with an agreement for a conference at Selenginsk. But then in 1688 the whole fabric of Mongol politics was transformed, leaving Selenginsk inaccessible to the Qing and the Qing court in its turn very much chastened and ready to make peace. Galdan, khan of the Dzungars, came out of western Mongolia to attack the Khalkhas, the closest allies of the Qing. The Khalkhas were driven far to the southeast; more than a hundred thousand sought refuge in Qing territory. Galdan was willing to ally with the Qing or with the Russians; but they wanted peace with each other, and neither wanted to encourage a vigorous new leader in Mongolia.

Ambassador Golovin finally met a Qing delegation in 1689 at Nerchinsk, east of Selenginsk. Having no language in common, the two delegations communicated by means of the Latin translations of two Jesuits from the Beijing mission and a Pole in the Russian delegation. In the famous Treaty of Nerchinsk, the Russians agreed to withdraw from the Amur Valley. The Mongolian frontier was not delineated, but arrangements were worked out for trade in Siberian furs for the Chinese market. The Russians could develop Siberia in peace, and Kangxi could turn his attention to the Dzungars. The emperor personally led an expedition in 1696 that crushed Galdan's power in a battle near Urga, near present-day Ulan Bator, and the vise continued to tighten on the people of the steppe.

In the dark of the short days at the end of 1688 troops of the tsar waited until Lake Onega froze to a good depth. Then they advanced across the ice to the Paleostrovskii Monastery, which sat on an island in the lake. On November 23, in bitter cold and only about five hours of daylight, the attackers breached the walls of the monastery, which had been occupied by Old Believers. The defenders retreated to the upper chapel, pulled their ladders up, and set it afire. When the fire had burned itself out, the tsar's troops surveyed the smoking ruins and withdrew across the ice; soon all was covered with fresh snow as the days grew even shorter. It was said that about fifteen hundred Old Believers had died.

The forests of northern Russia were formidable to seventeenth-century man. In the summer, boggy ground, swamps, and swarms of insects made travel difficult and miserable. It was easier to travel on skis, over the snow and frozen lakes, in the winter, but there were only a few hours of daylight, the cold was bitter, and a sudden storm when a traveler was far from shelter meant certain death. The beautiful and forbidding world of forests and lakes around Lakes Ladoga, Onega, and Vyg, between the Gulf of Finland and the White Sea, was one of the main theaters of the late-seventeenth-century confrontation between the Old Believers and the Russian state and state church, which they viewed as works of the devil, possibly already the rule of the Antichrist. The troubles had begun in the 1650s, when Nikon, patriarch of the Russian Orthodox Church, had decreed reforms to correct inconsistencies in the rituals of the church and to bring them into line with the practices of the Greek Orthodox churches. The most important of these changes was the requirement that the sign of the cross be made with three fingers instead of the traditional two. This was heresy for the devout Russian believer, for whom the communion of the faithful, the linking of God and man, was constantly re-created in the uncanny harmony of voices in the high, narrow nave of stone cathedral or wooden country church, in the icons glowing in the dim light, in every movement, every gesture of priest and worshiper. To change anything was to shatter this divine harmony. Moreover, since the fall of Rome and Constantinople, Russia was the Third Rome, the last home of true Christianity, and must not lose its true faith by trying to adjust to the practices of its debased contemporaries.

From the beginning those who rejected Nikon's reforms saw in them signs that the "time of suffering" had come, that the apocalypse was at hand. In the Last Days the faithful must preserve the true teaching, flee the evil world, and dwell in the desert to purify themselves and await the end. These ideas and impulses are almost as old as Christianity, and in Russia there already was a long history of solitary saints who found their "deserts" in the great forests and who sometimes gathered loose communities of hermit-monks around themselves. In the late 1600s this religious flight often mixed with a secular one, as peasants fled the new laws that bound them to their villages as serfs.

The first armed resistance to the state by Old Believers ended in 1675–76, at a monastery on an island in the White Sea. In 1667 the state had demanded absolute submission and begun a siege that ended, over eight years later, in the dead of the near-Arctic winter, in the sack of the monastery and the slaughter of all but fourteen of the defenders. During the long siege the monks had grown more radical in their rejection of state authority, refusing to pray for the tsar, condemning him in "terrifying" language, perhaps taking in some survivors of a crushed rebellion. The local people had sympathized with them and smuggled food to them, and some of the monks had slipped away before the end to spread their teachings. Even more threatening was the revolt of the *streltsy* in Moscow in 1682, when Old Believers were found to be in league with the rebels, and an Old Believer spokesman insulted the princess regent Sophia in person. The revolt was suppressed, but the court, alarmed by this combination of military revolt and religious dissidence, turned to total suppression of the Old Believers.

The Old Believers had nothing to gain by attempting to conciliate a state that was determined to crush them. They already were withdrawing into remote areas and had shown their determination to resist when cornered. If their resistance was overwhelmed, then martyrdom would be theirs, a martyrdom surely preferable to living on into the terrors of the Last Days as the tsar-Antichrist gained power. From the 1660s on there had been scattered instances of Old Believer congregations committing suicide by setting afire their wooden churches and forts, abundantly supplied with firewood, tar, and straw. The greatest spiritual leader of the Old Believers, the archpriest Avvakum, was burned at the stake in 1682. From a tradition of asceticism, of long, difficult exercises in the mortification of the flesh and the purification of the soul, it was a short and to many an appealing step to the swift, spectacular, and total purification of the roaring fire. Early in 1687 hundreds of Old Believers took control of the Paleostrovskii Monastery on an island in Lake Onega. This was a clear provocation, an effort to speed up the inevitable confrontation with the Antichrist. Local troops responded quickly and soon had the Paleostrovskii under siege. On March 4, 1687, the Old Believers barricaded themselves into the upper level of their chapel with plenty of hay and straw, pulled the ladders up after themselves, and set the chapel on fire. The soldiers had orders to take prisoners if possible and frantically tried to chop or shoot their way in; but the flames spread too quickly, and more than two thousand Old Believers were burned to death. There was another self-immolation that same summer, near the White Sea, in which it was said that several thousand died. Then one of the leaders of the Paleostrovskii occupation who had slipped away before the end quietly gathered new followers from the Old Believer settlements hidden in the forests and on September 20, 1688, led them to reoccupy the Paleostrovskii. They had plenty of time to prepare their defenses while the unsettled late fall weather kept the attackers off the lake. But then the lake froze, and the imperial commanders were able to move their men and cannons across the ice and up to the walls of the monastery. The same drama was played out as in March 1687, with the addition of some unwilling martyrs, monks whom the Old Believers had captured as they took the monastery.

CHAPTER 9

SURVIVORS AND VISIONARIES

I've been determined to get well, but still the illness lingers.
With no drink-brought flush, my face stays still more pale.
Another day, at rest, I'll still wonder whom to ask.
As always, Heaven fixes which way we must go.
Along the river the plum blossoms have fallen; so it is with my dreams.
The first returning swallow chances to find a mate.
I'm still riffling through documents, trying not to nap.
Somewhere in my papers a cricket sounds mi-mi.

The changing seasons, lateness in life, slow recovery from illness: These were conventional themes for a culture that took comfort in the slowing down of old age. The great scholar Wang Fuzhi was in his seventieth year when he wrote this poem in 1688. But he still was hard at work. Already having completed more than sixty volumes of some of the most brilliant, idiosyncratic, and difficult scholarship and moral philosophy in the later Confucian tradition, he was working on a set of commentaries on the history of the Song Dynasty, and another, the longest work of his life, commenting on a famous comprehensive history of China written in the Song.

It was altogether appropriate that Wang should be working in the twilight of his life on a study of history. For Wang, as for every follower of the rich tradition we call Confucian, history was the great teacher. Kong Qiu (551–479 B.C.E.), whom the Jesuits and their European readers in 1688 already were calling Confucius, a Latinization of Kongfuzi, "Master Kong," had claimed to be not a creator but a transmitter of institutions and ceremonies established by the sage kings of remote antiquity and by the founders of the Zhou Dynasty, who had lived about five hundred years before him.

The Confucian gentleman knew his texts had all the answers to the problems of society, morality, and above all government. If only a ruler would employ him, Confucius himself had said, he could set things to rights. But what if the times and the rulers were evil? Then there might be no choice but to withdraw and preserve one's integrity and the inherited teachings as a recluse. Wang Fuzhi was living out a particular version of this role, that of the minister of a fallen dynasty who refuses to serve the new regime. In 1644 mounted Chinese rebels had occupied Beijing, capital of the Ming Dynasty, driving the last Ming emperor to suicide in the imperial garden. After only ten weeks the rebels themselves fled in the face of a massive invasion by the Manchus, who occupied Beijing and proclaimed their new Qing Dynasty, claiming that they had come to avenge the death of the last Ming emperor and to restore order to the whole empire. This they did in a remarkably short time; Canton (Guangzhou) was permanently in Qing hands as early as 1650, and the last pretender to the Ming succession was driven from the southwest into Burma in 1659. Wang Fuzhi had taken an active part in efforts to organize a Ming Loyalist regime in the south to resist the Qing conquest. The regime in which he was a junior official was a miasma of all the corruptions and conflicts of late Ming politics, supported by armies of former peasant rebels against the Ming and others of former military allies of the Qing.

Withdrawing from this hopeless situation after about a year of active service and four years of interest and intermittent contact, Wang went to live a life of scholarly retirement in his native Hunan Province. There he lived quietly for over forty years, traveling little, seeing a few students and friends. Many men of his generation refused as a matter of principle to take office under the Qing; they thought it disloyal to do so if they had once served or received honors from the Ming. Wang went further, refusing to adopt the changed robes of the Qing scholars and officials or the Manchu-style queue—shaved front of head and long braid down the back—which the Qing had imposed on all Chinese men. This imposition had been deeply resented and occasionally resisted, until the new rulers made it clear that if you kept your hair, you would lose your head. The provincial officials in Hunan almost certainly knew about Wang's Ming dress and hairstyle, but out of respect for his scholarship and perhaps because he had protectors in the local elite, they chose to look the other way.

Wang Fuzhi was a lifelong student of the *Yi Jing* (older spelling *I Ching*), a mysterious and enormously influential work, part divination manual, part guide to the subtle harmonies and interplays of action and passivity, success and failure, light and darkness, an understanding of which is supposed to make possible a life of wholeness and integrity. In 1652, when Wang considered for the last time getting involved in the messy politics of Ming resistance, he had turned to the *Yi Jing* not as a predictor of the future but as a divinatory source of moral insight. A first divination had suggested that no harm would ensue even if he had to deal with bad men and that he might meet with his prince, but a further step had yielded a configuration that offered no hope of anything good. It had been in the 1650s, not long after his final abandonment of hope for Ming Loyalist resistance and before his fortieth birthday, that Wang wrote his most searching and innovative works of philosophy. The first of them was a commentary on the *Yi Jing*, in which he made his most radical break with the Confucian faith in the relevance of high antiquity. Many scholars simply believed in the perfection and unchanging relevance of the institutions of early Zhou and the teachings of Confucius. But where had those teachings come from? Wasn't it possible that changing conditions would call for different teachings and institutions? Wang built on the *Yi Jing* commentaries to argue that all Ways (*dao*), including the Way of the Former Kings, had to be understood in relation to concrete situations—that is, their contexts of institutions and practices. The concrete situations were primary; if they were in order, there was no need to worry about the corresponding comprehensive Way. Sages knew this, but most striving scholars did not; common people dealt with it better than intellectuals. There are many potential Ways that have never existed; new ones will be called forth as concrete situations change. Thus, although Wang spent his life studying the Confucian classics, which all other Confucians revered as the unchanging standards of social and political life, his deepest insight called for openness to the emergence of new situations in which traditional ways of life would have to be questioned and altered.

In another work of the 1650s Wang had made a generalization about structures and moral practices of Chinese history that drew on the experience of alien conquest in his own time. In so doing he gave a radical rationale for the rejection of Qing legitimacy:

But when the families of things became clearly defined and the lines of demarcation among them were made definite, each was established in its own position and all living things were confined within their own protective barriers. . . . It is not that [Heaven and Earth] made these different types because they favored separation and division, but because under the circumstances it was impossible for all things to cooperate and avoid conflict otherwise. . . . [T]he Chinese in their bone structure, sense organs, gregariousness and exclusiveness, are no different from foreigners, and yet they must be absolutely distinguished from foreigners. . . . If the Chinese do not mark themselves off from foreigners, then the principle of Earth is violated. And since Heaven and Earth regulate mankind by marking men off from each other, if men do not mark themselves off and preserve an absolute distinction between societies, then the principle of man is violated. . . . There might be abdications, successions, and even changes of the Mandate of Heaven, yet never should a foreign dynasty be allowed to interrupt the succession [of Chinese emperors].

Staying sober and worrying a bit about the time he spent napping, Wang Fuzhi in 1688 was still at work on his largest single work, a set of reading notes on the eleventh-century history by Sima Guang, the *Comprehensive Mirror for the Aid of Government*, and another set of notes on the history of the Song dynasty; these were completed in 1691, the year before his death. In the notes on the *Mirror*, Wang argued that there was still much to learn from the classics and the teachings of Confucius. But "ancient institutions were meant to govern the ancient world and cannot be generally followed today . . . and because what is suitable today can govern the world of today but will not necessarily be suitable for the future, the superior man does not hand it down to posterity as a model."

Wang's works were unknown and unpublished until the middle of the nineteenth century. Their circulation at that time owed a great deal to the support of conservative reformers struggling with a world of steamboats and European incursions. Wang could not have imagined these developments, but his principles of modifying institutions to fit changing concrete situations and defending China against foreign invasion seemed deeply relevant. Still later young Hunanese in the early years of this century formed a society to study Wang's works. One of the members for a time was Mao Zedong.

In the tenth lunar month of the twenty-seventh year of Kangxi (1688), the famous painter Shitao presented to his friend Ding Peng a fine hanging scroll of a mountain landscape, with a small house tucked among trees below great cliffs, a seated figure barely visible in the house. The subject and the feeling expressed in it, that even such a small creature as man could find his place and be at ease among the awesome forces of nature, were at least seven hundred years old when Shitao painted this scroll, and they had inspired many of China's greatest paintings. Equally long-lasting was the creative tension between observation and portrayal of nature on the one hand and revelation of the character of the artist on the other. In Shitao the urge to self-expression seems to dominate. Chinese painters built their images of rocks, trees, and plants out of a vocabulary of repeated dots, dashes, circles, and leaf outlines that can be clearly seen on close examination but that blend into a convincing representation of a real landscape when one steps back. However, in the painting given to Ding Peng in 1688 and in many others, Shitao's dots and circles remain dots and circles no matter how one looks at them, and the cliffs are built of strokes that remain virtuoso demonstrations of brush and water-base ink. And the shapes! In the cliff that looms highest an arbitrary diagonal separates one band of upward-thrusting shapes from another that reaches out horizontally. In the foreground a mass of rock seems off-balance, its surfaces and crevices in discord. The viewer of the painting becomes not a gazer of tranquil eye and fixed position but a walker, perhaps a scrambler and stumbler, through an unfamiliar stretch of mountains, shrinking from unexpected dropoffs, wary of unstable cliffs looming above, awed by the powers of earth that care so little for man and move him so deeply. It is as if Shitao's restless and insistent drawing, his piling up of forms created by the expressive energies of the Chinese brush, have tapped the very energies that built the mountains and thrust the rocks in different directions.

Written on the painting are Shitao's note sending it to Ding Peng "for criticism" in 1688 and a poem dated 1679:

> Like angry lions clawing the rocks,
> Thirsty horses dashing to the spring,
> Wind and rain gather round,
> The clouds take myriad forms.
> Beyond the bounds, another realm,

Landscape by Shitao, given to Ding Peng in 1688

Knowing neither pain nor cheer.
Passions flow into brush and ink.
Beyond the brush and ink, a true tranquillity.
It makes the connoisseur exclaim,
"Nothing like it's to be seen."

The cataclysm of the Qing conquest, which gave many people opportunities for military adventure, political maneuver, and commercial
wealth, had wrenched Shitao from a destiny of idle, closely circumscribed
comfort and thrust him into an unsettled life, largely dependent on the
patronage of others. He was born in 1641, scion of a line of princes of the
Ming imperial house that had been settled for more than two hundred
years in the remote southwestern city of Guilin, whose landscapes of water
and misty peaks had fascinated Chinese artists for a thousand years. The
Ming princes were required to live quietly on their estates and not meddle
in politics or military matters. These princes, untrained and out of touch
with the country around them, became, simply by the mystique of their
imperial descent, the focal points of efforts to rally the forces of resistance
to the Qing conquest, with its Manchu core and many Chinese allies. The
evanescent resistance effort of which Shitao's father was the figurehead
was, like quite a few others, destroyed not by Qing forces but by a stronger
Ming Loyalist force, the one that was supported (and then betrayed) by the
first of a succession of Fujian sea lords. Shitao's father was executed; the
son's life seems to have been in little danger as he grew up quietly in
ambivalent and overlapping circles that included both obdurate Ming Loyalists and some of the most prominent Chinese who had gone over to the
Qing. Like several other scions of the Ming house and Loyalist intellectuals, he shaved his head and took the vows of a Buddhist monk in order to
make it clear that he had no worldly ambitions. In 1679, when he painted
the landscape he later gave to Ding Peng, he was living not far from the
Huangshan Mountains, where many wonderful scenes like this one can be
found. We should not expect ever to be able to match this painting to a
particular view; like most Chinese painters, Shitao frequently absorbed
many views and later in the studio painted the landscape in his mind's eye.
In 1680 he moved to the Nanjing area, where in 1684 he met the Kangxi
emperor, then on his first great southern tour. There followed a series of
connections with the court of the conquerors that were to lead Shitao to a
long stay in Beijing in the 1690s and access to some of the great collections
of paintings assembled by Qing grandees. In 1688 he was living in
Yangzhou, a thriving commercial and cultural center.

Shitao was a painter and a writer about painting of immense talent,
ambition, and originality. Most Chinese painters either followed and developed the style of an earlier master or elaborated a distinctive personal style
that gives most of an individual's paintings a family resemblance. Shitao

sometimes tried to see what he could do in someone else's style and once confessed that he had not been able even to approach the effects of the austere landscapist Ni Zan. But more often his paintings were like no one else's and were so different from one another that they seem to be the work of a dozen different painters. This extraordinary variety in style is a central principle in Shitao's famous *Record of Remarks on Painting* (*Hua Yu Lu*). Styles of painting all have their origin, he said, in a primordial, undivided One Stroke. The individual can grasp this One Stroke for himself, and once he has done so, his refusal to be limited to any one style will give rise to many styles, each fully realized in itself, without any special effort. Each painting will represent the external structure and also seize the internal powers and movements of mountains, rivers, people, birds, animals, grass, trees, and buildings. Shitao's essay drew on over five hundred years of sophisticated critical writing about landscape painting but carried it to a new level of intellectual ambition, echoing basic ideas of Confucianism, Chan Buddhism, and especially Daoism, so that the One Stroke began to sound very much like the undivided primitive Way out of which all particular beings arise.

The One Stroke produced the many styles, and the many styles, always individual and coherent and right, begin to form in the mind of the viewer not One Style but a world of constant surprise and irreducible diversity. Shitao no doubt was aware of the Indian origins of the Buddhist teachings he studied for many years but otherwise left no evidence of any interest in a world outside the world that was China. But in his artistic genius and in his ideas he came as close as anyone to the kind of art needed to encompass the world of 1688. The historian seeking to sketch a world tries not to be confined by any style, any set of questions but to follow hunches, to let one thing lead to another. Like Shitao letting the One Stroke appear in many forms, he hopes to avoid system and to put before his reader many pictures of a world, reflecting the unconfineable variety, splendor, and strangeness of the human condition.

CHAPTER 10

AT THE COURT OF KANGXI

In 1688 the empire of the Great Qing was at peace. People in the know heard about the continuing uncertainties of relations with the Russians, the rise of Galdan of the Dzungars, and the flight of the Khalkhas toward the Great Wall, but all that seemed far away. At the Wuhan cities in the middle Yangtze Valley there was a mutiny of troops threatened with demobilization, but it was quickly put down.

Older people remembered very different times. Fifty years before, the northern China plain had been ravaged by huge bands of mounted rebels, pursued by Ming imperial troops who were almost as much out of control. A bloodthirsty rebel had paused briefly in his rise to power over the riches of the Sichuan basin. In the rich rice lands of the lower Yangtze Valley, a general loss of control and incursions by the northern rebels had set off violent uprisings by tenants and bondservants. The south coast was in the hands of sea lords who supported the dynasty largely on their own terms. And on the northeast frontier of the empire a people who had long been tributaries to the Ming court, the Jurchen, had reorganized themselves and given themselves a new name, Manchu, and were taking and holding Chinese cities.

In 1644 the northern rebels had taken Beijing, only to be expelled ten weeks later by the Manchus, who proclaimed that they had come to restore order, to avenge the martyred last emperor of the Ming, and to establish their own Great Qing Dynasty. The violence of the Qing conquest was immense but brief; the Qing was in control of most of the empire by 1650. In the 1670s a rebellion of some of the senior Chinese generals allied to the Qing threw several provinces into turmoil but ultimately failed. The last opponents of Qing rule, descendants of the late Ming sea lords holding out on Taiwan, surrendered in 1683.

Confucians, with a few exceptions like Wang Fuzhi, thought of the moral teachings of their master as something that anyone could learn, even if he was not Chinese. They knew that a number of surrounding smaller states—Korea, Vietnam, and the Ryukyu Islands—were deeply influenced by Confucian culture. They knew that Japan had been so influenced in the past, and although they knew little of the Japan of the 1680s, they would not have been at all surprised by the spectacle of the reigning shogun earnestly studying the *Yi Jing* and trying to impress a less violent code of conduct on his warrior ruling class. The Manchus drew on a Central Asian heritage of statecraft not altogether different from that of the Mughals and the Ottomans, but from before 1644 they also had sought to present themselves as heirs, though not uncritical ones, of the Chinese political tradition.

In 1688 the ruling Qing emperor was in the twenty-seventh year of his Kangxi reign period; although this is actually a "year period" used to count the years in a reign, even contemporaries sometimes used it to refer to the emperor himself, and so do we. Manchu was Kangxi's first language but he had a good Chinese education and took his Chinese learning seriously. We have extensive records of his daily deliberations with his ministers, and it is no surprise at all to find in them such hoary Confucian clichés as "Governing is a matter of men, not of laws." Thus we find the emperor and his ministers taking a great deal of time to consider various candidates for appointments and their relative strengths and trying to find the appropriate way of disciplining an errant bureaucrat without destroying his future usefulness.

The imperial examinations, key to the channeling of elite energy and ambition into the service of the imperial center since about 1000 C.E., also received a good deal of attention. In April 1688 hundreds of scholars gathered from all over the empire for the metropolitan examinations in the capital. They already had passed through the narrowest gates in the system. Examined by local education officials, they had been awarded a local designation of "official student," which gave them social standing and some tax exemptions but no qualification for office and was not permanent; they had to keep studying and were periodically reexamined. The next step was the most difficult, as many hundreds of scholars gathered every three years in each provincial capital to be locked in long rows of examination cubicles and to write for several days on topics of classical learning and contemporary statecraft. The gathering of the candidates in a provincial capital was a time of great excitement. The candidates exchanged views on scholarship and politics. The common people watched for the lists of successful graduates and bet on which names would be on it. The ratio passing this examination at any sitting might be as low as two or three in a hundred. Those who passed were qualified for low-level office and for the metropolitan examination. Not all of them were from wealthy families; often someone would contribute to the travel expenses to Beijing of a poor graduate, esteeming his scholarship and hoping to be remembered if he became a high official.

The metropolitan examination was held at the imperial Confucian temple, east of the palace compound. Again the scholars were locked in cubicles for a series of essay assignments. After a certain number had been selected to receive the degree of *jin shi*, "presented scholar," there was a final step called the palace examination, for which the emperor approved the questions and participated in the evaluation. It determined the ranking of the successful candidates. Those who received the top ranks would be instantly famous, eligible for immediate appointment to high academic posts in the capital, and were expected to have brilliant careers ahead of them.

On April 28, 1688, the examiners presented the Kangxi emperor with a list of the 176 men who had passed the metropolitan examination and ten of the papers they ranked highest. The emperor was well prepared. He asked about the character of each of the leading candidates, sometimes directing the question to a councillor who was from the same area. He recognized the paper of one Zha Sihan even before the seals were broken to reveal the name; he said he had seen samples of Zha's calligraphy. Zha was a member of an eminent family from Zhejiang, in the southeast, a family with some taints of Ming Loyalism but a great deal of prestige. After the emperor had examined several of the papers and discussed their merits with his councillors, he raised Zha from fourth place to second. But that left the first three places all going to men from Zhejiang, and he thought that not suitable, so he juggled the rankings a bit more. The next day the new *jin shi* were ushered into the huge court before the Hall of Supreme

Harmony, and performed their *ketous* (old spelling kowtow; three kneelings and nine prostrations) before the emperor, almost invisible on his throne in the shadows of the hall.

But despite the Confucian clichés there was more to governing than judging men and encouraging their scholarship and natural goodness. People lived on the land and drew their livings from it. Their rulers had to draw enough revenue from them to be able to keep order, defend them against bandits and invaders, teach the teachable, build up reserve stocks of grain for famine years, and maintain transport canals, irrigation works, and flood control systems. They also had to keep the burdens of tax and labor service light and equitable. When Chinese statesmen discussed these problems, they found it altogether natural to refer to the strengths and weaknesses of the various systems Chinese rulers had tried out since the founding of the Han around 200 B.C.E.

One set of policy challenges had an even longer lineage. Before 2000 B.C.E. the great statesman Yu was supposed to have rescued the world from a great flood by digging channels so that the water could run off into the ocean. Then he had been chosen as the best man to succeed as ruler and had regularized the kinds of goods each region should present as tribute. When a grand secretary mentioned the classical text *Tribute of Yu* in a debate in 1688, the emperor remarked that such an allusion to ancient times was what you would expect from someone who didn't really know anything about the subject at hand. But in fact Yu's wisdom in digging channels so that the waters could drain away, his assembling masses of workers, and his own doggedness in the struggle against the waters still were relevant to those who were trying to deal with the problems of the Yellow River and the Grand Canal.

The Yellow River flows down out of plateaus covered with fine loess soil. Untamed, it changes course frequently as it deposits its huge burden of silt on the North China plain. Since before Confucius's time China's rulers have sought first to drain parts of that plain for cultivation, then to channel the Yellow River. The result has been that its silt is deposited mostly between the dikes, and its bed eventually has risen above the surrounding plain. In Ming and Qing times the situation was compounded by the importance of the Grand Canal, which brought the rich rice surplus of the lower Yangtze to the capital, interacting in complicated ways with the Yellow River, the Huai River a bit farther south, and a series of shallow lakes on the floodplain. The whole system requires constant monitoring and centralized management. These were less and less available in the last decades of Ming. The mouths by which the Huai emptied into the ocean silted up. Lower channels were not kept dredged, so that river and lake beds built up and floods became more frequent. A major effort to get the system under control was inaugurated in 1677 with the appointment of Jin Fu as director general of the Yellow River. Jin superintended a major effort to dredge channels and build new dikes. But still there were floods, and some of his policies aroused controversy.

Thus it was that on April 8 and 9, 1688, determined to get to the bottom of the whole situation, the Kangxi emperor assembled in his presence all the major officials involved in Yellow River policy. Yu Chenglong, governor of the metropolitan province, was the most vigorous critic of Jin Fu. He accused Jin of failing to dredge the key river mouths, allowing floodwaters to ravage rich areas between the Huai and the Yangtze. Levies of labor had been excessive. Jin had converted land that was in private hands but not properly listed on the tax rolls into garrison fields, normally used to finance military establishments but here to support the water projects. The common people wanted to kill and eat Jin Fu, Yu said. Jin replied that all he had done was to crack down on abuses of power by the local landed elites. The emperor was very much in control of the debate, asking detailed questions, exposing his ministers' ignorance, reminding them that he had walked on some of the key dikes on his southern tour. He drove home over and over the need for a comprehensive view, for not just going along with the local people, who didn't mind releasing water that would flood fields in the next county. When he caught an official in a major error or contradiction, the official fell onto his face in a ketou. Finally it was clear that Jin Fu would have to take the blame for his adoption of the unpopular garrison field system and for his failure to clear the key river mouths and would be dismissed. But the emperor suspended the further punishments that had been proposed for him; we shall wait six or seven years, he said, to see if anyone else can do a better job.

On his second tour of the south in 1689 the emperor reexamined the river system, saw how much Jin Fu had accomplished and how enormous the challenge was, and restored Jin to his office, which he held until his death in 1692. Jin had been vulnerable in 1688 because he was associated with the grand secretary Mingju, who had just fallen from power. The emperor knew when he had to let the political winds blow, but he also valued competence and hard facts, especially in dealing with the great intractable river.

All early modern rulers understood the importance of ceremony in communicating favor and disfavor and projecting their own majesty; in this, Kangxi was very much the contemporary of Aurangzeb and Louis XIV. But in China the centrality of ceremony in Confucian thought added extra layers of care and self-consciousness. Kangxi, steeped from childhood in Chinese values as well as in those of his Manchu ancestors, presented himself as the gracious rewarder of a good minister and a filial grandson.

On August 9, 1688, the Kangxi emperor received in audience the sea-pacifying count, sea-pacifying general, commandant of water forces of Fujian Province Shi Lang. In 1683 Shi Lang had led the forces that conquered Taiwan, extinguishing the last organized center of organized resistance to Qing rule throughout China and incorporating Taiwan into the Chinese Empire for the first time. At the audience the emperor removed his own collar, lined with the special imperial dragon satin, and had it placed around Shi's neck. On August 10 the emperor received Shi again, at the Qianqing Gate, a great verandalike structure, often used for informal and working audiences, behind the formal audience halls of the Beijing palaces, and gave him some dishes to eat from his own dinner.

These already were gestures of very special favor, carefully recorded. The emperor never missed a chance to show his ministers how well he treated those who served him well and to remind them how often his judgment of men and political situations had been better than theirs. The emphasis on the ruler's evaluation and employment of ministers was one of the fundamentals of Confucian statecraft, but the touches of personal recollection and self-congratulation were highly individual and characteristic of Kangxi's style as a ruler. So was his way of reminding an official that he knew that man's weaknesses and remembered his mistakes but was allowing him to continue in office nonetheless. A loose imperial rein, a proper sense of gratitude on the part of the official, and a keen sense of being always on probation, always watched were the lot of the bureaucrat or general under Kangxi. After the second audience the emperor bestowed on his aged general the signal honor of a summons into the private areas of the residential Qianqing Palace, usually off limits to all except the emperor, his ladies, and the court eunuchs. The following conversation was recorded:

Emperor: Do you have anything to memorialize?

Shi: Your minister has served as commander of water forces for Fujian. It was only by means of the Awesome Majesty and Immense Blessings of Your Imperial Majesty that the maritime frontier was pacified. I have nothing with which to trouble Your Majesty.

Emperor: Previously you served as an Inner Court High Minister for thirteen years. At that time, because you are a Fujian man, there were those who belittled you; it was only We who knew you and treated you generously. Thereafter the Three Feudatories rebelled and oppressed our people, but one by one they were pacified, and only the sea bandits remained like wandering spirits, sneaking away to take Taiwan and to afflict Fujian. If We wanted to do away with these bandits, no one but you would do. Thus We made a decision, based on Our own convictions, to give you a special promotion and appointment. As it turned out, you were able to exert your strength and exhaust your mind, determined not to fail in your duties, zealous and unmindful of yourself, so that bandits who had been impossible to put down for sixty years were wiped out without any remaining resistance; this really is your accomplishment. More recently, there have been those who said you were presuming on your merit and becoming proud, and We heard something of this. Now you have come to the capital, and there have been people who have said We should keep you here and not allow you to go back. But We have considered that when the bandit disorders were at their height We used you and did not mistrust you; now that All Under Heaven is at peace, should We mistrust you and not allow you to go back? Now you are commanded to return to your post; henceforth you must be more careful, in order to preserve your meritorious name. In the past, when officials of high merit sometimes have not been able to continue without blemish to the ends of their careers, it has been because they were not careful; you must exert yourself in this way. You also must maintain harmony between soldiers and people, and keep your region at peace, in order to fulfill Our intention to love the soldiers and give solace to the people, and in order to preserve the ideal image of a meritorious minister.

Shi: The pacification of the sea bandits relied entirely on Your

Majesty's uncanny strategy and penetrating calculations. It was the plans that were transmitted to your minister, that made success possible; how could your minister have had the strength? Your Imperial Majesty has set up troops to protect that people; how would your minister dare not to imitate the Sage Compassion and keep harmony between troops and people? Moreover, since Fujian is my native place, your minister will be sure to devote himself to pacifying it. Your minister has received the Heavenly Grace of the Emperor in great abundance, being named an Inner Court High Minister, then granted the rank of Count with right of inheritance. All Under Heaven will be ruled by the Imperial Dynasty for ten thousand, one hundred thousand years, and your minister's descendants will enjoy good fortune without end. Also I have received the favor of Your Imperial Majesty removing an item of Your Majesty's clothing and putting it on your minister, giving Your Majesty's own food to your minister to eat; these are special favors without precedent since ancient times. But your minister is just a solitary individual, simple of mind and hasty of speech, so that I offend many people; for completing my career safely I depend entirely on Your Imperial Majesty. Your minister is old and his strength is spent. The affairs of the border region are weighty; I fear that my spiritual energy will not be sufficient to manage them.

Emperor: In generals, wisdom is to be esteemed, not strength. We employ you for your wisdom; how could it be a question of strength of hands and feet? You must exert yourself in your charge.

Shi Lang lived until 1696. In 1688 his influence still counted for something in coastal Fujian and even supported new ventures like the envoys to Madras that same year whom we shall meet later in this book, but he was spending more of his time in retirement at his country estate and had to share power in the ports with representatives of the new system of maritime customs collectors and other branches of Kangxi's bureaucracy.

At the end of their interview, according to the imperial diarists, the emperor took note of Shi Lang's age and gave a special order to an imperial guardsman to take his arm and support him as he departed.

A far longer and more serious drama of ceremony and politics already had begun at the beginning of 1688, with the illness of the grand dowager empress. At dawn on January 3, 1688, the Kangxi emperor led an immense procession of princes, dukes, lesser nobles, and high military and civil officials from the inner residential palace through all the gates and courtyards of the Forbidden City of Beijing, then more than a mile south through the streets of the city to the immense park of the Altars of Heaven. All went on foot, including, in a rare gesture of humility, the emperor himself.

The Round Hill Altar of the Altars of Heaven is an elevated marble terrace, devoid of structure or ornament except for the marble railing that encircles it; it is surrounded in turn by two more railings on lower terraces. Only fourteen days before, the emperor had come there in person at dawn to perform the great winter solstice sacrifice to High Heaven, which was the most awesome moment in the annual ceremonial round of the imperial system. Since about 1000 B.C.E. Chinese rulers had called themselves Sons of Heaven and had claimed to rule by the Mandate of Heaven. Heaven's mandate, its favor to a particular ruling house, was not immutable; it would be lost, and the dynasty would fall, if its rulers failed to provide effective government and to set good moral examples in their own conduct. It was such a "change of mandate," in Chinese eyes, that had led to the fall of the Ming and placed Kangxi's father on the throne in the Beijing palaces in 1644. The emperor thus appeared at the Round Hill Altar beneath the cold dawn sky as a dependent, almost a supplicant, not in control, acknowledging the ultimate moral precariousness of his position. Perhaps as old, though not as clearly visible to us in the early stages of its history, was a sense that when the Son of Heaven paid homage to Heaven, he became the sole and essential pivot among the realms of Heaven, Earth, and Man. The proper succession of the seasons, timely rain for the crops, timely planting by the farmers all depended on the maintenance by imperial officials of a correct calendar and on the proper performance by the emperor or his delegates of a regular round of ceremonies marking turning points in the cycle of the year. I doubt that many of Kangxi's subjects were seriously worried that the days would not get longer if the winter solstice ceremony were not properly performed, but here too there were echoes of hazard, of responsibility, of things that could go wrong.

Both in the winter solstice ceremony and in the special ceremony on January 3, details of rank—the insignia, badges, and sashes of rank, the proper places to stand, and the proper sequences of motion—surrounded a simple basic act. The emperor was alone on the top terrace of the altar, all others well behind him or on lower levels. He performed a full *ketou*—

three kneelings, each followed by three prostrations to the pavement—before a tablet bearing in gold letters, Chinese and Manchu, on a deep blue ground, the words "Sovereign Heaven, Lord on High." A ceremonial usher read out the text of the imperial prayer, and the emperor performed another *ketou*.

But the purposes of the two ceremonies were quite different. On December 25, 1687, the emperor's beloved grandmother the grand dowager empress Xiaozhuang had fallen seriously ill. Immediately the emperor began to spend almost all his time in her sickroom, never undressing, sleeping near her bed, preparing her medicines himself. On December 31 he sought to remove baleful influences and propitiate the cosmic powers by ordering a reduction of the sentences of most criminals in the empire. Now he had come, on foot, to plead with Sovereign Heaven to grant additional life to his grandmother. This was the prayer that was read out:

Ah! In the twenty-sixth year of Kangxi, the cyclical year *ding mao*, the first day of the twelfth month, the cyclical date *yi si*, I, your Minister, the successor Son of Heaven, dare to proclaim to Sovereign Heaven, the Lord on High, saying: Your Minister has received the assistance of Heaven, and has served his Grandmother, the Grand Dowager Empress, received her protection for long years, and relying on her was able to find peace and tranquility. But now suddenly she has fallen gravely ill, and within the space of ten days it has been seen that it is very grave, and that might become critical at any time. Your Minister took no rest day and night, putting aside thoughts of bed or of food, mixing her medicines myself, seeking doctors and prescriptions everywhere, but nothing had any effect. In the Palaces all were sorely afflicted, and no one knew what to do. This humble one considered that the Heart of Heaven is compassionate and loving, that there is no place not covered by its canopy. All the more should your Minister, this insignificant person, devote himself to her. Moreover, your Minister, this insignificant person, in the past was blessed with her kindly care. I recall that at any early age I lost my parents, and took refuge at the knee of my grandmother. For more than thirty years she has nurtured me, taught and admonished me, so that I have come to maturity. If it were not for my grandmother, the Grand Dowager Empress, your Minister certainly never would have been able to become what he is today. Such has been her boundless mercy to me, that in my whole life it would be hard to repay it. Now that matters have come to this dangerous point, I have dared to cleanse myself and choose a day, and respectfully lead all my ministers, calling out and imploring to the Vast Arch of Heaven, humbly beseeching it to consider with pity and sincerity, to look down in calm reflection, so that this grievous illness may quickly pass away and she may live to a ripe old age. If perhaps her Great Portion is exhausted, this Minister wishes that his years may be reduced, some of his years transferred to add to the long line of the Grand Dowager Empress. For this I prostrate myself here below on the Altar, imploring your Vast Assistance, overcome with prayerful beseeching.

The echoes of this ceremony were as long and as deep as those of the winter solstice rite. All traditional cultures respected family hierarchy, but nowhere was filial piety so central a social value as in China. Every classically educated Chinese would have recognized the echo of the story of the great duke of Zhou, about 1000 B.C.E., when his nephew the king was mortally ill, imploring Heaven to take him instead.

But the Kangxi emperor was Manchu, not Chinese. Although by 1688 he had acquired a quite respectable Chinese classical education, presented himself as a patron of the Chinese tradition, and shown a genuine personal interest in parts of the classical heritage, the first language of his court was Manchu, and the text of his prayer was prepared in both Chinese and Manchu. Also, the grand dowager empress was Mongol, a member of the imperial Borjigit clan, descendants of the world-conquering Genghis Khan and his brothers. She and her aunt had been married to Hung Taiji, the pre-conquest second emperor of the Manchu ruling house, who had played a key role in building its power and finding places in it for powerful Chinese and Mongol allies before the beginning of the conquest of China. In those distant days visits to the Manchu court had been occasions for vast gatherings at the imperial yellow tents set up far out on the grasslands, with much feasting, hunting, and horse racing.

Even if the emperor had wanted to abandon his Manchu heritage and become a purely Chinese emperor—and clearly he did not—he could not have done so without alienating the Manchu grandees of his court and its Mongol vassals. At the beginning of 1688 important Mongol princes were on the brink of rebellion against Manchu suzerainty, and the prospect that they might ally with the Russians was especially frightening to the Qing. But filial piety was not just a Chinese ideal. As the emperor remarked to his officials a few weeks later, "Who does not have family ties?" Manchus, Mongols, and Chinese might have somewhat different ideas of blood ties, but demonstrative love of an elder would appeal to all of them. In this particular case the Chinese could see the emperor setting a good example of a key traditional virtue, the Manchus would note his special reverence for a symbol of the glorious continuity of the Great Qing from preconquest days on, and the Mongols would appreciate that it was one of their own whom he was attending so anxiously.

There also was a more immediate political agenda. Since about 1679 the court had been dominated by officials allied with the Manchu grand secretary Mingju. In these years many officials seemed blatantly interested in making fortunes for themselves, there were frequent stories of bribery in connection with appointments, and the emperor sometimes found his selection of officials constrained by the choices Mingju and the others put before him. One possible counterweight to the power of Mingju was an increasing reliance on the Chinese scholar-officials who already were submitting memorials criticizing the corruption and mismanagement of Mingju's associates; but their protests were rooted in a purely Chinese tradition with no place in it for Manchus and Mongols, and their criticisms frequently were idealistic and impractical, uncomfortably close to targeting the emperor himself. Moreover, the emperor did not like the scholars' intricate politics of cultural attainment and personal connection. Another possible counterweight to Mingju was the power of Songgotu, Manchu chamberlain of the imperial bodyguard, uncle of the empress, an extremely capable man who had been an early supporter of the emperor in the 1660s but had been deprived of most of his power in 1679. Still, Songgotu's relation to the empress gave him an especially close relation to the emperor's thirteen-year-old heir apparent. It would not be wise to allow the court to be completely dominated by a grandee whose power reached so close to the throne, especially if the boy already was showing signs of the willfulness and instability that eventually led to his deposition and imprisonment. The emperor's extraordinary demonstrations of anxiety over his grandmother's illness would raise his own prestige in the eyes of all important elements in his court, increasing his own power rather than shift his dependence from one group to another. It would also give the heir apparent and anyone who might be tempted to support him against his father a lesson in filial piety.

This is not to say that the emperor's anxiety and grief were playacting.

His father had died when he was seven, and his mother when he was nine, and his grandmother had taught him, nurtured him, and supported him when at the age of fifteen he decided to take power for himself and dismiss his regents. He loved her, and I think he really believed that he never could have become the capable and powerful ruler he was without her.

On January 12 and 14 the high ministers knelt outside the gate of the grand dowager empress's palace and urged the emperor to take a little more rest. He refused. Court business had almost come to a halt; the emperor held only one work audience with his ministers in these weeks. The grand dowager empress died at about midnight, January 26–27. The emperor "beat his breast, stamped his feet, and wailed, calling out to Heaven and challenging Earth, crying ceaselessly, eating and drinking nothing." By midmorning the grandees and ministers had assembled and urged him to moderate his grief; the classics counseled that mourning should not be carried to such excess as to harm the health of the mourner, and this was all the more important for the Son of Heaven, on whose person the minister and people depended for so much. The emperor replied by noting that ruling emperors had almost never observed the canonical twenty-seven months of mourning but had "converted months into days," remaining in full mourning for only twenty-seven days. In his reading of history the emperor had found only one exception, in the late fifth century C.E. But because his father and mother had died when he was young, he could not even remember them clearly, and he never had had a chance fully to demonstrate his filial piety. He intended to stay in mourning for the full twenty-seven months.

The ministers immediately protested that this was impossible. There does not seem to have been any insuperable barrier to the emperor's carrying out his political functions, answering memorials, making appointments, approving sentences, and so on, while he was in mourning, as long as he moderated his demonstrations of grief and preserved his health. The real difficulty was with his *ceremonial* responsibilities. Among the ceremonies the emperor normally performed in person were many "of good omen," including the winter solstice ceremony and the regular rites of homage in the Imperial Ancestral Temple, which the emperor could not perform in mourning dress, which was of ill omen. If these ceremonies were not properly carried out, said the ministers, "then certainly the spirit of the grand dowager empress will not be at peace in Heaven." The emperor continued his weeping and wailing night and day; his ministers saw that he was weak, his face drawn. Moreover, they were expected to attend and assist him in his ceaseless mourning. February 2 was the first day of the Chinese Lunar New Year, ordinarily the year's most festive day. But now there were no festivities, and the emperor only grudgingly gave himself and his officials a day of rest from mourning before the coffin. Then the mourning began again, and the argument about "converting months into days" continued. "How can I eat my words?" asked the emperor at one point, but finally on February 6 he had to give in and abandon his plans for twenty-seven months of mourning.

On February 12 a huge procession accompanied the coffin of the grand dowager empress out of the Forbidden City to a temporary resting place in the northeast part of Beijing. In the deep cold the emperor followed the coffin on foot, mourning bitterly, and in the crowds of officials who knelt and mourned as the procession passed by, many feared that he was endangering his health. He wanted to find temporary quarters near his grandmother's coffin. His ministers persuaded him that dynastic precedent required that he return to the Forbidden City; he agreed but decided to spend his nights not in his usual comfortable quarters but in a tent set up by one of the inner gates, perhaps a bit out of the north winds off the steppes but still very cold.

The emperor normally had a working audience with his high ministers almost every day, but since his long walk to the Round Hill Altar on January 3 he had had only one in a month and a half. On February 24 he went back to work, turning at once to the intractable problems of flood control along the lower Yellow River. Then on March 9 he pronounced a long diatribe against self-serving officials who formed cliques and lower officials who kept quiet and did not speak out against faction and corruption. He ended by dismissing Mingju and his closest associates from their offices. The change was so sudden and came so soon after the emperor had resumed political activity that it may reflect a realignment of political forces at court. It seems likely that some important part of Mingju's power must have been based on a relation with the grand dowager empress or her household, so that her death left him vulnerable. The emperor continued to sort out the new political situation, dismissing some Mingju allies and pardoning others and placing Songgotu in charge of extremely important negotiations with the Russians. The appointment conferred considerable power on Songgotu and kept him thoroughly occupied and often far from

Beijing for the next year and a half, while the emperor continued to strengthen his own position.

In May the emperor accompanied the coffin of the grand dowager empress to the Eastern Tombs, about sixty miles east of Beijing; his ministers called this an unprecedented demonstration of filial devotion. He was away from the palace for twenty days. In June he went again, his ministers protesting that he should not exert himself in the summer heat. In November he went yet again, to accompany the tablets bearing all the titles of the grand dowager empress. The Chinese monarchy was sustained by a rhetoric of conscientious and paternal care for the welfare of the common people but was in fact so isolated from them that it comes as a bit of a shock when a direct encounter with them is recorded in the Diaries of Imperial Activities. As he left Beijing in November, the emperor observed that there were corpses lying in the ditches. It is not stated whether they were evidence of violence, disease, or famine. The great horror, to common people thoroughly imbued with the patterns of filial conduct the emperor was so ostentatiously following, was that the corpses lay without proper burial. The emperor ordered that five ounces of silver from his private treasury be given to the local headmen for the purchase of coffins and the proper burial of the corpses. The headmen gave thanks: "The Sage Ruler loves the common people, and his mercy extends even to corpses by the roadside; truly this is a benevolent government not equalled even in ancient times." The people crowded to the road, calling out, chanting, weeping as the emperor passed by.

CHAPTER 11

THE JESUITS AND CHINA

On March 11, 1688, the people of the northwest quarter of Beijing lined the streets to watch a funeral procession that was far more modest than that which had carried the coffin of the grand dowager empress from the Forbidden City a month before but that had its own points of interest and singularity. It included a delegation of high officials of the imperial court headed by Tong Guowei, whose family members were said to "fill up half the court." Kangxi's mother had been a Tong. Now a daughter of Tong Guowei was one of the most important of the imperial consorts. A family of bicultural origins, the Tongs had made the most of their ability to function effectively both in Manchu and in Chinese society. They had gained power as agents of the court in the provinces during campaigns against the rebellious Three Feudatories in the 1670s.

While the officials watched, the great varnished coffin of the deceased was brought out into the street and placed under a silk canopy of white, the color of mourning. Sobbing mourners prostrated themselves before the coffin as the procession formed. First came a band of musicians, followed by a group carrying a great tablet bearing in gold characters the name and titles of the deceased: Nan Huairen, president of the Imperial Board of Astronomy. Then there were many flags and banners and a large cross, carried between two rows of solemn Chinese Christians, each holding a lighted candle and a handkerchief to wipe away tears. There followed a large picture of the Virgin Mary and the Infant Jesus holding the world in

His hand. A portrait of the deceased accompanied an elegy composed by the emperor and written on a banner of yellow satin, both surrounded by a crowd of Chinese Christians and Jesuit missionaries, all in mourning dress. The coffin swayed along, borne by sixty men, accompanied by the eminent delegates of the court and a host of courtiers and officials on horseback. Fifty cavalrymen, impressive in their silent good order, brought up the rear.

From the first missionaries down to our own day, any foreigner who wants to fit into Chinese society takes a Chinese-style name. It should reflect in some way the sound of his European name as well as something of the values and commitments he brings to China. Nan Huairen was Ferdinand Verbiest, a Flemish Jesuit. *Nan* reflected a syllable in his personal name. *Huairen*, "Cherish Benevolence," proclaimed his allegiance to the highest and most demanding of the Confucian virtues, requiring complete selflessness, compassion for others, and constant moral self-examination, surely a Confucian virtue that a Jesuit would have no qualms about espousing for himself and his Chinese converts.

Verbiest had been a most worthy successor to his Jesuit confreres Matteo Ricci and Johann Adam Schall von Bell. All three were expert in the very delicate art of using science, technology, and secular learning in the service of the Chinese imperial court to negotiate a space of tacit tolerance for Christian missionary activity in the empire. Ricci had made a profound impression on some eminent late Ming literati, and his renown, his learning, and the European clocks he presented had won him enough of a foothold at the late Ming court that on his death in 1610 the emperor had granted a plot of land for his burial, where several other Jesuits later were buried. It was toward that cemetery in Zhala, outside the northwest gate of the city, that Verbiest's coffin was being carried. Schall had skillfully navigated the crosscurrents of the last years of the Ming, peasant rebellion, and Qing conquest, then had won the affection and favor of the young Shunzhi emperor, father of Kangxi and the first Qing ruler in Beijing, only to be imprisoned and almost executed in the last years of his life, after Shunzhi's death. Under Ming and Qing he had demonstrated the superiority of European computational and observational astronomy and had been placed in charge of the important work of preparing the imperial calendar for each New Year. He too was buried at Zhala.

Born in 1623 in a village near Kortrijk in western Flanders, Verbiest had been educated by Jesuits except for one uncomfortable year in the Jansenist-dominated University at Leuven. After his Jesuit novitiate and ordination he had made some efforts to go as a missionary to South America but then had made his decision for China in 1657. By 1660 he was in Beijing, never to leave it again except when he accompanied the Kangxi emperor on two expeditions beyond the Great Wall. Schall's death had been followed by several anxious years when three Jesuits in Beijing languished in house arrest while all other missionaries were confined in Canton. Then, on Christmas Day 1668, court eunuchs had abruptly summoned the Beijing Jesuits to answer the young emperor's questions about astronomy and the calendar. Stunned by the lively intelligence and curiosity and the political mastery of the sixteen-year-old Kangxi emperor, the Jesuits had demonstrated the superiority of their astronomy in repeated tests, so that their rivals and critics were dismissed and they were restored to favor and to responsibility at the Board of Astronomy.

The emperor's interest in the Jesuits, and in their learning and technical skills, was authentic and personal. Over the next twenty years the Jesuits often had ridden off at dawn to a suburban palace to give the emperor a lesson in astronomy, physics, or mathematics. The emperor had learned a bit of Western music and delighted in several elaborate fountains and mechanical toys the Jesuits made. They had supervised the casting of some small cannons for use against the rebellious feudatories in the south. They had made a few converts in the bicultural court society, endured the embarrassments of visits to their church by cynical courtiers and palace ladies, and done their best to answer the emperor's rather sharp questions about what seemed to him to be the contradictions of their teaching of the Holy Trinity. They had served as interpreters for Portuguese and Dutch embassies and now were involved in the negotiations with the Russians. The Jesuits found much of this secular activity distasteful and at odds with their missionary vocations, but their successes after 1668 had led to permission for other missionaries to reside in the provinces. Their good standing at the court did much to ensure that provincial officials would treat the missionaries well, and by 1688 a fitful discussion had begun that was to lead in 1692 to a formal imperial declaration that Roman Catholicism was not in conflict with good order and cultural orthodoxy and that Qing subjects might legally convert to it.

At the cemetery the missionaries read the prayers and performed the graveside ceremonies of the Church of Rome and then knelt while Tong Guowei read the imperial edict praising Verbiest's services to the Qing and expressing the emperor's sadness at his death. Father Thomas Pereira replied, expressing the Jesuits' grief and also their immense gratitude for the favor the emperor had shown them by sending the edict and such eminent delegates. The Jesuits later learned that the emperor had been pleased by these expressions of gratitude and had bestowed new honorary titles on Verbiest and a gift of silver toward the construction of a monument over his tomb and the engraving of his edict on a marble tablet.

Five of the Jesuits who knelt at Verbiest's tomb that March day in 1688 were newcomers, having reached Beijing just too late to receive Father Verbiest's blessing before he died on January 28, 1688. (The most probable reason for the six weeks' delay of Verbiest's funeral was that no such public event could take place while the emperor was in mourning for the grand dowager empress.) The five newcomers all were French, and their arrival just after the death of the last of the pathbreaking court Jesuits makes these first months of 1688 a transitional point; up to this time the Jesuit mission in China had drawn its priests from all Catholic Europe but had been under the control of the Portuguese crown, which claimed patronage over all Catholic missions in Asia under the post-Columbus treaties dividing the world between Spain and Portugal. The French priests, although a welcome infusion of talent and manpower, represented a direct challenge to that Portuguese monopoly. Their learning and literary abilities also were to give some new turns to old arguments about the appropriate Catholic attitudes toward the heritage and values of Chinese civilization.

The story of the Jesuit encounter with Chinese civilization from Ricci on illuminates some of the global intersections in the early modern world. The expanding net of European sea voyages led to encounters with previously unknown peoples, many of whom the Europeans fitted into well-established human types. They considered the peoples of the Americas and sub-Sahara Africa to be as savages, occasionally noble, but more often cannibals or otherwise subhuman. The Muslims of the Indian Ocean were nothing new, simply "Moors," followers of the epileptic impostor Muhammad, enemies of the Christian God. Hindus and Buddhists were worshipers of idols, often of the devil, and believers in a doctrine of transmigration of souls they probably had learned from the Pythagoreans. But the experience of China did not fit into categories derived from the European and Mediterranean past. China's bureaucracy of learned men, who claimed to draw their moral guidance not from God or gods but from a hallowed past of sage rulers and teachers, and the good order, populousness, and wealth of the country had no precedent in earlier European experiences of alien peoples. Ricci, deeply impressed by the learning and moral seriousness of his intellectual Chinese friends, as they were with his, became convinced that large elements of the Chinese elite tradition were compatible with Christian belief or could be made so without fundamental change. Confucianism, in particular, could be treated as a secular or civil tradition in a synthesis analogous to Saint Paul's linking of early Christianity with Hellenic culture or to the Renaissance mixes of Catholic fervor with adulation and study of the Greek and Roman heritage in which Ricci and his confreres were steeped.

Ricci's accommodations to Chinese ceremony and terminology never were without opponents even within the Society of Jesus, but they were debated among the missionaries in a nuanced and fairly open-ended manner until Manila-based Dominicans and Franciscans entered the China missions in the 1630s and soon took their condemnations of the Riccian accommodations straight to the Roman Curia. The baffled Curia, with no independent sources of knowledge of China, agreed with whichever side had last presented its explanation of Chinese realities and issued contradictory directives that settled nothing. Conferences among the missionaries confined in Canton in the late 1660s had led only to tenuous new understandings, and even these were challenged when the gifted Dominican polemicist Domingo Fernández Navarrete slipped away from Canton, made his way to Europe, and mounted a skillful campaign against the Riccian accommodations in books and in lobbying at the Holy See. Verbiest sought to rebut Navarrete's views. Nothing was settled in 1688, and the next fifteen years saw an eruption of "Rites Controversy" polemics in Europe. A papal legation sent to Beijing to reassert papal control over the practices of missionaries and converts in China outraged Kangxi and shattered the fragile goodwill that Verbiest and his confreres had built up.

In the 1680s, however, despite the jurisdictional confusion and the simmering quarrels over the Riccian accommodations, China seemed to hold much promise for the growth of Catholic missions. Promoters of a French role in the missions soon made plans to send a party of French Jesuits to China. These missionaries were to be completely independent. To improve their welcome in Beijing, they were to be chosen for their ability in mathematics, astronomy, and related fields. Moreover, in a wonderfully baroque use of the passion of the age for facts and maps, their refusal to submit to other church authorities was to be explained on the grounds that they were going not as missionaries but as scientific observers, collecting geographical and astronomical data for the Academy of Sciences.

Six Jesuits sailed from Brest early in 1685 on the ships that carried the Siamese ambassadors, the sieur de Chaumont, and the abbot of Choisy to Ayutthaya. In 1687 five of them went on to China on a Chinese junk, arriving at Ningbo in July. Kangxi, delighted to learn of the arrival of Jesuits who knew mathematics and astronomy and brought scientific books and instruments, summoned them to the capital. Thus it was that the five French newcomers to Beijing were among the prominent mourners at Verbiest's funeral. For one of them, Jean-François Gerbillon, his mission to collect geographical information was about to expand beyond his wildest imaginings. A high-ranking delegation, led by the redoubtable Songgotu and by the emperor's uncle Tong Guogang, was about to set out to attempt to meet the Russian envoys who had spent the previous winter at Selenginsk. The Russians now were overcoming the linguistic barriers that had inhibited earlier communications with the Qing court by regularly bringing with their envoys a Polish secretary or two who would translate each communication into Latin, to be translated into Chinese and Manchu by the Jesuits in Beijing. Thus it was thought necessary that two Jesuits should accompany the Qing envoys. One would be Thomas Pereira, who had been in Beijing for fifteen years and had won special favor by teaching the emperor Western music. Gerbillon would be the other.

Early on the morning of May 30, 1688, Gerbillon, who had been in China for less than a year and in Beijing for four months, joined in an imposing procession of seventy or eighty officers and about a thousand cavalrymen that set out from the capital to the north, seen off by the emperor's "eldest son." This probably was the thirteen-year-old heir apparent, whose instabilities of character and morality may already have contributed to the emperor's emotional displays of filial piety before and after the death of the grand dowager empress.

For every day of his four-month journey through the steppes, Gerbillon, scientific investigator dispatched by the Academy of Sciences, as much devoted to the augmentation of knowledge through the careful observation of particulars as were Rumphius and others whom we shall meet later in this book—Hans Sloane, Claude Perrault, Locke, Leibniz—noted down the distance and direction of the day's progress, the nature of the country, its animals, plants, and people. In the first days he described the great fortresses that guarded the valleys to the north of Beijing and the immense wall that linked them, which "descends to the precipices, and climbs to the top of inaccessible rocks." Impressed by the feats of construction, he thought the results added little to the security provided by the mountains themselves and found many points on it meagerly garrisoned.

On June 2 the expedition reached the city of Baoan. "This city has two walls, entirely of brick. The land around it is the best and most fruitful we saw in all this valley, the grains and other crops are very fine, although the land is a little dry. The Chinese have discovered the secret of watering their fields by making the water of springs in the vicinity run through canals which they have dug; they draw the water from these canals manually." At the next town a rich merchant gave a banquet for Tong Guogang, and Gerbillon was told that even Uzbek and Persian merchants came there. This zone was thoroughly controlled by the Qing. Local officers came to pay their respects to Tong Guogang and Songgotu. By imperial command local people regularly brought cattle and sheep to feed the expedition.

On June 7 Gerbillon saw his first Mongol camp and wrote down a full description of the construction of a yurt and a more cursory description of the apparent poverty and uncouthness of the people. He predictably had no use for the lamas—senior monks in the Tibetan Buddhist tradition, often believed to be reincarnations of a godlike figure or holy teacher—toward whom "the Mongols display a veneration beyond all expression." He was convinced that the Qing court's cordial treatment of them was solely for the sake of Mongol politics and asserted that in Beijing they quickly became accustomed to wearing fine clothes and bought the prettiest women slaves "on the pretext of marrying them to their slaves." From June 15 to 17 the party camped near Huhhot, then already a major Mongol center and today the capital of China's Inner Mongolian Autonomous Region. Gerbillon accompanied Tong Guogang and Songgotu to the principal Lamaist temple, and was appalled by their reverence toward the young man who was venerated as a reincarnated Bodhisattva. They prostrated themselves before "the pretended god," who placed his hands on the head of each and had each touch his prayer beads. The "Living Buddha" wore a long robe of fine yellow satin with a multicolored border, not unlike the vestments of a Catholic priest, which completely covered his body; when he reached out for a cup of tea, Gerbillon could see that underneath the robe his arms were bare and he had only a plain red and yellow monastic robe thrown over his shoulders. The meal that followed included some decent rice and soup, but also some disgusting dried fruits, oily cakes, and half-cooked chunks of meat. They toured the temple, parts of which seemed clean and well decorated, and saw a child also venerated as a Living Buddha.

Gerbillon was regularly measuring the height of the sun and calculating his latitude. He commented frequently on how cold it was at night and how hot in the middle of the day. Leaving Huhhot, the party struck nearly straight north, hoping to make contact with the khan of the Khalkhas. The scattered trees and cultivated fields that had been seen from time to time on the road to Huhhot disappeared. There were many rabbits, antelope, wild goats, pheasants, and wild geese, and the soldiers hunted every day. Gerbillon was delighted to be served a delicate pheasant egg omelet. The party split up to follow three separate routes. Now they saw a few Khalkha camps, which seemed even more impoverished than those of the Mongols farther south. Finding enough water for the expedition's hundreds of horses and camels was a daily worry.

On July 8 the party came across a miserable camp of twenty-five to thirty Khalkha yurts. Some of the people had come from farther north, fleeing the invading forces of Galdan of the Dzungars. Even the senior lama, brother of the Khalkha khan, was said to be fleeing to the south. The next day the column turned back south to rejoin the other two so that the commanders could consult about this new situation. By July 22 they had rejoined Songgotu and his column and had received orders from the emperor that they were to turn back to Beijing and write to the Russian ambassador at Selenginsk to make new arrangements for a meeting. This was a great relief; the weather was very hot, the horses were growing tired and thin, and the unsettled conditions to the north added immensely to the risks of an attempt to reach Selenginsk that summer.

As the party made its way back toward Beijing, they learned that orders had gone out to all the Mongol vassals of the Qing to mobilize their forces against the Dzungars. Some of them also were to join the annual imperial hunt, north of the Gubei Pass, which this year would have even more than usual the air of a military exercise. On August 12 Gerbillon witnessed one of the more low-key days of the hunt, in which a double circle of soldiers and servants gradually closed in while frantic hares tried to find a way out, even trying to run between the men's legs; 157 hares were killed in less than three hours. On August 29 he was able to examine and describe a wolf and some antelope that had been killed on the hunt. The route now led through much better country, then a difficult gorge, and there were apricots and sour wild cherries to be picked along the way. On September 27 they caught up with the imperial hunting camp. Gerbillon was deeply impressed by its orderly layout, with the guards and high-ranking officers' tents nearest that of the emperor, which did not seem a great deal larger or more splendid than the others but had a gold ornament on its highest point. The high officials and the Jesuits went out to wait beside the road and greet the emperor as he returned from the hunt after dark; His Majesty greeted them courteously, remarking that they must be very tired.

The party now continued on its way toward the capital. The mountain scenery was pleasant and less daunting than farther north, and there were even some wild grapes and wild pears near the road. The road was much more commodious because this was a route the emperor often took on his hunts. The party returned to Beijing on October 6; the emperor arrived on the eleventh. On December 9 the Jesuits gathered at the tombs of Ricci, Schall, and Verbiest for a further ceremony ordered by the emperor, at which his mourning edict was read aloud in Manchu.

The adventure was wonderful, the glimpses of the splendor of the imperial court fascinating, the information collected would delight the Academy of Sciences, but Pereira and Gerbillon had had only one or two occasions when they managed a bit of discussion of religion with the great men in charge of the expedition and had had to grit their teeth as they saw them groveling before a Living Buddha. The Jesuits' purpose in leaving behind their families and the comforts of their native lands and making such long and dangerous voyages was to save souls. The favor of the imperial court was essential to the safety and continuity of the mission enterprise, but the fruits seemed to come so slowly. Beijing court society had produced a few distinguished converts, including some Manchus of the imperial clan and some Tong relatives. It was said that there were some eighty thousand converts in the Shanghai area, which had been the home of Ricci's first significant convert. Other centers of Catholic growth were much smaller but could be extremely robust; the area around Fuan in Fujian Province, ministered to by Dominicans from Manila, had many zealous converts, and they and their descendants were to remain steadfast through many troubles in the eighteenth century. But there were never enough missionaries, and they were too conspicuously foreign, too vulnerable to suspicion of foreigners even when official policy was benign, too likely to die before their language learning and acculturation reached a level where they could interact with people effectively. Missionaries shook their heads at their converts' difficulties in learning Latin, and many of them were convinced that the Chinese character simply was not suited to the rigors of priestly life, but slowly the missionaries came around to the idea of a native priesthood.

Thus it was that on August 1, 1688, three Chinese—Liu Wende, Wan Qiyuan, and Wu Li—knelt before Bishop Gregorio Luo Wenzao in a church in Macao and were ordained priests in the Society of Jesus. Luo himself was a singular figure, educated and ordained by the Manila Dominicans, going along somewhat hesitantly with their opposition to the Riccian accommodations to Chinese tradition. Wan had been received into the society at Hangzhou, where there had been a solid Christian community since late Ming times. Liu had come into the orbit of the missionaries as an official in the Board of Astronomy in Beijing and used the Western name Blaise Verbiest. Wu Li was the kind of convert the Jesuits dreamed about, a poet and painter admired in the best circles of creativity and connoisseurship, a participant in the moral and intellectual ferment of the early Qing who had found in Christianity, as the Jesuits had argued since Ricci's time, the supplement to and completion of his Confucian quest.

Born in 1632, Wu Li was too young to have taken an examination degree under the Ming before 1644, so he was not bound by any formal ties of obligation to the old dynasty. But opportunities for advancement through the examinations were limited in the early Qing, and in any case his real interests were in painting and poetry, for which by the 1660s he was associating with some of the most famous masters in the empire. In the 1670s Wu Li joined in intellectual and literary circles that were especially interested in Song Dynasty poetry, with its vivid observations of mundane realities, and in poems and plays with historical themes, which had special resonances to men who had lived through the dramas of the Ming-Qing transition. Wu also associated with men who sought to give concrete expression to Confucian values through local meetings for moral exhortation and the study of classical texts. But for some the gap between utopian dreams of social and cosmic harmony and the present dusty realities was too wide, the conventional stories of the rise and fall of dynasties too full of delusion and chicanery. Such men needed a "single lord" to follow and worship, a new way of understanding the origins and nature of the world.

Most participants in these quests turned from Confucianism to Buddhism, or vice versa, or tried to revive some strand of Chinese popular religion and hero worship. Wu Li became, in 1679, one of the handful who made the astonishing leap to commitment to an obviously foreign faith. He at first planned to accompany Philippe Couplet, S.J., to Europe but then remained in Macao, becoming a novice in the Society of Jesus in 1682. A series of his poems from these years are vivid evidence for his skills as an observer and describer: the little white houses of the slave quarters, the Chinese fishermen coming in at night, the slaves singing and dancing to a guitar at a church festival, Wu and his European confreres struggling to converse with each other and sometimes having to write things out in their different scripts. He also expressed his growing understanding of his Christian faith in poetry. One poem begins as a conventional Chinese expression of sympathy for the hard life of a fisherman, then notes that lately Catholicism has come to his city, and some friends of the fisherman's have changed their job: "[T]hey now are fishers of men." It ends with a wry naturalistic touch, worthy of the best Song poets, as the fisherman realizes that converts keeping the fasts of the church will be better customers for his fish.

The Jesuits had made some risky accommodations with Chinese culture, and some of their critics were convinced that Chinese Christians under Jesuit tutelage were crypto-Christians at best, with no sense of the terrifying drama of the death and resurrection of the Son of God and the salvation He offered to each sinner. Such accusations cannot survive a brief acquaintance with Wu Li's Christian poems:

> By nature I have always felt quite close to the Way;
> When done with chanting my new poems, I always concentrate my spirit.
> Prior to death, who believes in the joy of the land of Heaven?
> After the end, then comes amazement at the truth of the fires of hell!
> The achievements and fame of this ephemeral world: footprints of geese on
>   snow;
> This body, this shell in a lifetime of toil: dust beneath horses' hoofs.
> And what is more, the flowing of time presses man so fast:
> Let us plan carefully about the ford that leads to the true source.

And perhaps it was in connection with his ordination on August 1, 1688, and his own first mass that he wrote:

Again he washes his hands,
and then turns around.
He prays that he and all assembled sinners
may be washed clean with not an iota left:
only then may they not betray
Jesus' compassion.
Why does he make the sign of the Cross over and over again?
The holy death took place nailed thereon.

The Jesuits risked all to change China. Many Chinese were respectful, and some converted. Chinese specialists in computational astronomy recognized and adopted the Jesuits' superior techniques. Many Chinese painters, although not the most ambitious and culturally pretentious ones, tried to learn something of Western techniques of shading and perspective. But the religious and cultural impact of the missionaries' message remained limited and local; Wu Li's conversion was not the beginning of a great trend. Ricci had stumbled on a time of exceptional cultural openness and deep questioning of received modes of thought, but by 1688 most Chinese intellectuals had resolved their tensions in ways that had nothing to do with a foreign religion. China's culture was changing, self-critical, but it had no unquenchable thirst for novelty, no principled quarrel of ancients and moderns, before about 1900. A thirst for new facts and new places was not absent, but it was not as widespread and obsessive as in the culture of seventeenth-century Europe. Whereas China's vast publishing industry rarely put out anything that offered a connected picture of the distant lands from which the traders and missionaries came, in 1688 Europe, and especially France, there was a wave of publishing about China that crested about 1700 and continued far into the eighteenth century. The anti-Christian polemics of Voltaire and other masters of the Enlightenment ironically owed much to the accounts of Chinese ways in the writings of the Jesuits.

In the middle of 1687 the learned world of Europe gained new access to the heart of the Confucian tradition with the publication in Paris of *Confucius Sinarum Philosophus*, a splendid folio volume of more than five hundred pages. In 1688 a long synopsis in the *Journal des Sçavans* and reviews in the *Bibliothèque Universalle et Historique* and in the *Acta Eruditorum* and a French synopsis by Jean de la Brune, *La Morale de Confucius, Philosophe de la Chine*, spread knowledge of this great work in the European intellectual world. This magnificent book contained full translations of three of the "Four Books," the texts at the heart of Neo-Confucian intellectual life that claimed to present the teachings of the Master himself and his immediate disciples. It also contained a brief life of Confucius. A chronological summary of more than three thousand years of the Chinese monarchy took up more than one hundred pages. The dedication of *Confucius Sinarum Philosophus* to Louis XIV was followed by a Preliminary Declaration of more than one hundred pages, which claimed that this work was intended not "for the amusement and curiosity of those who live in Europe" but for the use of missionaries. This was a bit disingenuous; the splendid book was meant to publicize and glorify the Jesuit mission enterprise in the courts and elite circles of Europe and to justify its approach to China. But it was true that the translations the book contained were the product of about eighty years of collective effort, as one generation of missionaries struggled to understand the texts that were so central to the lives and convictions of the educated Chinese whom they were seeking to attract to Christianity and then used the results of their efforts to teach newly arrived missionaries, who later might try their hands at improving the translations.

The Preliminary Declaration was an important statement of the approach to the Confucian heritage the Jesuits had been developing ever since Ricci's time. It argued that there were passages in the classical texts in which Heaven seemed to have consciousness, to care for mankind, and to infuse in man a moral conscience. There was a smaller number of references to the Lord on High, which seemed even more like intimations of the One God. But the Song Dynasty Neo-Confucian commentators, systematizing an organic naturalism that also was powerful in Chinese culture since early times, had insisted that the Lord on High was simply a synonym for Heaven, and Heaven was just a way of referring to the patterned order of a cosmos that ran itself and did not need a transcendent deity as establisher of order or object of worship. Ricci, encouraged by critics of Song thought in late Ming times, had emphasized the passages with glimmerings of an ancient knowledge of God. He also argued that the Song commentators had systematically suppressed evidence that the ancient Chinese, down to somewhat after the time of Confucius, had known and worshiped the True God. The greatest cause of the loss of that ancient knowledge, he said, was the coming of Buddhism in the first century C.E. The teaching he brought would remove that Buddhist taint, already widely criticized among Confucian intellectuals, and would supplement Confucian earnestness in self-cultivation and moral action with knowledge and worship of the True God.

This risky formula, which cast foreigners as explainers to a sophisticated elite of the real meaning of its classical texts, offended some Chinese intellectuals, intrigued some and led small numbers to the great leap of conversion. In the Preliminary Declaration it was reflected in descriptions of the "pure simplicity of the golden age," in which the sage emperors worshiped the Lord on High or an active, beneficent Heaven, and in demonstrations of gratuitous distortions of these passages by the "Modern Interpreters"—that is, the Song commentators. The translations themselves occasionally may be seen giving a twist toward anticipation of Christian ideas. For example, the phrase "bright virtue" appears several times, referring to a deep potential for virtuous action that can be "brightened" or developed. But in one passage the Jesuits translate it as "rational nature," and in another they build on assertions that this virtue is received from Heaven to find in it intimations of the Christian concept of the immortal soul. The result is an obscuring of the uniquely Chinese sense of the moral potential of man rooted in his organic relations to the world around him. In its place there is a concept of "rational nature" so narrowly based in abstract discussions of the soul and the rational nature of man that it could be easily cut away from its moorings in the Christian drama of sacrifice and redemption and used to support Enlightenment rejections of Christian orthodoxy.

In early reports on China around 1600 European readers had gotten glimpses of Chinese wisdom and a strong impression of the prosperity, populousness, and good government of the empire, but not a concrete sense of people and events. That changed abruptly after the collapse of the Ming, as accounts of the "Tatar Conquest" by missionary eyewitnesses began appearing. First impressions of a collapse of a civilization comparable to the fall of the Roman Empire soon yielded to an understanding that despite the many brutalities of the conquerors and the tragedies of heroic but vain Ming resistance, a new and effective order was rapidly emerging. Most of this writing took the form of narratives that focused on rulers and other individual actors. Speeches and actions might be melodramatic, but they were not exotic; these were actors in a kind of drama all too familiar in seventeenth-century Europe. Some of the reports depicted the Manchus as brave warriors imposing order where the "effete Chinese" could not, a vision that owed as much to European views of leadership and virtue in their own society as to the realities of early Qing China or Chinese ideals of scholar-official rule. The *History of the Two Tartar Conquerors of China* by Pierre Joseph d'Orléans, S.J., published in French in 1688, was an excellent representative of this genre, particularly rich in its portrayal of the Qing court as seen by the Jesuits. It included notes drawn from two imperial expeditions beyond the wall when Ferdinand Verbiest had followed the emperor, who showed the foreign priest much favor and studied the constellations with him.

A much more distinctive contribution to European knowledge of China was made by the *New History of China* by Gabriel de Magalhaens, published in 1688 in both French and English translations; the Portuguese original text has never been found. Magalhaens probably finished his book about 1675, when he was in his sixties and had been in China for thirty-five years. He had taught in the Jesuit establishments at Goa and at Macao before his arrival in 1640 at the lovely and cultured city of Hangzhou beside its famous West Lake. But soon he was sent off to aid Luigi Buglio in Sichuan, making the long and daunting trip up the Yangtze just in time to join Buglio in harrowing adventures as captives first of a monstrous rebel and then of the suspicious Manchu conquerors. Once settled in Beijing in 1648, Magalhaens stayed there until his death in 1677 except for one trip to Macao. He kept his distance from the court favor seeking of Schall and Verbiest.

Magalhaens's book contains good examples of the expositions of Chinese history and philosophy found in most Jesuit books, but it is particularly noteworthy for its sense of movement through the vast empire and its capital and its engagement with their ambiguities. The author gives an excellent description, probably drawing on his observations on his trip to Macao and back, of the Grand Canal and its sluice gates, where great grain barges were winched up to a higher level of the canal by hundreds of men straining at huge capstans. His section on the capital is especially notable for its account of the imperial palaces. He takes his reader with him on a walk, starting well to the south of the gate we now call Tiananmen, describing what is seen as one emerges from each grand gate into each new courtyard. People told him it had been much more splendid under the late Ming, "yet there is that in it still which serves to fill the imagination, and display the grandeur of the empire." He describes fully the "ordinary audience" ceremony, at which capital officials gathered to prostrate themselves in the greatest of the palace courts before the emperor, far away in the shadows of his throne hall. If we count the courtyards he and his reader traverse on their imaginary walk up the central axis of the palaces, he has reached fifteen by the time he emerges from the north gate of the palace compound, crosses a wide avenue, and passes through another triple gate into a vast open area that is left unpaved. It adjoins stables for some of the emperor's horses and is watered to keep the dust down when the emperor is about to go riding. Beyond the next gate is a fine park with five artificial hills built up out of the earth removed to make the lakes to the west of the palaces; this park and these hills still are to be seen in Beijing. They "are covered with trees to the very top, planted with an exactness of symmetry, every one with a round or square pedestal, wherein several holes are cut for the rabbits to burrow and hares to sit in, of which those little hills are very full. The park also has many deer, goats, and birds, and the emperor often comes there to relax and watch them." Louis XIV, lord of Versailles, was not much for reading, but I should like to think that somehow he read or heard a bit of these descriptions and was envious.

The lord of Versailles also would have understood the most startling aspect of Magalhaens's description of the Chinese politics of his time.

To be a viceroy, or governor of a province, before a man can have his commission sealed, will cost him twenty, thirty, forty, and sometimes threescore, sometimes seventy thousand crowns [ounces of silver]. And yet so far is the king [emperor] from receiving a farthing of this money that he knows nothing of the abuse. Only the grand ministers of the empire, the *colaos* or counsellors of state, and the six supreme tribunals of the court are they that privately sell all offices and employments to the viceroys and great mandarins of the provinces. On the other side, they to satisfy their avarice and reimburse themselves of the money laid out for their preferments, extort presents from the presidents of territories and cities, who repay themselves upon the governors of towns and boroughs, and they, or rather all together, make themselves whole again, and replenish their purses at the expense of the miserable people. So that it is a common proverb in China that the king unwittingly lets loose so many hangmen, murderers, hungry dogs and wolves to ruin and devour the poor people, when he creates new mandarins to govern them. In short there is not an viceroy, visitor of a province, or any such like officer, who at the end of three years of his being employed, does not return with six or seven hundred thousand and sometimes a million of crowns.

The Kangxi emperor certainly was very much aware that men sought office in order to get rich. He must have known a good deal about the ways those seeking appointments sought favor in the capital. Magalhaens's picture of a constant and systematic sale of offices gets only scattered support from Chinese sources from the time, but he spent a great deal of time listening to people of all conditions in the capital. His own experiences of China, perhaps his own misgivings about his confreres' enthusiastic pursuit of court favor, may have led him to believe the worst about the society around him. If Wu Li proves that some Jesuit converts were real Christians, Magalhaens proves that the fathers themselves could be respectful of Chinese culture and awed by the majesty of the court without becoming starry-eyed Sinophiles. Neither side of this great encounter feared ambiguity or complexity. That is why we continue to learn so much from it about the early modern world.

CHAPTER 12

KANAZAWA, EDO, NAGASAKI

In the first days of the eleventh month of the first year of Genroku—late November 1688—people walking in the clean and orderly streets of the Japanese city of Kanazawa occasionally were accosted by beggars dressed as lepers. Noticing that the beggars did not in fact have the missing fingers, ears, and noses of lepers and remembering what time of year it was, the stroller might give the beggar some money and receive in return a charm that would ward off the fearful disease.

The Japanese cycle of the year offered up great events for everyone: New Year, the Girls' Festival, the Boys' Festival, the summer Star Festival, and the Festival in Honor of Ancestors. In a society carefully and thoroughly divided into occupational and status groups, it was fitting that many of these groups also had their own separate festivals. The smiths had theirs on the eighth of the tenth month, and the merchants held theirs twelve days later, decorating their shops, offering discounts, giving small presents to regular customers. Beggars were another status group, with their own headmen recognized by the government; in 1688 they were upset by the number of people begging who were not part of their recognized groups. In fact, there were *two* separate groups of recognized beggars, and the sham lepers of the beggars' festival were not from the main group but from a smaller, separate group, tenaciously independent, with their own living area behind the Shinmei shrine, called the *monoyoshi*, "beggars who bring good fortune." In addition to begging they produced sandals and rain clogs for sale and cared for lepers. On auspicious days throughout the year they assembled outside prosperous households and showered the residents with blessings and good sayings if they got some food or money but insulted them if nothing was forthcoming.

In their carefully controlled and sanctioned discourtesies, their sham confrontations with real horrors, the public rituals of the "beggars who bring good fortune" were typical of the kinds of ceremonial outlets and expressions that have helped make life bearable amid the exacting social roles and carefully modulated expressions of emotion in Japanese society. Kanazawa itself was in many ways an excellent example of what was happening to Japan in the seventeenth century. In 1688, with about one hundred thousand residents, it was one of the twenty largest cities in the world. Like most Japanese cities, it was relatively new, standing where there had been only a small settlement until the 1540s. The oldest stone walls of the castle that dominated the city, seat of the Maeda family of daimyo (territorial lords), were less than a hundred years old.

The beginnings of the new Japan of the seventeenth century, which many historians now see as the direct ancestor of the sophisticated, productive, and highly organized Japan of the 1990s, can be most easily traced to the efforts of daimyo to build for themselves coherent structures of military power, political control, and economic activity from the 1550s on. Several superdaimyo attempted to put together alliances under their own hegemony that would control all Japan; finally, in the early 1600s, one of them, Tokugawa Ieyasu, succeeded. He and his heirs ruled as shogun (generalissimo), nominally appointed by passive, ceremonial emperors, until 1868. Daimyo allied with them, and even some of their defeated opponents, were placed in charge of substantial province-size pieces of the country, with wide autonomy in their internal administration and no taxes from these areas to the Tokugawa. Their loyalty was assured by the military predominance of the Tokugawa and their most loyal allies and by the requirement that daimyo leave their families as hostages in the shogunal capital at Edo (modern Tokyo, itself a new urban creation of the seventeenth century) and reside there themselves in alternate years. The Maeda had never sought hegemony for themselves but had astutely built up their power as energetic allies of the most promising contender. They were rewarded by the Tokugawa with successive grants that added up to the largest non-Tokugawa domain in Japan, reliably dominating a wealthy area valuable to any contender for power but not really a strategic key to the country, across the mountains from Edo and the other main cities, near the west coast of the main island.

The daimyo had worked energetically from the late 1500s on to devise political institutions that would strengthen their control of people and resources within their territories. They compiled registers of residents, their landholdings, and their tax obligations. The previously fluid distinction between samurai (warriors) and commoners was turned into a fixed hereditary one, and commoners were forbidden to carry weapons. Samurai, the hardest element to control, were subjected to harsh regulatory codes and were forced to move to the castle towns of their lords and live on stipends drawn from the daimyo's unified land revenue. Unique among the arms-bearing elites of the early modern world, samurai had no conflict of interest between their tax-collecting and landholding functions, no independent economic base from which they could challenge their lords. It is no accident that the disciplined and loyal salarymen of modern Japan look back on the samurai with fascination and respect.

Merchants and craftsmen, especially those most vital for warfare, were given monopoly marketing privileges and grants of land for workshops and warehouses in order to induce them to settle under one daimyo rather than under his rival. More peaceful crafts and commerce also were encouraged, as were land reclamation and agricultural improvements that could improve the daimyo's tax base. In the unsettled years just before and after 1600 all this was done to strengthen the daimyo's fighting capacity, and down into the 1630s there were enough worries about the stability of the new order that every lord wanted to keep his defenses as strong as possible. As the Tokugawa peace continued and solidified, the habits of thorough control and constant efforts to maximize the wealth and power of the daimyo's realm became engrained. The system of hostage residence in Edo turned out to be a huge drain on daimyo funds, reinforcing the search for new sources of revenue. The disciplined samurai showed themselves to be as effective in maintaining an orderly and efficient administration as they had been in killing enemies of their lord.

The results, by 1688, included a good many new houses and other signs of prosperity in the countryside. In the growing cities, all residential land was assigned by the daimyo's local governors, all people were organized into mutual security groups, all residential areas had watchmen and locked gates at night, and there was a great bustle of trade and crafts production. Most singularly, in a world of war and dangerous city streets, Kanazawa and other Japanese cities, administered by men brought up on tales of reckless personal courage and constantly practicing their skills with the world's finest swords, were the safest in the world of 1688. Japan had not seen open warfare in more than seventy years.

A final singularity: The two beggar groups were hereditary outcast groups. There were other such groups that engaged in "unclean" occupations like tanning hides. But all spoke the same language and were of the same race and culture. Japan was effectively closed to foreigners from 1640 on. In Edo, Kyoto, or Osaka, an occasional Dutch or Korean embassy could be seen. But not in Kanazawa, which may have been the biggest city in the world of 1688 with no foreigners at all. There had not been any for decades, and there would be none for at least 170 years to come.

Keeping order in Edo was a much more daunting task than it was for the lords of Kanazawa. Edo also was a new city. In the 1590s Tokugawa Ieyasu, allied with Hideyoshi, the supreme military leader of that decade, conquered the rich plain around what we now call Tokyo Bay. He began to build a castle on a new site, overlooking a small fishing village named Edo. After he had consolidated his grip on all Japan, he made Edo the seat of his *bakufu*, "tent government," his headquarters as shogun, supreme military dictator. The shoguns were formally appointed by the emperors, who descended in unbroken lineage from the sun-goddess. The emperors resided in the ancient capital of Kyoto and were well treated and generously supported by the Tokugawa but had no power. The Tokugawa shoguns promulgated general codes of conduct for all daimyo and their subordinate samurai and sent occasional spies or inspectors to the realms of the daimyo, but generally allowed them to make policy and to administer their realms as they saw fit. However, all daimyo served at the pleasure of the shoguns, who might move them to new realms or dismiss them entirely. The difficulty with the latter course was that it left their loyal samurai masterless, and masterless samurai—*rônin*, "wave men"—were easily drawn into crime, subversion, or rebellion.

By 1688 the process of consolidating Tokugawa supremacy had been through a period of quiescence and had revived somewhat. The *bakufu* had become a substantial bureaucracy of samurai, administering the large domains that the shoguns held directly and keeping close watch over the rest. A key instrument of control was the system that required daimyo to leave family members in Edo at all times and to spend every other year residing there in person. The shape of the city reflected its complex structure of power. In its center was the enormous Edo Castle (since 1868 the Imperial Palace), behind great stone walls and multiple moats, where the shogun and his household lived. Nearby were the mansions of the major daimyo who had been early allies of the Tokugawa and who occupied the highest offices in the *bakufu*. Then there was a zone of the more modest residences of the Tokugawa retainers called housemen and bannermen. Still farther away were the estates of the "outer" daimyo, who had not been so close to the early Tokugawa or had even actively opposed it; they did not have access to official posts in the *bakufu*. Their Edo estates were parts of their own realms; within their walls they administered their own house law, not Tokugawa law. There were many residences and shops within the imposing precincts of Buddhist temples and Shinto shrines, which also enjoyed a large measure of administrative autonomy. The commoner quarters too were broken up by walls and gates. The imposing wooden gates, still such a notable feature of temples and other survivals of traditional architecture, might serve as a master metaphor for a society of rapid growth, aesthetic refinement, and thorough control.

In 1688 Edo was one of the largest cities in the world, with a population of more than nine hundred thousand. Commoners, the vast majority of that population, were under the jurisdiction of two magistrates. Each month one of them was on duty, receiving instructions from his superiors at the castle, registering petitions, and hearing lawsuits; the other kept busy behind closed doors resolving cases that had come to him the month before. The magistrates controlled a small force of constables and patrolmen, fewer than three hundred for the whole city. There also was a large hierarchy of nonsamurai local elders, reaching from the three hereditary city leaders down through the neighborhood chiefs to the common citizens. These last were organized into groups of five families, which kept in touch with the neighborhood chiefs and were jointly responsible for the conduct of all their members. Each residential quarter, whether commoner or samurai, was responsible for night patrols to prevent crime and watch for fires. Each maintained and manned its own gatehouse and guardhouse. Edo had more than nine hundred such guardhouses. Beijing had household registration systems; Amsterdam and Istanbul, we shall see, had night patrols; no other metropolis of 1688 had Edo's full range and rigor of methods of control.

The rulers of Edo wanted everyone in his or her proper place, ranked and registered. But the city grew and changed all the time. Shops edged into streets. Seasonal warehouses became permanent. Along with the threat to public order, uncontrolled building increased the danger of fire in a city almost entirely built of wood. In 1657 fires had swept across large parts of the city, destroying the central structures in Edo Castle and, by official estimate, 160 daimyo estates, 350 shrines and temples, 750 residential areas of bannermen and housemen, and 50,000 merchant and artisan homes. In order to lessen the danger of another such fire, the authorities laid out several new residential quarters that reduced crowding in the existing ones and designated some burned-out areas as firebreaks, not to be rebuilt. One firebreak area was Edobashi, Edo Bridge, created by landfill in the early seventeenth century, a prosperous merchant quarter until 1657. (Its big riverfront lumberyards must have made especially spectacular fires.) Residents allowed to rebuild in a part of Edobashi were required to maintain guards and patrols to keep people out of the firebreak area. This was a heavy financial burden, and the residents sought to offset it by leasing plots in the firebreak area to seasonal merchants, such as the sellers of the pine branches and bamboo cuttings favored for New Year decorations. Soon there were teahouses, used-book dealers, fortune-tellers, and many more. But they were allowed to put up only modest stalls, with no living quarters attached, so they could be quickly broken down and hauled away in case of fire or if the shogun was going to pass by on the river. By 1688 shipping agents and fish wholesalers were nearby, pressing for access to choice riverside sites in the firebreak. The reurbanization of Edobashi went much further in the eighteenth century.

Edo was a great city of consumers, but not a center of fine craft production compared with the old capital of Kyoto and its mercantile neighbor Osaka. Literary and cultural trends tended to start in Kyoto and Osaka and then reach Edo in vulgarized forms. The result was that Edo was at least the equal of London or Paris as a center of pleasure seeking and the quest for social respectability through conspicuous consumption.

The daimyo spent great sums on performances within their estates of Nô dance dramas, refined, ceremonious, subtle, piercing in their portrayal of the human condition. They also built magnificent landscaped gardens, such as the famous Kôrakuen built by Tokugawa Mitsukuni, daimyo of Mito, head of one of the highest-ranking branch houses of the shogunal family, patron of Confucian studies. He had been assisted in the design of the garden by an erudite Ming Loyalist refugee from China who had brought Chinese classical learning in its full development to Mitsukuni's academic and publishing projects, and whose very presence in Japan suggested to some Japanese that men of loyalty and integrity no longer were at home in China but still were honored in Japan.

That was all very well for the earnest, the refined, and the culturally pretentious. But Edo swarmed with samurai—Tokugawa housemen and bannermen and retainers of the daimyo—with time on their hands and with literate commoners with various degrees of newfound wealth. (The lumber merchants were among the richest.) For them there was plenty of entertainment of broader appeal. Prostitution was legal in one quarter, the Yoshiwara, which was supposedly off limits to samurai. But everyone jostled in its narrow streets, ogled the cheaper girls, and told stories about the famous refined and reclusive beauties, usually kept by high-ranking samurai or rich commoners. Books were on sale of wonderful black-and-white prints depicting all kinds of amorous escapades, the lively lines of the moving bodies setting off the geometrical patterns of furnishings and clothing. They were called *shunga*, "spring pictures," and they owed something to phallic/fertility elements in Japanese religion. Some claimed to be books of instruction for sexual beginners. But they might well have alarmed as well as aroused the uninitiated, breaking completely from the elegance of line of the rest of the print to show a towering bushy tool aiming at an equally exaggerated bushy cleft.

There were kabuki playhouses in at least three districts of the city; the first listing and ranking of kabuki actors that has come down to us is from 1687. Kabuki performances were as great spectacles as Nô, and much more plot-driven. Despite plots that often told a noble tale from Japanese history, the kabuki theaters could not shake, perhaps did not want to shake, an air of decadence and sensuality. Earlier in the century the women who had acted in them had had a bawdy reputation. After women were banned from the stage, female roles were taken by young men, many of whom attracted the homosexual attentions of the wealthy and powerful. In Edo in the 1680s kabuki plays that presented contemporary political dramas, with all the names changed but clearly recognized, were very popular, and a few plays that portrayed the suicide of lovers who could not marry because of class differences were beginning to appear.

Fully equal to the kabuki as an art form in Edo was the *jôruri* puppet theater. Chikamatsu Monzaemon, not yet at the height of his fame but already a powerful and successful playwright, wrote for both, and some of his greatest work was for the *jôruri*. The puppets were about three feet tall, beautifully designed and articulated. Their manipulators frequently were visible; the artificiality of the figures and the magnificence of their costumes and the patterns they formed were essential to the experience. The chanter of the text was the key expressive artist. The most popular *jôruri* producer of the day was Yamamoto Tosa-no-jô, who was criticized by the more refined for his disconnected plots, uninspired language, and frequent inclusion of brothel scenes.

The shogun who presided in Edo Castle in 1688 was Tokugawa Tsunayoshi. He was called the Dog Shogun, and many stories were told of his torrent of edicts forbidding cruelty to dogs and other animals and his savage punishment of violators. It was speculated that he had been under the influence of a Buddhist monk opposed on religious principle to the killing of living things or that since he had been born in the Year of the

Jôruri puppets, their handlers, and the chanter

Dog, he felt a special obligation to protect dogs. There is no question that the people of Edo were aware in 1688 that their lord was especially concerned about "compassion to animals"; one collection of *bakufu* documents records nine edicts on the subject in 1687 and one in 1688. But later stories of his bizarre actions owe much to the hostility of high-ranking *bakufu* bureaucrat families to his use of personal favorites in government.

Tsunayoshi's attention to domestic animals seems to have begun in 1686 with new rules on the registering of dogs and their owners. Several edicts in 1687 elaborated on this policy. Others forbade the abandonment or turning loose of sick horses. One order exiled a daimyo whose cook had drowned some kittens. Although we should not discount the regular references in these edicts to "compassion toward animals," we also can begin to see the importance of these policies for order and public safety in the great city. Dogs, many of them large breeds trained for hunting or guarding, were breaking loose and terrorizing the ordinary people in their flimsy houses and open shops, while sick horses wandering crowded streets posed a clear threat to public health and safety.

Moreover, these policies were part of a larger effort by Tsunayoshi to tame and civilize the samurai. He was the first shogun who had no high degree of interest or training in warfare. He was a serious student of Confucianism who in the 1690s gave a series of lectures on the *Yi Jing*. In 1684 he cracked down on gangs of housemen and *rônin* who were causing trouble in Edo and two years later did the same to gangs of commoners. "Compassion toward animals" was part of the milder, more civilized ethic he was trying to promote. People who were cruel to animals often treated people the same way. The samurai saw that they couldn't mistreat even dogs, much less commoners.

Tsunayoshi pursued these policies until his death in 1709. Students of Tokugawa Japan sometimes have a hard time putting together the bizarre tales of the Dog Shogun with other images of that time. The year 1688 was the first of a new "year period," designated Genroku, which has become a byword among historians for the emergence of an urban, consumer-oriented culture, of the arts of peace. But peace, luxury, and lectures about compassion could go only so far. In 1701, in Edo Castle, a daimyo drew his sword on a rude *bakufu* official. He was ordered to commit suicide. Two years later forty-seven of his samurai, now *rônin*, broke into the Edo mansion of the official who had provoked their lord, killed him, and in their turn were condemned to commit suicide. But the tale of the loyalty of the forty-seven *rônin* was widely retold and helped preserve the spirit of the samurai through the long centuries of peace.

In 1688 Nagasaki, at the upper end of a long, narrow bay on the western side of the southern island of Kyushu, had been at the vortex of Japan's extraordinary relations with the outside world for more than a hundred years. From the 1540s on, Portuguese traders had begun to probe for trading opportunities, soon followed by Saint Francis Xavier, who found in the Japanese a sense of honor and a capacity for single-minded warriorlike commitment that appealed to him both as a Jesuit and as a Spanish hidalgo. In the political and cultural turmoil of Japan in the late 1500s, lords of competitive domains were eager to attract the trade of the Portuguese to their own ports and found that it was easier to do so if they were hospitable to the Jesuits.

Some Japanese of all classes found in the religion preached by the missionaries a set of coherent and disciplined responses to the moral and intellectual disorder of their times. By 1580 there were more than one hundred thousand Christian converts in Japan. In that year a daimyo granted Nagasaki to the Society of Jesus as a feudal fief. But only seven years later the rising superdaimyo Hideyoshi had grown worried by the danger of Christianity as an advance guard for Portuguese and Spanish power and attempted to expel all the missionaries. From 1612 on, under the Tokugawa shoguns, laws against missionary activity and the practice of Christianity by Japanese grew steadily more severe. In 1622 and 1623 almost one hundred missionaries and converts were executed, most by crucifixion, in Nagasaki and in Edo. Other Japanese Christians chose to emigrate; they did much of the work on the facade of the grand Church of São Paulo in Macao, drew the concern of the Spanish in Manila, formed a royal bodyguard in Ayutthaya, and even settled in Batavia. Many Christians in Japan remained steadfast in the face of brutal tortures. In the late 1630s everything came to a head around Nagasaki. Nearby, at Shimabara, Christian peasants rose in rebellion and were crushed. The shogunate concluded that the Portuguese were irremediably involved with the missionaries, expelled them, and executed almost every man of an embassy sent to plead for reconsideration.

The Dutch, who had been trading at Hirado farther north on the coast of Kyushu, were transferred to Nagasaki and confined to Deshima, an artificial island built for just this purpose. The Chinese also were limited to trade at Nagasaki but not so tightly confined. Foreign trade in Japanese ships, which sometimes had been carried on by Japanese Christians and which often led to contacts with Christians abroad, had been more and more tightly regulated in the 1630s and was now strictly prohibited. The consequences of this voluntary withdrawal were immense; a maritime Asia with an active Japanese presence in 1688 would have been profoundly different from the actual situation.

Nagasaki thus became by far the most important window on the world for a political elite that was terribly conscious of the dangers of involvement with that world. Nagasaki was under direct control of delegates of the Tokugawa shoguns, not part of any daimyo's domain. The shogunate rejected a few appeals from Ming resistance regimes for assistance against the Qing conquerors and kept abreast of the developments in China by systematically questioning the captains of every arriving Chinese junk. A few Chinese settled in Japan and became bilingual and bicultural interpreters. Nagasaki had two fine Chinese Buddhist temples. Chinese sailors sought the pleasures of the port, especially the beautiful women with their unbound feet. The Dutch had to send an embassy every year to pay homage to the shogun in Edo, but otherwise they were largely confined to Deshima, their artificial island. Prostitutes came there to serve them. Interpreters learned their language. Japanese artists have left us a few vivid pictures of their strange dress, the weird colors of their hair, their uncouth manners, and their little orchestras of Asian slaves.

In the decades that followed the expulsion of the Portuguese and the confinement of the Dutch and the Chinese to Nagasaki, the shogunate continued to be concerned with the possibility of some revival of Christian or other maritime threats to Japanese security. It also sought to get under control the fluctuations in supplies of copper, silver, and gold, all produced in Japan, that resulted from their export. In the 1670s they recognized that efforts simply to prohibit the export of one metal or another were hard to enforce and instituted a more comprehensive system of tightly controlled bloc trade, with all prices set by the Nagasaki officials. No other political system in the world of 1688 engaged in such thorough monitoring and effective control of its foreign trade; Japan, internally a collection of pacified but well-organized and competitive ministates, faced the external world as a single highly unified polity, just as Japan has done so often, in war and in peace, in modern times.

Following Shi Lang's conquest of Taiwan in 1683, the Qing rulers legalized maritime trade from Fujian and Guangdong ports at the beginning of 1685, in time for ship captains to make their spring voyages to Japan. By the end of the year eighty-five junks, more than three times a typical annual figure for the previous decades, had reached Japan. The rush brought reminders of all the reasons why Japan was wary of foreign contact. A Portuguese ship arrived from Macao, bearing fifteen shipwrecked Japanese; the Portuguese were kept under strict guard and sent away as soon as possible with orders never to return. A Chinese ship brought a Chinese book that was found to contain information about Roman Catholicism; the Chinese responsible were executed, and their ship and goods burned. The Qing conquerors of Taiwan sent two officials to Nagasaki, probably to look for former opponents who had not yet surrendered. The *bakufu* sent special commissioners to Nagasaki to question them and order them to leave, with a warning that the Qing never should send officials to Japan again. The Dutch noted signs that the Japanese feared that the huge number of trading junks could provide cover for a surprise Qing attack on Japan.

In 1685, as the tide of Chinese imports rose, the *bakufu* and the Nagasaki officials kept these security concerns in the background and took more direct action to control the size of the trade, ordering that Dutch imports be limited to the value of three hundred thousand ounces of silver annually and Chinese to six hundred thousand. In January 1686 Japanese officials ordered the junks remaining in Nagasaki Harbor to leave before the Lunar New Year. They did but remained nearby, attempting to evade the restrictions by smuggling. Some Japanese smugglers were caught and executed. Some of the ships that had been ordered to leave came back in again after the New Year and were allowed to trade under the quota for 1686. In the spring and summer of 1686, 112 junks arrived at Nagasaki. Some with small cargoes were allowed to sell everything; those with larger cargoes, valued up to one hundred thousand silver ounces each, were allowed to sell only goods worth a maximum of twenty-five thousand ounces. Thus these restrictions still allowed large numbers of junks to come, sell some goods legally in Nagasaki, and then withdraw to outer waters and smuggle the rest.

The rush to trade with Japan continued to grow, with 136 junks in 1687 and a staggering 192 in 1688. The smuggling continued, as did the executions of Japanese engaged in it. On August 9, 1688, the Nagasaki authorities announced that of the 165 Chinese junks already in harbor, only 120 would be allowed to break bulk and participate in the sale of goods up to the six hundred thousand ounces' total limit; the rest of the junks, and presumably those that arrived after this, would have to leave at once with their hatches still sealed. In September it was announced that henceforth only 70 junks per year would be allowed to trade, a specific number from each home port or region: 10 from Jiangnan, 12 from Ningbo, 13 from Fuzhou, 6 from Canton, and so on. Moreover, a walled residential compound was to be constructed for the Chinese, somewhat like the famous Deshima of the Dutch but, to judge from a surviving bird's-eye image, less completely isolated from the rest of the city. The compound was completed, and the Chinese moved into it in 1689. They were not allowed out in the city, and their cargoes were taken from them and stored elsewhere. These were of course measures to enforce strictly the 1685 quantitative limits, but we may also see in them efforts to deal with the threat to Japanese security (or at least tranquillity) presented by the arrival of so many foreign ships and sailors. The quantitative limits on imports apparently had been set to enable the Japanese to balance imports with exports other than gold and silver, and they were largely successful in preventing exports of precious metals. The struggle to repress the smuggling trade went on for many years. The only effective solution was the encouragement of Japanese "import substitution" industries, especially in silk. The quotas governing the Chinese trade fell even lower in the eighteenth century.

CHAPTER 13

SAIKAKU AND BASHÔ

Ihara Saikaku's *The Japanese Family Storehouse* (*Nippon eitai-gura*), published in 1688, begins:

Heaven says nothing, and the whole earth grows rich beneath its silent rule. Men, too, are touched by heaven's virtue; yet, in their greater part they are creatures of deceit. They are born, it seems, with an emptiness of soul, and must take their qualities wholly from things without. To be born thus empty into this modern age, this mixture of good and ill, and yet to steer through life on an honest course to the splendors of success—this is a feat reserved for paragons of our kind, a task beyond the nature of the normal man.

But the first consideration for all, throughout life, is the earning of a living. And in this matter, each one of us must bow before the shrine of the Heavenly Goddess of Thrift (not Shinto priests alone, but samurai, farmers, traders, artisans, and even Buddhist bonzes), and we must husband gold and silver as the deity enjoins. Though mothers and fathers give us life, it is money alone which preserves it.

In the first chapter of this work Saikaku goes on to tell the story of a temple where pilgrims borrowed three, five, or ten copper coins for good luck as they left, always paying back double the number the next year. One day an ordinary-looking man asked to borrow a thousand coins. He disappeared before the astonished priests could collect their wits and wonder if they would ever get their money back. The man lent the coins to fishermen in good-luck strings of one hundred, always got them back with interest, and kept track of the compounding interest he owed the temple. After thirteen years he returned to the temple 8,192,000 coins. Saikaku concludes: "Those who inherit nothing from their fathers and whose fortunes, won by sheer ability, exceed five hundred *kanme* of silver, are known as Men of Substance. If their fortunes mount above a thousand *kanme*, we call them Millionaires. By interest alone such money grows to thousands on tens of thousands, and its voices swell in silvery songs to sing its lord's posterity ten thousand years of luck."

Saikaku's *Family Storehouse* contains many such stories of wealth gained through prudence, diligence, and cleverness. One man never neglected a detail that might lead to profit, stopping on the way back from a neighbor's funeral to pick medicinal herbs, pausing when he stumbled to pick up pebbles to use to light fires. A widow left with debts she could not possibly pay off by her own meager earning power decided to raffle off her house. She took in enough money to pay off her debts and get a new start in life. A hired farm girl won the raffle, getting a house of her own for a few coins.

Saikaku's book consists of thirty chapters, each containing several stories of this kind. Sometimes the connections among the stories in a chapter are clear, but in other chapters they are loose, perhaps no more than an association of words or names. Here we can see the continuing influence of the author's earlier devotion to the *haikai*-linked verse form, in which an image or word in one verse may be used in a quite different way in the next. Saikaku was famous in his own time for his immense fluency in writing haikai and for the density of their layers of allusion to literature and to contemporary realities. Some contemporary detractors called his style the Dutch style, "Dutch" apparently being used in his time for anything exotic and overblown, roughly as some of us might use "baroque."

Ihara Saikaku is the pen name of a man who inherited substantial merchant wealth early in life. Although he clearly knew a great deal about the Japanese business world of his time, he cannot have spent much time actively managing the family business, for he was an amazingly prolific writer. *Haikai* composition traditionally had been a group activity, with one artist writing the first poem, a friend writing another poem echoing and varying the words and attitudes of the first one, then other friends building on one another in a potentially interminable poetic jam session. Saikaku's first publication had been of a selected 300 from the 10,000 poems he and 150 others had composed during a twelve-day session. Thereafter he and other poets challenged tradition by writing strings of *haikai* by themselves. In 1683 Saikaku set a record that no one seems to have tried to break, writing 23,500 *haikai* poems in one day and one night.

By 1683, however, Saikaku already had turned the great flood of his literary creativity into some novel forms of prose, drawing on realms of experience that seldom appeared in earlier Japanese literature and writing for a widening audience of merchants, urban samurai, and probably a few prosperous, literate farmers. Although he did not have to sell his books to fill his rice bowl, his writing was very much directed to those who would buy them, not just to aristocratic patrons and connoisseurs. And although Japanese literature from the tenth-century *Tale of Genji* on is not prudish, Saikaku's writings about commercial and obsessive sex set a new standard for frankness and lack of sentimentality. His first prose work, *The Life of an Amorous Man*, published in 1682, tells the story of a man who "chose of his own to be tormented by love, and by the time he reached the age of fifty-four he had dallied with 3742 women and 725 young men." Many think his finest work is *Five Women Who Loved Love*, in which only one of the erotically obsessed heroines avoids execution, suicide, or the nunnery, and another exclaims to a warning vision of a Buddhist deity, "Please don't worry about what becomes of us. We are more than glad to pay with our lives for this illicit affair." Still other collections, including *Tales of Samurai Duty*, published in 1688, tell new stories and retell old ones of samurai demonstrating suicidal loyalty and obsessive pursuit of revenge, but without any of the admiration that had been expressed by earlier authors. The samurai dying for their lords, it seems, are just doing what they have to do, having been born in warrior households. So are the merchants never wasting a moment or a penny. So too, perhaps, are his erotic compulsives, driven by their lusts, showing themselves to have little depth of character or feeling or interest in the individuality of those whose bodies they enjoy.

It is as if in the new and highly differentiated social order of Tokugawa Japan, this amazing writer, with his keen sense of the emptiness of men's souls, no longer could sustain the old unified vision, common since the *Tale of Genji*, of the warrior-litterateur-aristocrat, his valor or his erotic obsession always tempered with Buddhist knowledge of the transience of all lives and loves. In its place Saikaku presents a world of distinctive types pursuing, with intelligence or stupidity, good luck or bad, the duties and obsessions fate has given them.

Near the end of *Family Storehouse*, Saikaku writes: "The world is a dreadful place. Never lend money casually, nor, when you marry off your daughter, leave the marriage broker to arrange matters as he pleases. There are enough ways of losing money even if you take proper care. . . . There is more money than there used to be, and both making it and losing it are done on a grander scale. Now, if ever, trade is an exciting venture. So let none of you risk slipshod methods in earning your livings." In another passage he describes the misery of the poor in a pawnshop: a man leaving in the rain after pawning his only umbrella, a woman pawning the family cooking pot, another pawning her underslip and enduring the leers of the men who can see through her thin dress. But even that far down there is hope; one poor man, out of work in Edo, simply watches the crowds passing by on the great Nihon Bridge. There is so much good work for carpenters in the building and rebuilding of the lavish daimyo mansions that at the end of every day crowds of happy carpenters and their apprentices cross the bridge, leaving a trail of shavings and scraps of wood from their bags. Our hero begins by picking up the scraps and selling them as they were, goes on to build up a flourishing chopstick-making business, and ends as a great timber merchant, owning a mansion, warehouses, and tracts of forestland.

Although most of Saikaku's tales of wealth made and lost came from the world of the cities, it should not be forgotten that much of Japan's urbanization had occurred in just a few generations before his time, and rural life was by no means as remote to him and his readers as it is to many city dwellers today. He drew two of his strongest images of the happy results of thrift and diligence from the country. One describes a poor farmer who scatters parched beans for luck every New Year's Eve. One New Year's Day he decides to plant one; miraculously it grows. He plants the beans from that plant, and continues to expand his bean plantings until they yield a nice income. The beginning miracle has a strongly Buddhist tinge; Buddhist teachings early and late are full of metaphors of the planting of seeds of merit and compassion that later bear holy flowers and fruit. The farmer now uses some of his income to have a stone lantern constructed to light the way for travelers on the main road at night. "Known as the 'Lantern of Beans,' it shines to this day. . . . All things grow bigger in

time, and our largest ambitions are not beyond hope of ultimate fulfill-
ment."

Saikaku chose to end his collection of often worldly and cynical stories
by telling of a farm household near Kyoto where grandfather, father, and
son and their wives all live in harmony, prosperity, and good health. "Living
thus in perfect contentment, worshiping the gods and holding the Buddhas
in deep reverence, their hearts came naturally to be endowed with every
virtue." When the grandfather reaches the age of eighty-eight, many people
come to him, as was customary for honored men of that age, to ask him to
cut for them a bamboo grain level. All the merchants who use these levels
prosper; one millionaire uses his bamboo level to measure out the silver he
is dividing among his three sons. Saikaku concludes: "Money is still to be
found in certain places, and where it lies it lies in abundance. Whenever I
heard stories about it I noted them in my great national stock-book, and, in
order that future generations might study them and profit thereby, I placed
them in a storehouse to serve each family's posterity. Here they now rest,
as securely guarded as the peace of Japan."

Matsuo Toshichirô, who signed himself Bashô, "Banana Tree," spent most
of 1688 on the road, visiting many famous scenes of Japan at their best
times, trying to be, as he believed all great artists were, at one with nature
throughout the four seasons. Sometimes he confessed that a well-known
place left him with no fresh inspiration. Already he was an eminent poet;
his best-known poem, the most famous haiku in all Japanese literature, had
appeared two years before:

An old pond.
A frog jumps in.
The sound of water!

Fond of conversation, forty-four years old, not in robust health, he had
been through years of rigorous meditation under a Zen Buddhist priest.
The most basic teaching of Buddhism is that everything we desire is illu-
sory and inconstant and that to desire, to cling to, to love things of this
world can only bring sorrow and endless reincarnation in this sorrowful
world. One can gradually liberate oneself from illusions and clingings, gain
more and more insight into the real nature of things, and eventually escape

altogether from the wheel of rebirth. Zen was a version of this teaching developed in China, Korea, and Japan from about 650 C.E. Its highly disciplined techniques of meditation under the direction of a master are meant to bring the disciple to a moment of enlightenment, a sudden vision of the reality underlying the illusions.

For Bashô, both meditation and his travels to view famous places were routes to inspiration. The artist was necessarily part seer, part shaman and could not expect insight if he cared for his own safety and comfort. The dangers and uncertainties of travel simply mirrored the fundamental inconstancy and unreliability of human life. There was a density of association around famous sights built up by previous visits by notable Buddhist priests. The most ordinary experience might bring insight, Buddhist and artistic. That splash of a frog may have brought a shock of enlightenment into the profound silence of his Zen meditation. He liked banana trees in part because their trunks were of no use; a quiet allusion to the *Zhuangzi*, a great Chinese text of the third century B.C.E., much appreciated by Zen Buddhists, in which the useless twisted tree is a metaphor for the "useless" man who survives and knows more than the "useful." Even a chestnut tree would lead him through the character for "chestnut" (栗, "west" over "tree") to thoughts of the western paradise and of reliance on the great Buddhist deity who dwelt there.

Many of Bashô's travels were uncomfortable and dangerous, but in 1688 he managed to spend Buddha's birthday among the civilized splendors of the ancient city of Nara. Nara had been the capital of Japan from 710 to 783, at the peak of Japan's enthusiastic assimilation of Buddhism and of Chinese models of government. Bashô loved the fine buildings of its temples, the multiple walls of its palaces, its cherry trees. The deer in its monastery groves are still one of its pleasures today, and to the Buddhist they bring thoughts of the Deer Park near Benares in India where the Buddha preached his first sermon, advising his disciples to follow a Middle Way, neither clinging to the inconstant things of this world nor engaging in the asceticisms and self-mortifications of Hindu holy men. In Bashô's response to the ancient trees and the gentle vegetarian animals, there was no distinction among the Buddhist, the aesthete, and the man. There is a haiku from the 1688 visit:

> By what divine consideration
> Is it, I wonder,

That this fawn is born
On Buddha's birthday?

In the fall of 1688 Bashô decided to take a trip to see the full moon rise over Mount Obasute near Sarashina village. This was the mountain, he said, where in ancient times the village people used to abandon their aged mothers. The Kiso road leading to the village passed over several high mountains. The Lord Buddha had taught the inconstancy and sorrowfulness of all things; surely this frail and aging poet taking a dangerous trip to view the waxing and waning moon in a place of great beauty but fearsome associations was a worthy disciple of the Buddha.

At one point Bashô and his companions met an old priest tottering along, carrying an enormous load. "My companions sympathized with him, and taking the heavy load from the priest's shoulders, put it together with other things they had been carrying on my horse. Consequently, I had to sit on a big pile. Above my head, mountains rose over mountains, and on my left a huge precipice dropped a thousand feet into a boiling river, leaving not a tiny square of flat land in between, so that, perched on the high saddle, I felt stricken with terror every time my horse gave a jerk."

Finally Bashô gave up riding and walked, still frightened and staggering. "The servant, on the other hand, mounted the horse and seemed to give not even the slightest thought to danger. He often nodded in a doze and seemed about to fall headlong over the precipice. Every time I saw him drop his head, I was terrified out of my wits. Upon second thought, however, it occurred to me that every one of us was like this servant, wading through the ever-changing reefs of this world in stormy weather, totally blind to the hidden dangers, and that the Buddha surveying us from on high, would surely feel the same misgivings about our fortunes as I did about the servant."

At Mount Obasute, Bashô wrote a poem:

A yellow valerian
With its slender stalk
Stands bedecked
In droplets of dew.

Hot radish
Pierced my tongue,

While the autumn wind
Pierced my heart.

Horse-chestnuts
From the mountains of Kiso
Will be my presents
To city-dwellers.

Bidding farewell,
Bidden good-bye,
I walked into
The autumn of Kiso.

PART IV

VERSAILLES, LONDON, AMSTERDAM

I n 1688 the attention of politically aware Europeans was focused on a splendid French court at the center of a powerful and aggressive state; on London, capital of a realm growing in power and wealth if only it could stop tearing itself apart over religion and the family quarrels of its monarchs; and on Amsterdam, commercial capital of Europe, at the center of a confederation of cities and provinces so intricately checked and balanced that it seemed incapable of decisive action. Surveying the politics of Europe more widely, one would think of the polycentric Holy Roman Empire; anarchically elective Poland; cautious, legalistic Spain; and many others. Observers from many other parts of the world—India, China, Russia, the Ottoman Empire—would have found these differences less striking than the singular fact that the European political world had no imperial center, no Beijing, no Agra, no Istanbul. The medieval holy Roman emperors had aspired to rule all Europe; but their power never had reached beyond the German and Italian lands and the Balkan frontier they held against the Ottomans, and now Vienna faced major rivals even within those territories.

The intense struggle for survival of each unit in this multistate system pushed all of the more adaptable of them toward new strategies for mobilization of allegiance, wealth, and manpower. This made the Europe of 1688 a cauldron of forms of political life new in Europe, such as centralizing bureaucracies, or new in the world, such as representative assemblies with real powers. It was generally accepted that rulers had the right to determine what religions would be followed in their realms. Cynical manipulation of religion by rulers and ruled, incitement of one faith against another, turned some entirely against orthodox Christianity and others toward deeper inwardness within it. Novel forms of mobilization of resources and human energy, like the Dutch East India Company and the Society of Jesus, spread European power and presence to almost every part of the world.

There were always new points of crisis on the great chessboard of European politics. In 1688 they included the election of a ruling bishop in Cologne and the birth of a crown prince in London. French armies moved. A formidable Dutch fleet set out down the Channel and landed an invasion force in England. By the end of the year the chessboard had a new configuration. That narrow Channel now divided the central antagonists. This configuration was to last from the end of 1688 to the fall of Napoleon in 1815.

CHAPTER 14

THE SUN KING AND THE LADIES

"Sire, Marly? Sire, Marly?" The gorgeously dressed ladies curtsy deeply and whisper under their breath as the Sun King passes through the great room. Much depends on whom he notices. He likes to have pretty women along, especially on one of his relaxing outings to the nearby Château of Marly. In the past he often would have had his eye on one or more of them as possible new mistresses. But now there is another presence at Versailles, modestly dressed and circulating in the crowd at some distance from him, for she is not the crowned queen. But she is the king's wife, and Madame de Maintenon is a considerable figure at the court. The king loves and admires her and has become monogamous.

In 1688 the Royal Palace at Versailles was quite new, and the vast complex was still expanding. The fine classical Trianon Palace at the far end of the gardens was completed in that year. From the grand entrance court to the Hall of Mirrors to the open colonnade of the Trianon, there were many vistas that suggested immensely magnified sets for some baroque opera. And so they were. In the culture and concept of ruling that had been elaborated by the princes of Renaissance Italy and now was being further developed north of the Alps, the distance between stagecraft and statecraft was not great. The ruler, the one actor who mattered, gauged the effect of his every word and gesture.

Louis XIV was Europe's greatest master of this theatrical statecraft, and Versailles was designed as his great stage. By 1688 Louis had worked for

more than twenty years to undercut the independence of the French nobility. He wanted them to hang upon the royal favor, so that instead of meeting in their castles and provincial capitals to hatch new schemes of
self-aggrandizement or rebellion they would spend months in uncomfortable lodgings at Versailles, weighing every bit of gossip, attending every
public appearance of the king, watching anxiously to see to whom he
would speak, who would be allowed to stand close to him, who would get
to hold the candlestick when he went to bed, and who would hand him his
dressing gown as he awoke.

Louis's entire life had taught him the importance of acting like a king.
He was born in 1638, a time of immense turmoil and confusion in France.
Low ebb came in 1651, when a Paris mob broke into the Louvre Palace and
demanded to see the young king; his mother had to agree, and he pretended to be asleep until she managed to get them out. He grew up hating
Paris and disorder. He built Versailles and other smaller palaces outside
Paris and rarely set foot in the Louvre. He got a poor formal education but
excellent mentoring in statecraft and the arts of court life from his first
minister, Cardinal Mazarin, who may have been married to his mother.
When Mazarin died in 1661, Louis immediately announced his intention
to be his own first minister, to make all final decisions himself. Soon he was
reminding his ministers that he was the state. Even earlier kings of France
had sometimes used the metaphor of the gleaming, life-giving sun—not
the sun at the center of the cosmos, which was not yet orthodox opinion—
as a metaphor for the monarchy. Louis made constant and emphatic use of
the symbol, cutting a splendid figure when he danced the role of the sun or
of Apollo, the sun-god, in a court ballet. All of Louis's life the formalities
and apparent gaieties of court life concealed hours of document reading
and council meetings by the king and his high ministers. By 1664 he had
the ideal detail-oriented, control-minded minister to assist him, Jean-Baptiste Colbert. By prodigious effort Colbert and his modest staff of clerks
and provincial appointees uncovered many unauthorized claims of nobility and other cases of fraudulent tax exemption, eliminated many useless
offices and other claims on the royal treasury, reduced the indebtedness
that weighed so heavily on the royal budget, and increased the efficiency
and honesty of tax collection. By 1671 net royal incomes had at least dou-
bled. Similar impulses to order, hierarchy, and centralization could be seen
in many spheres. Paris and other cities were brought under more effective
control, the lawcourts and provincial assemblies had their powers reduced,

controls on publication were elaborated. The nobles found that they had fewer chances to build counterforces in the provinces. If they wanted access to the many lucrative offices now directly at the king's disposal, and if they wanted their sons to earn their spurs in the king's growing armies, they had to forsake their power bases in the provinces and spend most of their time at the royal court.

If an orderly and prosperous France had been the goal of the policies of the young Louis and Colbert, they could have begun to relax, admire their handiwork, and fine-tune their policies about 1671. But they were even less interested in the comfort and security of the ordinary people than most seventeenth-century rulers. For them, prosperity and order were means to the end of being a prince: magnificence, prestige, precedence, and domination over other rulers. At first Spain was the great adversary, as a result of the long rivalry of Bourbon and Hapsburg, and the presence of Spanish territories on three sides of France (along the Pyrenees, in Flanders, and Franche-Comté to the east). It was expected that the feeble Carlos II soon would die without an heir, and Louis might be able to claim by way of his Spanish queen a share in the territories that bordered on France, in Spanish holdings in Italy, or even in Spain's vast American empire. Through skillful diplomacy, bribes and subsidies, and playing on common anti-Hapsburg orientations, the king wove a complex web of alliances.

But then French advances into the Spanish Netherlands (Flanders and Brabant, roughly modern Belgium) alarmed the Dutch. Louis pulled back but was deeply affronted by the check to his ambitions from a society of ordinary merchants and burghers, and Colbert resented continued Dutch domination of maritime trade. With the new royal incomes supporting the largest and best-trained army in Europe, Louis invaded and almost conquered Holland in 1672; the Dutch had to open the dikes to stop his armies. William III of Orange came to power; he was to devote his life to building a great alliance to stop Louis XIV. The fiscal strain of full-scale war was now so great that Colbert had to raise taxes and begin again some of the borrowing and other expedients he had worked so hard to eliminate. Louis had to moderate and then halt his advance in the Spanish Netherlands. He turned instead to slower methods, seeking judgments from his tame lawcourts that France had sovereign rights in some border territory and then occupying it. He occupied Strasbourg in 1681 without any such justification. Nothing was done that would provoke a declaration of war, but the continuing pressure caused a steady drift of German and other rulers toward a network of anti-French alliances. When the sovereign bishop of Cologne died in July 1688, both the French and the Hapsburgs made frantic efforts to influence the election of a successor. The candidate supported by the French won a majority, but not the two-thirds majority that his opponents claimed was required. French troops marched on Cologne; its German neighbors reinforced its garrison and reaffirmed old ties with William. French forces also besieged the important Rhine fortress of Philippsburg, and occupied a number of other German cities. The French campaign into the Rhineland was a fine example of military organization. Besieged by forces under the command of the dauphin himself, advised by Vauban, the finest fortifications engineer in Europe, Philippsburg fell on October 29.

There was another European crisis of concern to the Sun King. Ever since 1660, when the Stuarts had overthrown the regicides and regained the English throne, France had cultivated and subsidized English monarchs who seemed to share their religious and political views. Now it seemed that this patient effort was yielding excellent fruit; an open Catholic, James II, was king of England. The French court had little sense of the depth of English popular anti-Catholicism or the other political tensions that made James's rule so insecure. It seemed the longest of long shots that William of Orange would manage to secure Dutch consent to launch an invasion, make a successful landing, and claim the English throne in his wife's name. Certainly the Dutch would not have risked their regiments in the invasion if Louis's armies had been advancing through Flanders. But late in 1688 *Louis marched the wrong way*, northeast toward the Rhine, not north into Flanders. Seeing the French tied down in that direction, William of Orange was able to commit himself to the invasion of England. By the end of the year William had won and had all the power of England and the Netherlands at the core of his anti-French alliance. Louis now prepared for further interventions in Germany. In 1689 he was to invade the Palatinate, claiming that his sister-in-law had a right to a share in the inheritance of its territories, and his armies wreaked much havoc and destroyed the castle overlooking Heidelberg. But by then the powerful coalition against him was falling into line, and France was at war with most of Europe much of the time until 1715.

At the same time, Louis's quest for domination and glory had pushed him into a nearly complete break with the papacy. The difficulties were not primarily theological. The French church claimed extensive "Gallican" rights over church appointments and incomes in France; the papacy assented to only part of what was claimed. But the real crisis in 1688 was over the "franchises," the extraterritorial privileges of the ambassadors of foreign powers in Rome. Most of Europe's monarchs had modified or relinquished these privileges, but Louis had refused to do so, and now he had sent a career military officer with a thousand soldiers to occupy and fortify the French ambassador's palace in Rome. Late in 1687 the pope excommunicated the ambassador. In the fall of 1688 Louis sent troops to occupy Avignon, a papal enclave in southern France. It may be that only the death of the intransigent Pope Innocent XI in 1689 allowed the two sides to avoid a complete schism.

One of our best sources on the life of the court at Versailles in 1688 is the diary of Philippe de Courcillon, marquis of Dangeau. In 1688 the marquis already was fifty years old. Like many young noblemen at the time, he had gained some military experience abroad, in Spain, and soon was named colonel of a new infantry regiment. But his real talents were those of a courtier, not a commander. The Spanish-born queen mother, Anne, and Louis's Spanish queen, Marie Thérèse, liked to speak with him in their native tongue. The courtiers spent many evenings wagering gold pieces on simple card games, and Dangeau was *very* good at cards; he was rumored to have won a vast fortune in these games. He was not a statesman, not a member of any of the councils where the king spent so many hours reading dispatches and making policy, but he tells us a great deal about the daily life of the court.

News of many aspects of the world of 1688 discussed in this book reached the courtiers of Versailles: the upheaval in Istanbul, the Venetian campaign against the Ottomans and Morosini's election as doge while on campaign, the arrival of an opulent silver cargo at Cádiz, even the death of the duke of Albemarle in Jamaica. The courtiers commented on the presents, not very splendid, they said, that the king of Siam had sent to the king of France. There was much discussion of the conflict with the Holy See. In the fall everyone hung on the latest news from the siege of Philippsburg, with much talk about how well the dauphin and various nobles were doing. In November and December the reports from Holland and England were confusing and contradictory, then amazing and distressing, and finally disastrous. There is in fact far more in Dangeau's memoirs about events elsewhere in Europe than there is about life outside the court in France itself.

The main content of his jottings is the life of the court. The king and his brother went hunting or shooting almost every day. There were musical or dramatic performances many evenings, and a great deal of cardplaying. The king usually was present; he spent much time in council meetings and reading dispatches, but he also did a great deal of his royal work—judging people and signaling his favor and disfavor—in these apparently frivolous entertainments. He was always alert, his manners and carriage perfectly controlled. Newcomers to court required some time to get over being terrified of him. In March and April 1688 Dangeau noted the magnificent new costumes, red and blue accented with gold and silver, for the royal wolf-hunting parties. He meticulously recorded who appeared at court and who went where with the king, matters of great importance. So were royal appointments and grants. Here the mercenary structure of French court society shows through the glittering surface of diversion and ceremony. For every appointment, every grant, every death and inheritance, Dangeau records the value of the transaction. Thus on March 30, 1688, "M. de Montgou, colonel of the cuirassiers, is marrying Mlle d'Heudricourt. In support of the marriage, he will have a pension of 1000 écus from the King, and from the young lady 2000; in addition to that she has 22,000 écus in minted silver, and Madame de Miossens, her aunt, promises her 40,000 livres after her death." On April 8 "The King has given an augmentation of pension of 1000 écus to M. de Villette, commander of a [naval] squadron. Caillavel, captain of the guards, has received the government of Dax, vacant by the death of the late M. de Poyane; this government will bring him at least 1000 écus in income, and is in his home region." And so on.

A name that was almost always on Dangeau's lists of the king's companions for his excursions was that of the marquise de Maintenon. She had come into his orbit as the governess of his children by a previous mistress, the marquise de Montespan. She probably caught him at an age when, like many a middle-aged roué, he was ready to think about settling down a little and taking life more seriously. He married Maintenon within six weeks after the death of Queen Marie Thérèse in 1683. She did not have high enough rank to be made queen of France, and the marriage was kept secret but was widely suspected. Apart from believing in his own appointment by God, Louis had not been very religious. He was chronically at odds with the Holy See and had been mentored in politics by Mazarin, the great enemy of the politically "devout." But Maintenon was a serious Catholic, and under her tutelage he began to go to mass regularly and to fulfill his other religious duties. She could not intervene in her husband's governing too openly, but it was understood that he respected her judgment and might say to her with respect and affection, "What does Your Solidity think?" In 1688, Dangeau records, the players of Italian comedies were warned that in the future they must avoid all double's entendres in their dialogue.

The marquise de Maintenon sometimes is blamed for the most famous, or infamous, of Louis's actions in the 1680s, the revocation of the Edict of Nantes in 1685, which withdrew all toleration of Protestantism and led to the emigration of many thousands of Huguenots to Holland, England, and even South Africa. But although Maintenon must have rejoiced in the religious "unification" of France, as most French Catholics did, she by no means brought about a policy that was well under way before she gained influence over the king. In 1688 toleration as a matter of principle was an idea still on the far frontiers of intellectual discussion; even the broadminded rulers of the Netherlands believed that they had an obligation to forbid the publication of works that impugned the fundamentals of Christianity. In France Catholics and Protestants long had been in conflict as political forces and as blocs in local society, with much violence and deep hatred on both sides. Louis was predisposed to see any bloc of subjects with special privileges, like those granted Protestants under the Edict of Nantes, as an infringement on his sovereignty and the unity of his realm. Some eminent and earnest Catholics and Protestants were groping at the time for formulas that would lead to a reunion of Christianity, by which the Catholics among them certainly meant some kind of reunion with the Roman Catholic Church, even if somewhat modified. But these projects tended to be under the patronage of the Hapsburg holy Roman emperors, and had no more appeal to the French court than did projects for total submission to the Holy See. The result was that although there were men of high principle involved in efforts to convert French Protestants to Catholicism, the main thrust of the effort was as political and cynical as the diplomacy of Louis XIV and his gradual occupation of small territories along the Rhine. Dozens of decrees barred Huguenots from any activity not expressly permitted by the Edict of Nantes, even the practice of midwifery. A special fund was set up to make payments to new converts to Catholicism. Mob violence and the prosecution of Protestant ministers on flimsy charges led to the horror of the quartering of royal troops in the houses of recalcitrant Protestants, which gave the word "dragonnade" to French and the verb "to dragoon" to English. Very large numbers of Protestants gave way and became at least nominal Catholics. Others fled the country.

By 1685 Louis's court was so full of stories of wonderful conversions, with none of the details of terror and compulsion, that it was easy for him to conclude that the work of religious unification was almost done and that his final revocation of the old privileges would be a matter of form. That was not entirely true, and since Protestant laymen now were forbidden to leave France, many sneaked out by land or by sea. They took with them their wealth and their skills in industries and trade, contributing to the prosperity of every Protestant state. They carried more and more terrible tales of persecution, confirming the Protestant princes and elites in their determination to oppose French power, and creating the largest black blotch on the shiny image of the court of the Sun King. For 1688 few records can be found of anti-Protestant activity in France; by then all had nominally converted, fled, or gone far into hiding.

Madame de Maintenon was responsible for the Sun King's involvement in a project that did not directly challenge his male worlds of sieges and wolf hunts, or the mercenary glitter of Versailles, but sought to provide a counterweight of modest and devout solidity in the aristocracy at large. The Royal House of St. Cyr was a boarding school for 250 daughters of poor nobles, with preference given to children of those who had died or been disabled in the king's service. Girls entered it between the ages of seven and twelve. All wore modest brown dresses with lace trim and white lace caps, the whole trimmed with ribbons, red for the youngest, green, yellow, then blue for the oldest. Each of the teachers, who were not nuns, had under her charge a quasi family of girls for whom she worked out a schedule of lessons in reading, writing, religion, and quite a lot of fine needlework. Madame de Maintenon was seriously interested in education; she had had an anxious youth and had spent some good and important years caring for the king's bastards. Having persuaded the king to found and endow St. Cyr, she was able to work out there her vision of an education for young women that would be cheerful, religious but not of the convent, and would value charm and beauty. Some graduates might choose to become nuns, but many others would become good wives and participants in the most pleasant and serious kinds of salon conversations. For the carnival season in the spring of 1688 the girls performed for each other scenes from the Bible and from the works of Corneille and Racine. At the end of the year rehearsals were under way for one of Madame de Maintenon's great moments of triumph, the performance on January 26, 1689, by the girls of St. Cyr, in her presence and that of the Sun King, of a splendid new drama by Racine, *Esther*, retelling the Old Testament story of the humble, devout, and virtuous woman who ascended to the side of a powerful king.

But by that time Madame de Maintenon already found much to worry about at St. Cyr. It was too close to Versailles, and a visit there became a popular diversion for the courtiers. The teachers and the girls of course were very much excited by all the attention. On December 10, 1688, the king abruptly dismissed the young superior of the school, who seemed to be especially caught up in the excitement of court favor. Madame de Maintenon found it very hard to chart a middle way between the petty restrictions of convent life and excesses of unladylike cleverness and boldness; gradually the convent won out, and in the 1690s all teachers had to take final vows as nuns.

Madame de Maintenon's Christianity was a nice complement or corrective to excesses of male control, but no threat. It was not always so when women turned to God. In 1688 Madame de Maintenon was given many anxious moments, and the Sun King at least a few annoyed ones, by the strange figure of Jeanne de Guyon. Already as a girl inclined to a life of constant internal prayer, she had turned further inward in response to the abuse heaped on her by her husband and mother-in-law through twelve years of marriage, embracing her suffering as her "cross." After her husband died, she was able to devote herself altogether to internal prayer and most of her modest means to charities for converts from Protestantism in the Geneva area. She moved through a time of utter spiritual desolation to a way of "bare faith" that was beyond visions and enthusiasms. She began to write and was amazed by some of the things she found in her own writings. In addition to spells of illness, which she embraced as a special cross, she developed a childlike simplicity and a special devotion to the Child Jesus. Many who encountered her were disconcerted by the outward manifestations of this mix of mysticism with maternal themes (although she was not a good mother) and a deliberate, childlike passivity. Bishops were fascinated by her deep sayings but then wanted her to move on. When she arrived in Paris in 1686, she had just published her most famous work, *A Short and Easy Method of Prayer*. Prayer of the heart needed no forms and no words or only very familiar ones like the Our Father and could be continued by anyone in any condition at any time. Madame de Guyon aroused great interest in devout circles in Paris, but soon many were alarmed. Her teachings seemed too close to the quietism of the Spanish Jesuit Molinos, who had been arrested in Rome in 1685. The differences from other Catholic teaching may seem slight to the outsider, but the difficulty was that any teaching that encouraged a belief that the individual soul could reach God without the mediation of the church seemed to threaten the authority of the church. Since all involved were and hoped to remain in communion with the Church of Rome, the debates did not reach into the lives of ordinary individuals the way the Catholic-Anglican-Puritan struggles did in England. But they did represent something basic: a collision between the determination of the king and his bishops to enforce religious discipline and the unquenchable Christian impulse to inwardness and singularity represented by Madame de Guyon. And of course the very idea of a woman's daring to write about God was offensive to many.

In 1687 there were public attacks on *A Short and Easy Method of Prayer* that eventually led to its being placed on the Index of Prohibited Books in 1689. A priest who was Madame de Guyon's close adviser was arrested. Then on January 29, 1688, she was arrested and confined to the Convent of the Visitation, where she had no sympathizers, was treated quite severely, and embraced this new cross of passive suffering. But some of her supporters had ways to reach Madame de Maintenon, who, after her own careful investigations, was impressed by Madame de Guyon's devoutness and not convinced that she posed any threat to orthodoxy or public order. Madame de Guyon was released from her arrest on September 13, 1688. The controversy over Quietism, like others among French Catholics, continued in wordy vehemence for years to come.

The marquis of Dangeau tells us that there were a number of days in 1688, beginning in January, when the king and a small party went to the far end of the great park of Versailles to the Trianon. Here there had been a small, delicate palace of singular beauty, covered with ceramic tiles. It now had been razed, and the king was going to watch the last stages of the construction work on a larger and more austere structure, the Grand Trianon, which still stands. It is especially notable for its tall columns of tan marble veined with pink, the severe classical shapes nicely setting off the random play of the warm colors, and for the black and white diamond pattern of the pavements in the courtyard and colonnades. It was a fine place for a stroll in good weather and one of the finest of the great stage sets for the Sun King. Somehow the king and his party were even able to eat an occasional meal at the Trianon, brought in, as were all the king's meals, from kitchens far away. Some wonder if he ever had a hot meal. It was only on November 13 that Dangeau recorded that the building was "completed and furnished." On December 3 an Italian comedy, presumably shorn of doubles entendres, was performed there in the presence of the king and most of the court. On December 18 an opera was performed there by the musicians and dancers of the Paris Opéra, on the twenty-seventh a ballet. By then the French court knew that the queen and infant son of James II had fled and were safe in France and that James had been turned back when he tried to flee England. On December 30 and 31, 1688, and January 1, 1689, Louis and his court were entirely occupied with the elaborate ceremonies, marred only by one dispute over precedence between two dukes, for the induction of three ecclesiastics and twenty-four lay nobles into the Order of the Holy Spirit.

CHAPTER 15

A FAMILY QUARREL AND A
GLORIOUS REVOLUTION

T he drama of England in the last two months of 1688 might be
described as a complex baroque improvisation for two kings, a
polyphony of peers, choruses of invading soldiers and rioting Londoners,
and an obbligato for printing press. On October 10 William of Orange
issued a Declaration of his reasons for his planned invasion. It listed all the
"crimes and abuses" of James's reign, saw in them a grave threat to the
established Protestant religion in England, but blamed all this on the king's
"evil counsellors" and called only for the summoning of a free Parliament.
The infant prince of Wales was labeled an impostor, but William denied
any intent to seize his father-in-law's throne. Sixty thousand copies of the
Declaration were printed, and their distribution in England by various
channels began at once. By the end of October William of Orange had
assembled at The Brill near Rotterdam a formidable invasion fleet and an
army of at least twenty-one thousand, including all the crack Dutch regiments hardened in long years of confrontation with the forces of Louis
XIV, and an abundance of cannons, supplies, and horses most unusual in a
seventeenth-century expedition.

The fleet made a magnificent show as it sailed in fine weather on October 30, but it soon encountered a severe storm. Barrels broke loose and
rolled around belowdecks, and five hundred to one thousand of the four
thousand horses were killed, suffocated below battened-down hatches or

their skulls smashed where they were tied against the sides of the ships. The fleet returned to Dutch harbors, was put back into sailing condition with amazing speed, and sailed again on November 12. It was not clear where it was going. Some of William's leading allies were in the northeast of England, which seemed a likely landing area. But surprise would be greater with a landing elsewhere, and the northeasterners might be able to secure that area on their own. On November 13 the fleet sailed with all flags flying through the Strait of Dover, crowds watching from the cliffs on both sides. The "Protestant wind" that was speeding it forward also was holding the English fleet in its ports, but even when it put to sea, its admiral pursued the invaders slowly, perhaps trimming his political sails.

The east wind was threatening to drive the fleet beyond good harbors on the east coast of Devon toward well-defended Plymouth, but then it shifted, the invaders anchored at Tor Bay, and a fisherman named Peter Varwell carried the small, slight William to the beach and lodged him overnight in his cramped little house. It was November 15 by the Continental calendar, but by the old calendar still in use in England, it was November 5, Guy Fawkes Day.

The first day ashore had been lively, with drums beating, flags flying, and a very happy proprietor at the local alehouse. Several days later at the first town, Newton Abbot, bells were rung and Prince William's Declaration was read. But the daily work of William's army was a slog in the cold late-autumn rain through the narrow, muddy lanes of Devon. On November 9 they formed up into a regular parade, with kettledrums and flags flying, to enter the cathedral town of Exeter. William ordered that there be no more prayers for the prince of Wales at services in the cathedral. Outlays for the army's cloth and provisions made William popular, and he seemed determined to keep his troops under strict discipline. There were several reports of men being hanged for stealing a chicken. In a speech at Exeter on November 15 William used the royal "we" for the first time. On the twentieth he set out again, in terrible weather, with much sickness in the ranks. But there was also good news. Key nobles in the west country had come over to his side, and his allies in the northeast had taken York, Nottingham, and Newcastle. On November 24 King James's trusted commander John Churchill and the duke of Grafton appeared before William at Axminster. William used the words of King David—"If you be come peaceably unto me to help me, my heart shall be knit unto you"—and Churchill answered with another Old Testament passage: "Thine we are, David, and on thy side, thou son of Jesse. Peace, peace be unto thee and peace be unto thy helpers, for thy God helpeth thee."

On November 26 William took a day off to go deer hunting. He had more copies printed of his Declaration and a speech at Exeter. He passed the village where his advance guard had gotten into one of the two episodes of combat of the entire invasion, with a total death toll of perhaps fifteen on both sides. On the morning of December 4 he stopped outside Salisbury at Wilton House, seat of the earls of Pembroke, to see the famous paintings by Anthony Van Dyck. The house was magnificent, built by a nephew of the great Inigo Jones, an appropriate seat for a family that had made astute use of positions close to the throne for almost two hundred years, living in the highest style and patronizing the arts. There is a local tradition that Shakespeare and his company gave the first performances of *Twelfth Night* and *As You Like It* there. The most splendid of the Van Dycks was of the fourth earl, gentleman of the bedchamber to James I, and his family. The later earls of Pembroke showed some of the options open to the landed aristocracy in the Restoration years. The seventh earl had been convicted of manslaughter and confined in the Tower and had run so deeply in debt that many of the contents of Wilton House had to be sold after he died in 1683. His brother, the eighth earl, a man of deep learning, patron of John Locke, participated in the great debates of 1688–89, served William and Mary in many high offices, revived the family fortunes, founded the famous Wilton Royal Carpet Factory, and bought many fine books and works of art.

Amid all the splendid paintings and the symmetrical stage set rooms of Wilton House, William would have been especially intrigued (if it was there, not in the earl's London house, and on view) by a smaller, square Van Dyck of the three young children of Charles I. On the left was the future Charles II, old enough to wear miniature adult clothes. On the right was Princess Mary, future wife of William II of Orange and mother of William III himself, in a miniature lady's dress. In the center, in infant's long dress, was the future James II, William's future father-in-law and object of his deliberate advance across the kingdom.

Later that day William made a full-scale formal, triumphal entry into Salisbury, which James had left only ten days before. His troops marched on unopposed, stopping briefly to wonder at the sight of Stonehenge and discuss many odd explanations of it. On December 6 he reached Hungerford, and there on the eighth he received envoys sent by King James to attempt to negotiate a settlement. Time was on his side. The king was desperate. Peers and county leaders all over the kingdom were beginning to come over to William. James might still make something out of the general deference to the monarchy if there was a settlement. William's strategy was to avoid at all costs meeting his father-in-law or moving toward an agreement with him.

There is no shortage of ways in which England's Glorious Revolution of 1688 has been explained to later generations. It was glorious in that it was almost completely bloodless and in the way it opened the way to the various forms of constitutional government we cherish today. The Declaration of Rights of 1689 established an elected Parliament as supreme in the fundamentals of taxation and legislation and set clear limits to royal power. These beginnings were elaborated on in subsequent centuries not only by parliamentary governments of English heritage in London, Ottawa, New Delhi, and elsewhere but also by parliamentary regimes of varied language and much more mixed lineage in Paris, Prague, and Tokyo and by the non-parliamentary government of the United States.

The Glorious Revolution also has been called, rightly, the culmination of a family quarrel, as William of Orange drove his father-in-law from the throne. We have seen that it was a major turning point in European international relations, crystallizing a long century of Anglo-French conflict. It also was the culmination of a century of dramatic political change in England. English men and women of 1688 frequently expressed their political and religious allegiances by memorializing some great man or event of that century: Guy Fawkes Day was the anniversary of the discovery of a bizarre Catholic plot in 1605 to blow up Parliament; royalists, Catholic and Protestant, solemnly commemorated the anniversary of the execution of King Charles I in 1649; and many a frustrated radical yearned for the days of great dreams of liberty in the 1640s or even for the days of Oliver Cromwell.

The political upheavals of seventeenth-century England were shaped by immense changes in society and culture but above all by patterns of religion and politics that drew very large numbers of English men and women into deciding *for themselves* what their commitments to king and church were. Protestants could not rely on the authoritative guidance of a universal church. The Church of England was Protestant but hierarchical and under state authority. Those who found it too tainted by its Catholic heritage might try to purify it from within—the Puritan approach—or might reject altogether the idea of a church prescribed for everyone by political compulsion, the Separatist option. In any case every Protestant was in principle called upon to make an individual decision about these matters; his or her salvation depended on it. Debates about religion inevitably spilled over into politics; what were the rights of king and Parliament in making policy for the Church of England? Beyond that, almost everyone accepted the need for a monarchy with real authority, but the Parliament had ancient rights, especially the right to vote on taxation, and was becoming much more inclined to assert and expand them. Ideas of the rights of freeborn Englishmen made all these questions seem the business of anyone who could read or had any political awareness. A new insistence by monarchists on the divine right of kings, especially encouraged by the example of the French monarchy, further raised the temperature of debate. A flood of arguments and refutations arose in Parliament, great country houses, London coffeehouses, and print. Literate Englishmen confronted the terrible choices of politics and religion as members of congregations, societies, and sometimes mobs, but also as solitary readers of pamphlets, newspapers, and printed sermons.

A first major turning point in this drama came in 1629, when the Stuart king Charles I refused to let a Parliament dominated by Puritans interfere with his drive for anti-Puritan uniformity in the Church of England, dismissed Parliament, and managed to rule without it until 1640. Then, as both king and Parliament lurched toward more absolute forms of their claims to final power, civil war broke out. By the end of 1646 King Charles was a prisoner of the parliamentary forces. The wide front of opposition to arbitrary royal rule now splintered. Powerful religious impulses, including millennarian prophecies, led some toward the imposition of Puritan standards of behavior on the whole society and others toward dreams of radical equality and the rejection of all authority. Many who had resisted royal power were alienated by Puritan repression and attacks on traditional customs and social relations. This was the first important case of that modern phenomenon, the capture of a broadly popular revolution by an authoritarian elite, here, as so often, with a formidable army at its core. King Charles was executed by the parliamentary forces in 1649, his head held up to a silent, appalled crowd. The army repeatedly purged Parliament and arranged the appointment of Oliver Cromwell as lord protector of the new Commonwealth. Cromwell was an intelligent and competent politician who hoped to implement broad religious toleration at the head of a military dictatorship with a narrow political base and limited claims to legitimacy. After his death in 1658 it was only a matter of time until the right combination of military and parliamentary maneuvers led to the return of Charles II to his father's throne amid widespread rejoicing. The Restoration period under Charles II is famous for its radical reversal of Puritan moral repression, as the king led the way in the acquisition of mistresses and extravagant living. It was obvious that his court was oriented toward the France of Louis XIV and was sympathetic to Roman Catholicism. Dissenters from Anglican orthodoxy suffered under many legal disabilities.

The battles of the Civil War in the 1640s, the sieges of towns and castles, the families divided or deprived of their fathers had given way to sullen repression under Cromwell, then the reversal of the Restoration, and the uncertainties of confiscation and restitution of estates and the settling of old political scores. Paradoxically it was in the Commonwealth and Restoration years that foundations were steadily laid for the emergence by 1688 of an England of unprecedented prosperity, a far more important player in European international politics than it had been at the beginning of the century, with a broad elite accustomed to participation in the shaping of national policy. Religious differences and questions of the rights of crown and Parliament continued to arouse passionate commitment in these years. Landowners worked steadily to improve the productivity of their fields. Mercantilist policies to promote the foreign trade of the kingdom at the expense of that of rivals, especially the Dutch, began under Cromwell and were continued under Charles. Even the famous decadence of the Restoration had its economic uses, as the great peers of the realm and their sons spent all their incomes, and a great deal of borrowed money, on splendid country houses and on mansions and pleasures in London. London became a crucible of early modernity, with coffeehouses where political views could be aired and commercial deals made, a raffish and vibrant theatrical and literary life, and a constant succession of political rumors and dramas recorded in gazettes, pamphlets, and broadsheets.

The man at the center of the new/old order, King Charles II, was one of those rulers who give decadence a good name. His example of high living and many mistresses was avidly followed by many peers and their sons. Charles's brother, James, duke of York, was an open Roman Catholic.

Although personally inclined to Roman Catholicism, often in the pay of the king of France, and more or less committed to pro-Catholic policies, Charles knew that his people were rabidly anti-Catholic. He converted to Catholicism only on his deathbed. The concessions his father had made trying to stay on his throne were still in force; the monarchy had permanently moved quite a distance toward constitutional and parliamentary limitations. But not all of Charles's canny and cynical maneuvering could paper over England's deep divisions.

They came to the surface suddenly in 1678, under the immediate stimulus of fantastic revelations of a "Popish Plot" to assassinate the king, massacre Protestants, and install James as king with a council of Jesuits. The anticourt forces won a parliamentary election early in 1679, but when a bill was introduced to exclude James from the succession, King Charles stopped giving way to the extremists in Parliament and dissolved it. The exclusion proposal was truly revolutionary, an interference of Parliament in the affairs of the hereditary monarchy. The Exclusionists organized effectively and elected a majority in the House of Commons, but opposition grew, fueled by reaction against mob hysteria, the vicious executions of Catholic priests on trumped-up charges, and a deep-seated respect for the monarchy. The anticourt, often exclusionist forces controlling Commons began to be called Whigs; those supporting the monarchy, Tories. The polarization that was to produce the Revolution of 1688 had crystallized. Charles II now dismissed Parliament and governed without one until his death in February 1685. In the general prosperity, taxes that he had been granted for life were enough to sustain his government. His military forces were small. He was receiving large payments from Louis XIV of France. In 1682 he began to use his wide powers to remodel municipal corporations, removing political opponents and ensuring that they would elect procourt members of Parliament in the future. The Whigs were in deep disarray. Their most basic problem was that only a few radicals among them were antimonarchical, and if they opposed the succession of James, whom did they favor? James, duke of Monmouth, the king's bastard son, was popular but not an experienced or reliable leader. In 1683 some radical Whigs were implicated in a plot to assassinate the king and the duke of York at Rye House; some were executed, and the court grew ever stronger.

When James succeeded his brother in February 1685, his position looked strong. A new Parliament granted him life revenues equal to those his brother had enjoyed. A rising in Scotland, and another led by the duke of Monmouth, were quickly crushed. But James had nothing of his brother's cunning and deviousness. He made no secret of his Catholicism and even expressed publicly his hope that some day all his subjects would be reconciled with the One True Church. As a first step in that direction he sought some way to remove the barrier of the Test Acts that barred Catholics from positions in government or the army. He was angered when Parliament protested mildly against his desire to appoint some Catholic officers to the army. He appreciated the deep royalist sentiments of the Tories, saw the Church of England, to which most of them were deeply devoted, as a ceremonious and authoritarian structure not that different from the Church of Rome, and simply did not understand how their Anglicanism and their vehement anti-Catholicism went together. Rebuffed by Parliament and by the bishops of the Church of England in his efforts to win toleration for Roman Catholic worship and officeholding, he tried with some success to build bridges to Protestants outside the Church of England, who suffered from most of the same legal disabilities as Roman Catholics. He expressed his horror at the excesses of the anti-Protestant campaigns in France.

The Tories in Parliament were even more horrified by James's general toleration, which included some fairly extreme sects, like the Quakers. Moreover, although everyone recognized the royal power to "dispense" with the enforcement of a law in a particular instance, there were many doubts about the king's power to order a general suspension of a law that had not been repealed by Parliament. Despite his condemnations of the French anti-Protestant campaigns, it seemed to many of his subjects that he was seeking absolute powers like those of Louis XIV and that this was just what you would expect of a king who gave his allegiance to an authoritarian, absolutist religion. Moreover, James was using the solid life incomes Parliament had granted him to build up a growing standing army, much of it camped on Hounslow Heath near London. To James, a straightforward and thickheaded military man, it made sense to build up a more reliable army than the local militias that had had trouble even dealing with Monmouth's ragtag forces. To many of his subjects, the troops on Hounslow Heath, many of them Irish Catholics, looked altogether too much like the dragoons that had crushed French Protestantism. Not many understood the impossibility of any military force's imposing a religion that was followed by only 1 percent of the population.

James could get what he wanted without ambiguity if he could obtain the election of a docile Parliament that would repeal the Test Acts. The Exclusionist Whigs of the late 1670s had led the way in manipulating local politics to obtain, out of a diffuse system of local corporations and county elections, a majority of elected members of a given persuasion. Thereafter Charles and then James had used the powers of the crown to reshape corporations and obtain a docile majority. Now at the end of 1687 James began to demand of potential Tory candidates for county election to Parliament explicit commitments to support the repeal of the acts. Many of these men, his natural allies, resented the pressure and began to turn against him. But in the spring and summer of 1688 he continued his efforts.

In the seventeenth century death was never far away. If James died without a son and heir, his daughter, Mary, wife of William of Orange, would succeed to the throne. William's strategic opposition to the expansion of French power in Europe often was bolstered by Protestant anti-Catholicism. Holland was the great refuge of radical Whigs and Huguenots. James's suspicions of his son-in-law's support for the duke of Monmouth's invasion had been only partly allayed when William sent to England three English regiments and three Scottish that were more or less permanently stationed in Holland. In 1687 William pointedly refused to support James's efforts to win toleration for Roman Catholics in England and Scotland. James's second marriage to Mary of Modena had not been barren, but no son had been born. Thus reports at the end of 1687 that the queen might be pregnant were political intelligence of highest importance. A son born and brought up a Catholic might ensure decades of Catholic grip on the immense power and mystique of the monarchy. James, Mary, and their Catholic courtiers held their breaths in hope. Protestants waited in dread and began to seek extreme alternatives.

On April 27, 1688, King James repeated his 1687 Declaration of Indulgence suspending the Test Acts and ordered that it be read from all church pulpits in his realms. On May 18 a delegation of bishops confronted the king and told him that they would not do so, that he had no power to suspend laws of the realm in this way. The furious king waited three weeks and then, on June 7, had seven bishops sent to the Tower of London.

Europe was not the only part of the world of 1688 that had big cities, but Christian Europe and the Ottoman Empire's great capital of Istanbul were the only places where they were seen as the crucial locations for every act of political or religious significance, the stage sets for every drama of high destiny. Greek debates in the agora, Roman triumphs, medieval processions to the cathedral all had shaped this urban focus. Rulers feared the city mob, but they also courted it, mobilized it. The London crowd of the 1680s was passionately Protestant and capable of violent attacks on "papists" and their churches, but there was surprisingly little of such violence through most of 1688. The people made themselves heard in a different and very moving way in the crisis of the seven bishops. On June 8, the great diarist John Evelyn records, the bishops were "sent from the Privy Council to the Tower, for refusing to give bail for their appearance (upon their not reading the Declaration for Liberty of Conscience) because in giving bail they had prejudiced their peerage. Wonderful was the concern of the people for them, infinite crowds of people on their knees, begging their blessing and praying for them as they passed out of the barge, along the Tower wharf, etc." On June 10 Evelyn heard the cannon of the tower sounding and the church bells ringing to celebrate the birth of the prince of Wales. On June 15, when the bishops were brought to Westminster for the first phase of the legal proceedings against them, "there was a lane of people from the King's Bench to the water-side, upon their knees as the bishops passed and repassed, to beg their blessing. Bonfires made that night, and bells ringing, which was taken very ill at Court."

And so it was that right in the midst of these moving demonstrations of popular opposition to the royal policies the queen gave birth to a healthy baby boy. Almost immediately stories began to circulate that the royal birth was a fake, that someone else's infant had been smuggled into the lying-in chamber in a warming pan. It was so important to so many people to retain their implicit loyalty to the hereditary monarchy and at the same time to remove the threat of long-run Catholic rule that such stories would have circulated under the best of circumstances. The obtuse soldier king, deaf to his subjects' fervent anti-Catholicism and expecting that they would accept his good faith in such a personal matter, was baffled and offended. Moreover, he had blundered badly in allowing key Protestant witnesses, including his younger daughter, Princess Anne, to be away from London so that they could not be summoned to witness the birth.

The lines of communication between disaffected grandees in England and William of Orange had remained open. In April William told three important visitors that he would invade England if he received a formal request from important people. By the end of July he had such an invitation, signed by seven eminent men, including one bishop and two earls.

Many others, he was told, would support his cause but could not bring themselves to sign, even in code, such a document. Now it was up to William to secure the consent of the Dutch authorities and to prepare his forces.

Since early September it had been clear to King James that his son-in-law William of Orange was preparing forces for an invasion. Alarmed, dismayed, feeling betrayed, he lost his nerve. He spoke to the bishops in a conciliatory fashion but offered no firm change in policy. In August he had finally felt confident enough of the results of his pressure on counties and corporations to issue writs for a new Parliament, to convene on November 27. But now he first declared that Catholics would not be eligible for election and then simply withdrew the writs. He sought military forces wherever he could, bringing about four thousand troops from Scotland and five thousand from Ireland; the latter being mostly Catholic, this only served to raise London's anti-Catholic hysteria another notch. As soon as there was firm news of William's landing on November 5, he ordered several of his best regiments to march west and take up positions on the Salisbury plain. On November 11 a Catholic chapel was attacked at St. Johns, Clerkenwell. On November 12 the London mob demonstrated its advanced understanding of the role of the media in politics by stoning the offices of the king's printer. James took measures to restore order and waited until he was sure that the city would not rise behind him, and then, November 17–19, he went to Salisbury. William's forces were on the march. James's army would have stood a good chance if they had advanced to confront them, but his commander advised withdrawal. There was ominous silence from the west; neither nobility nor commoners were making any effort to keep their king informed of the movements of William's forces. The king suffered day after day from severe nosebleeds because of the terrible stress. He gave orders to withdraw. Lord John Churchill, one of his most trusted courtiers and commanders, rode west to join William. Prince George of Denmark, husband of Princess Anne, did the same. The cruelest blow of all was when Anne and her great friend Sarah, wife of John Churchill, slipped out of London to join their husbands and William.

On November 27 James summoned a council of peers and declared that he was determined to call a Parliament, to dismiss Catholics from office, and to appoint envoys to go to treat with William. The terms

William demanded for further discussion were harsh but might have been accepted if they had not reached James in the middle of a rising tide of anti-Catholic hysteria, brought on in part by an anti-Catholic "Third Declaration" in the name of William, which was a fake but did its work in stirring up the mob. James, surrounded by only a small remnant of Catholic courtiers, sent Queen Mary and the infant prince to France and then, on the night of December 11, burned the writs for a new Parliament and sneaked out of his palace, intending to flee the country. On his way he threw the great seal of the kingdom into the Thames.

News of the king's flight carried the anti-Catholic mobs to new heights. The new Catholic chapel in Lincoln's Inn Fields was pillaged, and all its furnishings were burned. Books were looted from the shop of the king's printer and burned. The Spanish ambassador's residence was plundered, and much damage done to the Florentine embassy and the papal nuncio's lodgings. A mob was already at work pulling down the organ and decorations in the Chapel Royal in the palace when soldiers arrived to drive them out. The red glow in the winter night sky reminded some of the Great Fire of 1666. Then the next day rumors spread across the city, and soon across much of the kingdom, that the Irish soldiers were slitting every Protestant throat they could lay their hands on. No Catholic was safe from the mob, but the "Irish fear" seems to have been the beginning of the end of the wave of violence.

In the meantime the peers and ministers of the kingdom and the council of the City of London had begun to meet to maintain some form of government in a kingdom that now seemed to be without a king. One of their chief preoccupations was law and order in the city: "Whereas the rabble are grown to an ungovernable height, we, the Peers of this Realm, being assembled with some of the Privy Council, do hereby direct and require you to use your best endeavors to quell and disperse the said rabble; and in case of necessity, to use force, and fire upon them with bullet." The peers also decided to send a delegation to William, but not yet to invite him to London, and to try to find King James and bring him back. They were hoping for an agreement by which James would agree with William on terms for calling a free Parliament. The City went further, sending a separate delegation that did invite William to London. But then King James was recognized before he could slip across to France, and on the sixteenth he was brought back to London, to much popular rejoicing, and quickly reestablished his court. The fear of disorder and the deep-seated deference to the ruling monarch were on his side. But William held all the other cards and knew it.

On December 17 William ordered his Dutch Blue Guards to march on London and secure the approaches to St. James's Palace. That night, in a pouring rain, the Blue Guards stood with matches burning, ready to fire if need be, while their commanders secured a peaceful withdrawal of James's guards. Three envoys sent by William arrived after midnight. James was awakened and told that William advised that he withdraw from London at once. He did so, under Dutch guard. William arrived at the palace, amid many signs of rejoicing, later the same day. James was lodged in a house facing the Medway estuary, the guard was deliberately relaxed, and early on December 23 he slipped away to France.

William had won. James's flight left the way clear to the throne for him and his wife. The terms were not clear. Had James vacated the throne? Abdicated? How could a Parliament be summoned without a king to summon it or a great seal on the summons papers? On December 26 William convened an informal council of peers and sympathetic members of Parliament. He clearly set the agenda for the meeting but also sought their advice. The Restoration of 1660 provided the necessary precedents. There would be a convention elected in much the same fashion as a Parliament in response to William's letters of summons.

The convention met on January 22, 1689. Radical Whigs, heirs of the Exclusionists of ten years before, were ready simply to declare William king. But many others could not tolerate the idea of a purely elective monarchy and wanted a role for Mary by hereditary right. Thus it was that the crown was offered to both of them. One peer said to another, "I look upon this day's work to be the ruin of the monarchy in England, for we have made the crown elective. But there is an absolute necessity of having a government, and I do not see a prospect of any other than this; we must not leave ourselves to the rabble."

The convention also passed a Declaration of Rights, which was presented to William and Mary at the same time as the offer of the crown. It was a comprehensive reassertion of "ancient rights and liberties," including freely elected and frequent Parliaments and many limits on pretended royal prerogatives. It became statutory as the Bill of Rights at the end of 1689. William declared that he was not taking the crown on conditions, but the Declaration was read at the beginning of the coronation ceremony of William and Mary on February 13. It could hardly have been clearer that

William and Mary had come to the throne by consent of their elected subjects and on terms set by them.

William was not a popular king, and resentment of his heavy-handed
rule probably helped solidify the English practices of limiting their monarchs' powers and asserting their "ancient rights." Under him, England
became the second most heavily taxed realm in Europe, after Holland, and
largely on the Dutch model of heavy excises and customs tolls. In 1689 and
1690 the continued presence of Dutch troops caused occasional resentment. The immense commitment of England's military and naval power to
the war against France was not universally popular, but John Churchill,
eventually the duke of Marlborough, won some brilliant victories on the
Continent. The financing of the wars was facilitated by the English public's
investment in new forms of funded public debts and in such quasi-govern-
mental bodies as the Bank of England and the East India Company. More
and more, profit and power walked hand in hand.

If James still was thinking about anything other than his own survival
when he fled his kingdom, he was counting on chaos; his burning of the
parliamentary writs and throwing the great seal in the river seem to have
been intended to make regular legal procedures impossible. Chaos did not
come, but James did try to return. In March 1689 he sailed to Ireland with
French support. The French were interested mainly in opening a second
front that would keep William's English forces from commitment to the
Continent, while James saw Ireland as a stepping-stone to Scotland and
England. Local Protestants at Derry refused to acknowledge his authority,
and a formal siege was begun. It was raised by forces sent by William in
July, and the relief of Londonderry is celebrated by Ulster Protestants to
this day. On July 1, 1690, William and James finally confronted each other
across the battle lines of their armies along the Boyne River. William's victory that day marked the end of James's hopes of return to England and
was decisive for the future of Ireland. That too, along with the noble heritage of the Declaration of Right, is with us yet.

CHAPTER 16

ECHOES ACROSS THE OCEANS

The great crisis of 1688 had echoes wherever Englishmen gathered, on the edge of the North American forests, on the islands of the Caribbean, and even in the ports of West Africa and India. Englishmen everywhere followed the gathering storm as well as they could, wondering how it would affect the outcomes of their own quarrels, which ultimately would have to be referred to London. Sometimes they had their own agents in London.

In the eyes of many in London, events in North America and the Indian Ocean were small matters compared with the assault on Spanish wealth and power in the Caribbean, the riches of the slave trade, and the rising sugar production of the islands. Jamaica was one of the newer English possessions in the Caribbean, but it was by far the largest and potentially the richest, and in 1688 it was the scene of the most improbable transatlantic echoes of the Glorious Revolution, in the singular person of its governor, Christopher Monck, second duke of Albemarle.

In the careers of George and Christopher Monck, father and son, first and second dukes of Albemarle, we can see just what could be accomplished by ability and guile in the maelstrom of the English Revolution. We can also see how vulnerable the ascendance of a noble family was to extravagance, personal dissipation, and changes of political fortune. The father, who had served Charles I as an able commander, had been imprisoned by the parliamentary forces and had agreed to serve them in Scotland or Ireland, but not against his old royalist comrades. He had passed the Cromwell years quietly in Scotland. In the crisis of 1660 he marched on London without revealing his intentions, then made a subtle and well-timed switch to Charles II, who rewarded him with a dukedom and immense gifts of crown lands. In 1669–70 the son's marriage to a grand-daughter of the duke of Newcastle was followed by the death of both parents. The young duke and duchess soon slipped from the controls his father had sought to leave over them and began to see how much they could spend of their immense fortune. The duke was a drinking, whoring, and brawling crony of James, duke of Monmouth, natural son of the king; one night one of them killed a beadle in a brawl at "a scandalous place," and they received instant royal pardons.

The young duke of Albemarle became a Knight of the Garter, took his seat in the House of Lords as soon as he was of age, and was a steadfast supporter of the king throughout all the twists and turns of the reign. But he showed little interest in politics or policy and less in religion or books. Hunting, horse racing, gambling, and contests of boxing, football, and so on between his retainers and those of other lords were his favorite pastimes. To accommodate his revels in London and to receive noble visitors in style, he paid twenty-five thousand pounds* for a great mansion, thereafter called Albemarle House. There and at his country houses he entertained many grandees, an ambassador of the sultan of Morocco, Prince William of Orange, and the king himself. He was one of the richest men in the king-dom, with an income of at least fifteen thousand pounds per year, but the expenses of entertaining were immense, and at his level of society people sometimes lost five thousand pounds in a single night's gambling.

The duke and duchess had no living child. Racing through their fortune at a fantastic rate, they had to sell Albemarle House in 1682. The duchess sank into poor physical and mental health, becoming depressed, anxious, sometimes incoherent. The duke was drinking more than ever and suffered from jaundice, indicating that his life of heavy drinking had damaged his liver. His position at court weakened after James II came to the throne; he had been a steady supporter of Charles's policies, including James's right to the throne, but he was also a firm supporter of the Church of England.

---

*Comparisons of sums of money in the seventeenth century and today are full of difficul-ties. According to one useful estimate, one pound in the 1680s would have bought goods worth nearly one hundred dollars today.

When James placed a Catholic in command of all his military forces, Albemarle refused to serve under him.

In the spring of 1686 court hangers-on were astonished to learn that the duke of Albemarle had accepted appointment as governor of Jamaica. What could such a great man want with such a distant and insignificant post? Some, especially in Devon, where he was lord lieutenant and had many admirers, thought it was intended as an exile for one who would not go along with the king's plans. Albemarle himself may have seen advantage in a few years away from a court where he would be in opposition and probably in danger. Moreover, a colonial governor might profit from bribery, manipulation of trade, and grants of land to his favorites, although hardly at a level to compare with the still-massive incomes from Albemarle's estates in England.

But Albemarle had another, more exciting reason for going to Jamaica. For several years he had been in touch with Captain William Phips of New England, who was fairly sure he knew where there was a rich and salvageable wreck of a Spanish silver galleon on the north side of the island of Hispaniola. A first attempt to salvage some of the treasure had failed. In 1686 Albemarle, with some fresh information about the location of the wreck, brought together a new set of investors and secured a patent under the great seal of his association's right to salvage it, and Phips set off with two ships and a few divers whom he had brought back from a voyage to the Indian Ocean. They returned to England in June 1687, bringing treasure worth more than six hundred thousand pounds; Albemarle's share was about ninety thousand. This is one of a small number of big success stories in the long history of search for sunken treasure on the Spanish Main. In 1686, when results were still unknown, Albemarle had every reason to go to the West Indies himself to keep an eye on the operation and attempt to enforce his patent. By the time he sailed from England in September 1687, it still was likely that more treasure would be salvaged, and with every Caribbean port full of talk of the treasure, there was even more reason to go there and defend his rights. In the end it does not seem that he ever got any additional treasure or income from the wreck.

Albemarle reached Port Royal on Jamaica on December 19. With him were his duchess—whose physical and mental health was not likely to be improved by tropical weather and food and the rough society of a half-pirate colony but whom he certainly was not going to leave behind to cause more trouble for him in England—and his recently designated personal physician, Hans Sloane. Sloane exhibited the fascination of the age with "natural history," especially with accumulating knowledge of, and objects from, remote parts of the world. He spent his months in Jamaica trying to keep his willful noble patient alive, treating many others of all classes and colors, collecting specimens of tropical plant and animal life, and having sketches made of his more perishable specimens that were to be the bases of the magnificent, meticulous engravings in his *A Voyage to the Islands Madera, Barbados, Nieves, S. Christopher, and Jamaica*, published in 1707. His collections were one of the foundations of what eventually became the British Museum.

Albemarle was no scholar, but having lived close to the centers of power all his life, he was expert at political ceremony and maneuver. The politics of the little colony was a competition between the interests of the planters, like Francis Price in Lluidas Vale, and those of the Royal African Company and associated commercial ventures. The planters wanted a steady supply of slaves at moderate prices; the company wanted to sell its imports wherever it got the best price for them, which frequently was on the Spanish mainland. Sir Henry Morgan, the famous old pirate turned pirate chaser, generally sided with the planters. Albemarle arrived to confront a colonial assembly dominated by men sympathetic to the company, and a council that had excluded Morgan from its deliberations. He had instructions to bring Morgan back into the council and in general to deal with the grievances of the planters. His opening speech to the assembly on February 16 was extremely brief and bland, but he soon made it clear that he expected it to stay at work and to pass some bills, which he proposed, for the better treatment of slaves and a revision in valuation of the Spanish real that would favor the planters. When the assembly did nothing, he followed the example of Charles II: He dissolved it, ordered a new election, and plunged into the campaign to secure an assembly more to his liking. He got a more tractable assembly, which passed the bills he had proposed, and brought Henry Morgan back into the council. (Hans Sloane's book contains, among its notes on more than a hundred patients whom he treated in Jamaica, a description of "Sir H.M.," as sallow, with a protruding belly and a badly disturbed digestion, refusing to cut down on his late-night roistering and drinking.) As in England, electioneering required a great deal of feasting and toasting of the electorate. By the end of the campaign the duke had a severe case of gout and then suffered a relapse of his old liver troubles that almost killed him.

He had scarcely begun to recover when, sometime in August, news of the birth of the prince of Wales reached Jamaica. Before celebrations could be held, Henry Morgan died and was widely mourned. Then, in the middle of the hurricane season, amid the fierce heat, downpours, and deafening thunder of early September, the celebration finally was held. We have no description, but can be sure that a great many huzzahs were shouted, volleys were fired, and above all toasts were drunk. The duke collapsed. Amazingly he survived and on October 1 wrote a businesslike letter to accompany a representative of the assembly who was going to England. Then on October 6 he died.

King James II, in his last month of rule, canceled all the new laws Albemarle had gotten through the Jamaica Assembly. In Jamaica, Dr. Hans Sloane embalmed the duke's body. He and other friends managed to protect the widowed duchess from all those who were convinced she must have a vast treasure in her household and to take her and her husband's body back to England in the spring of 1689. The duchess now seems to have been quite out of touch with reality. In 1692 she married a fortune seeker who presented himself to her costumed as the emperor of China. He died a few years later; she died at the age of eighty, in 1734.

Puritans as well as dissipated nobles found their echoes across the oceans. Increase Mather, minister of North Church in Boston, president of Harvard College, was most at home in his pulpit, at his writing desk, or on his knees pouring out before God his misery and worthlessness. But when he spent 1688 first a fugitive in his own land and then paying court to a Roman Catholic king, he seems to have suffered no sense of loss of self or distraction from his true vocation.

The central mystery and drama of Mather's Puritan Christianity were the Covenant between all-powerful God and unworthy Man. It could be maintained only by those who lived godly lives but recognized their own utter unworthiness and, prostrating themselves before a Righteous God, finally became convinced that despite their worthlessness, He had chosen them for salvation. The Covenant between God and Man was a matter not just of individual salvation but also of a Chosen People, who could break it by turning away from God as individuals or by not preserving a pure church of the Elect as the core, the saving remnant, of the Chosen People.

Of course the Chosen People might have to defend itself in worldly fashion against the assault of the ungodly, as the kingdom of Israel had done before it broke the Covenant irretrievably.

Increase was the son of Richard Mather, one of the leading ministers of the first generation of Puritans to establish themselves in Massachusetts Bay. Since he grew up in a minister's family and showed considerable intellectual gifts at an early age, Increase's choice of a career in the ministry cannot have been in much doubt. He experienced a long time of spiritual doubt that ended when "I gave myself up to Jesus Christ. . . . Upon this I had ease and inward peace in my perplexed soul immediately." In this hardworking frontier society, few could devote the hours and days to study and prayer that Mather did throughout his life, but no one could become a full church member without having had personal experience of his or her own worthlessness and of God's saving grace, an experience sufficiently vivid and specific that it could be publicly described to the congregation, all of whom had had to do the same thing before they were admitted to membership. Ordinary Puritans could be as inward and exacting in examination of their own spiritual states and those of their neighbors as Zen abbots or Jesuit novice masters. They had to be sure, each of them, that they were among the Elect, or the Covenant between God and Man might be lost. But they could not be permanently sure, and for Increase Mather and many others, life provided little respite from self-doubt and anguished meditation on "that body of sin which I bear about with me: pride, passion, sloth, selfishness, sensuality, earthly-mindedness, unbelief, hypocrisy." Puritans did not live lives of withdrawn contemplation, and they might be grateful for, moved by, the blessings of harvest and home or overcome by the immeasurably greater blessing of Jesus' life and death for the salvation of worthless sinners. Increase Mather almost always was moved to tears by the sacrament of communion. He frequently recorded that in the course of his prayers he was "curiously melted" by a sense of God's power and mercy. His father's first book had been entitled *A Heart-Melting Exhortation, Together with a Cordial Consolation.*

Increase Mather was among those who had been conspicuously at odds with the Governor Andros and the new royal government that London had imposed on Massachusetts ever since 1683. Edward Randolph, a leading figure in the royal government of the colony, had accused him of writing a seditious letter, but Mather had insisted that the letter in question was a forgery; when he went on to say that Randolph himself was the forger, Randolph sued him for defamation, but on January 30, 1688, the suit was dismissed, and Randolph was ordered to pay court costs.

In April 1687 James II had issued a Declaration of Indulgence abrogating the religious requirements for officeholding and the laws against non-Anglican worship, both Roman Catholic and Dissenting. Increase Mather called this "reviving news," and many in New England shared his optimistic assessment. At his suggestion the Boston ministers sent a letter of thanks to the king and then decided that Mather should go to London to convey their thanks in person and to take the opportunity to present their complaints against Randolph, the governor, and the royal government of Massachusetts. On March 13, 1688, "This day I was strangely melted in my spirit and persuaded that God would be with me in my going for England and that I should there do some service for Him and for His people." On March 22 he preached a farewell sermon, the text being Exodus 33:15: "If Thy presence go not with me, carry me not up hence."

Because Randolph was seeking to prevent Mather's departure by having him arrested again for defamation, he slipped out of his house on the night of March 30 in a wig and a white cloak. Later he heard that one of Randolph's men had recognized him but had felt powerless to lay a hand on him. He stayed quietly at a house in Charlestown and on April 4 boarded a ketch from which he transferred to a ship for England. While he was gone, his wife fasted repeatedly and prayed for his success and for relief for God's beleaguered Chosen People in New England.

From April 17 to 19 the ship was surrounded by icebergs, "one of them as big as Egg Rock at Lynn in New England and higher than that. It overset in our sight, having many gulls upon it." Off Cornwall the ship was boarded by some "barbarously uncivil" fishermen, who would give no directions until Mather gave them four half crowns.

Arriving in London on May 25, 1688, Mather was given excellent guidance by other Dissenters who saw opportunity in James's policies, including William Penn. He found the Catholics at court, including Father Petre, the king's confessor, very courteous. "How often did I think of that Scripture, 'They shall take up serpents, and if they drink any deadly thing it shall not hurt them.' . . . Those serpents, contrary to their natures, were so far from hurting me, as that they were very kind to me." On May 30 Mather waited on the king in the Long Gallery at Whitehall and read to him the address of thanks he had brought from New England. The king replied that he intended to seek from Parliament "a Magna Charta for liberty of con-science." Admitted the next day to the "King's Closet"—that is, his private apartments—he said to him, "Your Majesty's subjects in New England are a people that were persecuted thither on the mere account of religion. Inasmuch as Your Majesty has delivered them from the fears of a future persecution, they are transported with joy and dutiful affection to Your Majesty, and there are many hundreds of them who are desirous that I should assure Your Majesty of it." He then went on to inform the king about New Englanders who had been fined or imprisoned by the royal government because they refused to swear on the Bible and about other abuses of that government. He had three more such interviews; at the last, on October 16, the king told him "that property, liberty, and our College [Harvard] should all be confirmed to us." All this time, Mather recalled later, "Many a day . . . did I sit apart in my chamber in London, not only to pray for a blessing on my family, and that God would in His due time return me to them again, in all which he has been entreated by me, but to pray that liberty, and prosperity, and a good government might be restored to New England."

On February 17, 1689, "as I was praying alone in my chamber, I was marvelously melted and could not but with tears say, God has saved New England. The thing is done. God has done it. My God, and the God of New England has heard prayer and delivered that His people." He already was hard at work getting to know all the key men in the Convention Parliament and eventually William and Mary themselves; when he finally sailed for Massachusetts in 1692, he had obtained a new charter for Massachusetts Bay, complete with permission for that government to incorporate Harvard College.

In this time of grand visions and projects, there was another Protestant plan for a new beginning in America represented at the court of James II in 1688. The story of William Penn, Pennsylvania, and Penn's role as King James's adviser and ally on the issue of toleration offers a striking counter-point to the anxieties of Mather. In English eyes, Penn's Quaker beliefs and practices were more radical and less deserving of toleration than Mather's strict Calvinism. But Penn was more at ease in the snake pit of the court and in the intricate maneuverings of high politics than was Mather. By birth, experience, wealth, and power, Penn belonged at court. In 1688 he was at court almost every day and sometimes had hours of private conversation with the king. Quakers did not remove their hats for any authority, even the king; Penn seems to have dealt with the problem by going to court bare-headed. He had a fine carriage and a big house, where many with business at court came to call on one so obviously in royal favor.

The story of the two William Penns, father and son, also runs in baroque counterpoint to that of the dukes of Albemarle: a father who gained power through naval command rather than military, a son who knew how to dress well and spend money but preferred books and prayer to bearbaiting and who, instead of ruining his health and the family fortune, became one of the most creative religious and social leaders of his time. The father, Admiral William Penn, won notable victories against the Dutch for both Cromwell and Charles II, commanded an expedition that failed to take Hispaniola for Cromwell and took Jamaica instead—another counterpoint with the Albemarle story—and commanded the squadron that went to Holland to bring the future Charles II back to England in 1660. The younger William, despite his profoundly antiauthoritarian convictions, never lost his aristocratic tastes and habit of command and drew astutely on his heritage as Admiral Penn's son in his dealings with Charles II and with James, duke of York, whose special sphere of interest and power was the navy.

Admiral Penn had been granted estates in Ireland both by Cromwell and by Charles II. It was in Ireland that the younger William had his first encounter with the wandering religious teachers and the small, wary networks of religious enthusiasts that formed the Society of Friends, the Quakers. They were the most singular and enduring product of the wild religious enthusiasms of 1640s England, drawing on the deepest reserves of Christian spirituality to open visions of individual integrity and social peace and justice that seem as alive and elusive today as they did in 1688. They rejected all forms of religious authority and ceremony, sitting quietly in their meetings until someone was moved by the Inner Light to speak. They dressed soberly, refused to take part in warfare in any way, did not take their hats off in worship or as a gesture of respect to social superiors, allowed women to speak in meetings and to preach, addressed others as "thee" and "thou," and refused to swear oaths, thinking it presumptuous to call on God in support of an affirmation. Early Quakers mostly were people of modest education and social standing, little interested in sustained argument or theological subtlety, frequently moved by the Holy Spirit to interrupt church services, to preach on street corners, or to ride into a town calling out, "Woe to all sinners." Their disruption of church services, the excitement that accompanied their street preaching, and their refusal to swear oaths often landed them in jail. The presence among them of a son of a highly influential admiral was most unusual.

Young William Penn attended his first Quaker meetings in Ireland in 1667, standing silently in respect when he agreed with a speaker. He flashed his lordly ways to expel a soldier who came to harass the Quakers, was arrested, released, thrown out of his father's house, and arrested in London for writing a pamphlet that attacked all established churches and even found the doctrine of the Trinity unnecessary. In 1670 he was arrested for speaking on the street and in a famous trial completely outmaneuvered and outargued the inept judge and won an acquittal from the jury. In the 1670s he made two trips to Holland and Germany seeking ties with like-minded religious groups and continued to produce a stream of polemical pamphlets, overwrought in invective and excessive in erudition; a full bibliography of the works he produced during his lifetime, mostly short pamphlets, runs to 157 titles.

In the sectarian and anti-Catholic agitation of the 1670s the Quakers, seen by the court and by Anglicans in general as the most wild-eyed and rebellious of all Protestant sects, faced deepening hostility and repression. Admiral Penn had died in 1670, but the younger William was well known at court and always was given a hearing out of respect for his father. Still, he could not do much to ease the lot in England of his beleaguered people. A few Quakers had begun to settle along the Delaware River in 1675, and William Penn now was inspired to seek in America a grant of land where the Quakers could take refuge. Charles and James liked the idea; they could justify it to a degree as compensation for salary never paid to the admiral and show their broad-mindedness and generosity to troublesome subjects. If the colony succeeded, some of those subjects would be settled a long way indeed from London. Their generosity was staggering; the colony had an area of forty-five thousand square miles. William could not even object to their decision to name it Pennsylvania, since it was done ostensibly in honor of the late admiral. The charter did not give Penn powers as absolute as Lord Baltimore had in Maryland to the south, but still, he could shape things pretty much as he wished. And although he sold land at modest prices, he still made over nine thousand pounds, almost a million dollars at today's prices, most welcome since his tastes and way of life had little Quaker modesty about them and he was deeply in debt. Later the expenses of running the colony and some bad management decisions destroyed any profit from it; Penn's many talents did not include those of a businessman.

More important, Penn soon was talking of his colony as his "Holy Experiment," where Quaker pacific and antihierarchical principles could be put into practice. We should not be surprised to find such a marvelous combination—the heritage of holiness and the openness to experiment—inspired by the piety and the radical individualism of the Quaker way. In his first draft of a governmental structure the people were to elect their delegates to the assembly and give them specific instructions as to how to vote. The Frame of Government that ultimately was adopted still provided a broad electorate for the assembly; but voters could not instruct their representatives, and the assembly shared power with a smaller council.

Penn himself sailed for Pennsylvania in 1682. He found his little colony thriving and was delighted by the climate and the abundance of nature. These responses come through with his usual verve and the touch of a natural public relations man, in his *Letter to the Committee of the Free Society of Traders*, published in London in 1683. Even more striking than his catalogs of crops, animals, and native plants are his descriptions of the Delaware Indians, with whom he had several meetings and with whom he strove to deal on terms of friendship and equity: "For their persons, they are generally tall, straight, well built, and of singular proportion; they tread strong and clever, and mostly walk with a lofty chin. . . . Their *language* is lofty, yet narrow, but like the Hebrew. . . . But in liberality they excel; nothing is too good for their friend. Give them a fine gun, coat, or other thing, it may pass twenty hands before it sticks; light of heart, strong affections, but soon spent . . . they never have much, nor want much." He also described the oratory and procedures of their councils. Trying to fit them into the biblical story of mankind, he suspected that they were descended from the Ten Lost Tribes of Israel.

In 1684 a territorial dispute with Lord Baltimore seemed to require Penn's active presence at court, and he returned to England. He was an effective and well-connected courtier, and the dispute was settled largely in his favor. When Charles II died in February 1685, many were dismayed by the accession of an openly Catholic king, but Penn was optimistic about the prospects for wider religious toleration. "Pardon me, we have not to do with an insensible prince, but one that has been touched with our infirmities: More than anybody, fit to judge our cause, by the share he once had in it. Who should give ease like the prince who has wanted it?" That is, James, as a believer in a proscribed religion, could be counted on to have real sympathy for others in similar situations. Moreover, Penn's own influence at court was stronger than ever, since James as lord high admiral had had an especially close relation with Admiral Penn. Penn respected James because he practiced his religion openly, unlike his dissembling brother, and James respected Penn's directness of speech. Both were deeply serious in their religious beliefs and impatient with the hypocrisies and dissemblings of politics.

Penn wrote a series of pamphlets urging James to grant wide religious toleration. In 1686 he was sent by James to try to persuade William of Orange to support broader toleration, with no success. Penn had a hand in the decision to issue the Declaration of Indulgence in 1687, and he wrote another pamphlet to urge Parliament to ratify it. He was more concerned with the principle of toleration than with the ambiguities of parliamentary and royal prerogative. He knew that some Catholics had wild ideas of bringing England back under the Church of Rome, but he did not think the king was among them. He argued that in the long run it was in the interest of the king and of all English Catholics, who were, after all, less than 1 percent of the population, to adopt and stick to a policy of toleration. Neither he nor his king seems to have fully grasped the visceral force of English popular anti-Catholicism and the way it had been given new fuel by the persecutions of the Huguenots. Most historians have been baffled and dismayed by the spectacle of the great Penn "taken in" by what they see as the obviously insincere manipulations of James II. But more recent views of the rather inglorious ambiguities of the Glorious Revolution have disposed some to think that perhaps Penn knew what he was doing and that if the people of England had been willing to stomach a Catholic king and hedge him around with guarantees of religious freedom, they might have achieved in 1689 a more comprehensive toleration, including both Catholics and Quakers.

Through 1688, advising the king, trying to head off the disastrous measures proposed by the Catholic hard-liners, he also was juggling the affairs of Pennsylvania, where he was installing a new deputy who was not to the liking of the settlers; corresponding with the bishop of Ely about the difficulties of some Quakers in that area; and receiving a petition from some English landowners in Ireland condemning his consorting with the papists.

The Glorious Revolution was a disaster for Penn. He was charged with treason several times and spent long periods in hiding in the years that followed. He was in Pennsylvania again from 1699 to 1701, and he spent his last years back in England. His Holy Experiment was becoming a more conventional place, with more conventional problems, including settler-Indian conflicts, but it never entirely lost its Quaker heritage or the open and democratic political culture he had sought to foster.

CHAPTER 17

A HUNDRED YEARS OF FREEDOM

Amsterdam was one of the great cities of the Europe of 1688, a likely stop on the grand tour of a young gentleman, a crossroads port with ships and canalboats going off to almost all destinations. It was prosperous and impressive in its energy and good planning, but it offered almost nothing to the baroque fondness for broad avenues, long vistas across courtyards and gardens, palatial stage sets for regal ceremony and gesture. The traveler arriving at the docks along the Ij River walked or took a boat into a series of carefully laid-out semicircular canals, the key elements in the planned growth of the city in the late sixteenth and early seventeenth centuries and today still among the finest and most distinctive of European urban landscapes. The canals were lined with handsome, tall houses, many of them with hoisting devices under their high eaves so that trunks and furniture could be moved in and out of the upper stories. The visitor probably also would see the great East India House and its warehouses, redolent of the scents of Europe's richest spice trades; one or another courtyard of small charity houses; and the thriving Jewish district, especially its splendid baroque Portuguese (Sephardic) Synagogue, with its fine dark wood pews, pulpit at one end and Ark of the Torah at the other—the Sephardic arrangement—and an uncanny sense of calm and divine presence in the light from the high windows. In a city where militant Calvinist preachers had a considerable hold on public opinion and appearances, neither Roman Catholicism nor commercial sex could make such a public display of itself;

the visitor might also learn of a large house that contained a discreet but generally known hidden Catholic chapel or notice a tavern or music hall where a drunken sailor, apprentice, or farmer could lose his sexual inhibitions and perhaps his purse. He would be impressed by the general cleanliness, good order, and the safety of many streets even at night, which owed much to the citizens' watch groups that patrolled them regularly and also to the oil-burning streetlamps, more than two thousand of them, in use since 1670, the first in the world. (By 1688 several other cities had them, and the philosopher Leibniz had a scheme to bring them to Vienna.) Accustomed to the smells of any city full of horses and chamber pots, the visitor might still wrinkle his nose, if there was a northwest breeze, from the whale oil works.

Sooner or later the visitor was likely to be taken to the municipal House of Virtue, or workhouse. The public was admitted for a small fee to see the good work that was being done and probably to feel comfortably superior to the inmates. Here vagrants, beggars, and disturbers of the peace were confined and, it was hoped, taught how to live moral and productive lives. They had to listen to lectures or minisermons, drawing heavily on the Gospels and on the proverbs and other didactic parts of the Old Testament. They were supposed to be taught trades and paid, modestly to be sure, for their work. But the work in which most men engaged (there was a separate institution for women) required little skill and had little application outside the workhouse. The city council had given the House of Virtue a monopoly of the provision of powdered brazilwood to the local dyeworks. The wood, which yielded a red dye, was reduced to powder by teams of two men, pulling back and forth, hour after hour, a big rasp, about three feet long, with a handle on each end. The House of Virtue was known colloquially as the Rasp House. Inmates were subject to strict control, forbidden to fight or swear or use the nicknames and slang beloved of urban lowlifes. Those who would not reform might be whipped, often with a tanned bull's penis. Many visitors also reported a more serious lesson in the necessity for work, a cistern or small cellar that filled with water if not constantly pumped; the miscreant would be confined to it and told to pump or drown.

The "drowning cell" may have been just a story; but there are some fairly plausible sources, and the idea is well founded in Dutch attitudes and realities. All Amsterdam was built on pilings, just above or even below the waterline. Much of Holland was and is below sea level. From the late Middle Ages on, the region had been transformed, its habitable and productive area steadily increased, by diking and draining. The constant pumping required was done not by men or draft animals but by windmills. A polder (tract of land surrounded by dikes) poorly designed or carelessly maintained might be inundated in an hour. Dikes might be built to withstand ordinary conditions and then give way to a storm or flood worse than any seen in a century, and in the ultimate sacrifice for freedom the Dutch might open the dikes and flood their fields to stop an invader. They had done it to stop Louis XIV in 1672. The careful planning of dikes and drainage, investment in land reclamation, and constant coordination of water control in each polder produced an orderly and disciplined rural society and a form of capitalism that was not at odds with rural prosperity and actually created land. The canals and rivers gave the country a remarkable transportation network, far better than any country's roads in the seventeenth century.

So the resistant vagabond in the drowning cell was simply being taught to be a good Dutchman, to keep pumping or drown, to do his share for a country that was hardworking, uncommonly orderly and prosperous, and constantly aware of the fragility of all the works of man. All those little sermons pointed in the same direction, toward Calvinist fear of a righteous God, toward a life of prayer, Bible reading, and hard work.

Our visitor was likely to be baffled by Dutch politics. He knew something about elective monarchies and even republics, but where was the sovereignty among the Dutch? The state that exchanged ambassadors with other European sovereign states was the United Provinces of the Netherlands, but they did not seem to be very united. The stadholder, William III, prince of Orange (soon to be William III of England, Scotland, and Ireland), was not even an elective monarch, but a military commander and administrator formally appointed by the assembly of delegates of the provinces. When he came to Amsterdam, he did so not as a sovereign but as a respectful negotiator with its oligarchic rulers, likely to arouse suspicions if he arrived in too princely a state. If our visitor had entrée to some of the great houses along the canals, he might encounter an interesting variety of political opinions. Some would say that the United Provinces were an enduring union of sovereign provinces, others that it was Amsterdam and the other cities that were sovereign and that the provincial assemblies in which they met could not compel them to act against their own principles and interests. Amsterdam paid more than half the taxes of the entire United Provinces and usually took the lead in their politics. The central government of the provinces, such as it was, was in The Hague, which also was Prince William's residence. The lifeblood of Amsterdam was in the crowds of ships along the river, the East India House, and the other bustling warehouses that made the city Europe's most comprehensive source for luxury goods from all over the world. At the stock exchange well-dressed men kept out of the frequent rains under the arcades and bought and sold obligations of the city and provincial governments, shares in the East India and West India companies, and much more. The stock market always responded quickly to good and bad political news, never more so than in the uncertainties of the summer and fall of 1688.

Our visitor's Dutch informants might refer to library shelves lined with books and pamphlets on the intricacies of Dutch political principles and organization, but he would find that many of them were in Dutch, which few foreigners read. That was no obstacle to exchanging views with his hosts, who spoke and wrote excellent French. In their fine houses along the canals the great families of the city accumulated wealth through trade, rural landownership, investment in drainage projects, interest on their bonds, and the legal and illegal perquisites of their service as municipal officers. Well read, multilingual, often university-educated, many of them were tolerant by temperament and conviction, proud of the heritage of tolerance and "true freedom" for which they had fought for over a hundred years. Tolerance and freedom also were known to be good for trade. Amsterdam traded with peoples of all religions, and almost any-one could settle there and contribute to its wealth: Jews, Baptists, Luther-ans, even Catholics if they were willing to keep low profiles. This did not mean that these thoughtful people were all skeptics or religiously indiffer-ent. They might feel uneasy or unworthy with the blessings of prosperity or remind themselves how quickly flood or invasion, perhaps God's judg-ment on an unfaithful people, could destroy them. Of course death was never far away, even in a comfortable house in a safe and orderly city. Calvinist preachers always were calling for a "further reformation" of soci-ety and individual lives, for regular prayer, Bible reading, strict observation of the Sabbath, and so on; these calls increased, and met with more of a response from all classes, in moments of political tensions and uncertainty, such as 1688.

• • •

In 1688 the United Provinces of the Netherlands were engaged in their last enterprise as a European power of the first rank, the invasion of England. They looked back proudly on a little over a hundred years of freedom, counting from their formal political union in 1579 or perhaps as important from the "great alteration" that had brought Amsterdam over to the cause of independence in 1578. The Dutch polity had been born in particularist revolt, town by town and province by province, against the taxes and controls of the Spanish Hapsburg monarchy that then ruled all of what is now the Netherlands and Belgium. The United Provinces had grown out of their alliance in their struggle for freedom. They acquired an extra dimension of unity and fervor as they became associated with, though never completely identified with, the Protestant struggle against the Roman Catholicism that the Spanish defended so stoutly. They received magnificent political and military leadership from William the Silent, prince of Orange, and generations of his descendants, but always as stadholders, delegated administrators, appointed by and ultimately answerable to the provincial States of Holland and the other six provinces and to the States General, their general decision-making body, in which each province had one vote. The States of Holland, by far the most important of the provinces, discussed only those matters already approved by their Delegated Councillors, a sort of standing committee, and referred to the towns for discussion in their councils. The constitutions of the other six provinces were roughly analogous in pattern with many singularities. Everywhere in the United Provinces the real centers of politics—some said even of sovereignty—were the towns. The town council was typically an oligarchic body, something like a board of directors of a modern corporation or university, selecting its new members out of a stratum of qualified families, reaching out to take in outsiders only at its own pleasure. The common people had no vote but frequently made themselves heard in demonstration and threatened riot, especially in times of crisis. From the great revolt of the 1570s and 1580s down through the crises of 1618, 1672, and 1688, and on to the end of the United Provinces in the days of the French Revolution, Dutch politics had a singularly local style, the great conflicts being hammered out in dozens of towns and scores of permutations by grandees, merchants, and ordinary people who had known one another all their lives.

The Dutch had to fight off the finest armies of Europe, the Spanish, in order to keep their freedom. Two stadholders, Maurice and Frederick Henry, turned out to be military organizers and strategists of the first rank. The wealth and sophistication of the town elites, the Calvinist fervor of the preachers, and the centralizing military achievement of the stadholders all reinforced one another in time of war. But when the Spanish signed a truce with their former subjects in 1609, internal stresses emerged. Theological strife between Calvinist militants and advocates of a more tolerant church under greater state control, strikingly similar to quarrels in England at the same time, coalesced with constitutional controversies between Prince Maurice and the town and province localists. With support of the Calvinists and some of the towns, Maurice won; the great advocate of Holland, Johan van Oldenbarnevelt, was executed in 1619. With the expiration of the Spanish truce in 1621 Maurice and then his half brother, Frederick Henry, managed to find enough allies among the towns to wage successful war. Frederick Henry died in 1647 just as the war was winding down. His son, William II, disapproved of the peace being discussed and resisted moves to reduce military forces. He had used his alliances within the towns and the threat of military force to gain a dominant position when he suddenly died in November 1650. His only son, the future William III, was born in December.

The years that followed were remembered by the prosperous Amsterdammers as the glorious days of the "true freedom," when without a massive military threat on the land frontiers or an adult stadholder, the towns and provinces had their own way. In 1672 Louis XIV shattered this dreamworld with a massive invasion. Forts and forces had been sadly neglected. Even when the dikes were opened, the polders filled slowly. Large parts of the United Provinces were occupied by the French. In many towns there were big, but generally nonviolent, demonstrations against the ruling groups that had allowed things to come to such a terrible state. The leading figure of the "true freedom" regime, Johan de Witt, was torn to pieces by a mob in The Hague. William III was named stadholder. He now proceeded to use all his prerogatives and powers, and all the popular indignation that was on his side, to purge town councils of the partisans of the old regime. But he was not a sovereign, every town was different, and it was slow work. Some writers reminded him, perhaps with a glance across the Channel at England in the 1670s, that if he pushed too hard, he might create two permanently irreconcilable parties. In 1678 and again in 1684 Amsterdam

won the ratification of terms of peace with France of which William disapproved. In 1684 he turned from constant conflict with the towns to conciliation, never undertaking a major initiative without the cooperation of
Amsterdam. The caution and feel for the intricacies of human interaction
that William learned in these struggles, as well as his iron determination to
forge a Protestant coalition that could resist Louis XIV, carried him to his
triumph in London at the end of 1688. At the same time, some new key
figures who were more conciliatory emerged in Amsterdam. One of them
was Nicolaas Witsen.

The well-dressed, shrewd-looking men who return our gaze from the
endless group portraits of the leaders of seventeenth-century Dutch society are not very easy to get to know across the centuries. Few of them mis-
behaved as spectacularly as the young dukes of the reign of Charles II.
Dutch politics only occasionally manifested the polarization and extreme
risk that produced such memorable and dangerous personalities in England. The many-leveled system of dispersed sovereignty and collective
decision making called for men who could listen to one another and move
carefully toward a new consensus.

Nicolaas Corneliszoon Witsen was an outstanding member of this political and cultural elite, a man of real learning both historical and contemporary, a key figure in the intricate minuet that led to Amsterdam's surprising
commitment to Prince William's risky venture in 1688. The Witsens had
been members of Amsterdam's ruling elite since the upheaval and change
of government in 1578, in the founding days of the independent Netherlands. Nicolaas's father, Cornelis, is a bold central figure in one of the finest
of the collective portraits, van der Helst's *Dinner for the Civic Guard*. He
played a major role in the city's break with William II in 1650 and was
burgemeester in 1653. Nicolaas, born in 1641, accompanied his father in the
1650s on a mission to England, where they were received by Cromwell
and shown the pillow and the ax used in the execution of Charles I. Witsen
had an excellent classical education, followed by studies at the University
of Leiden, some of them with Jacobus Golius, professor of Arabic and an
early investigator of other non-European languages, including Chinese.
Witsen received the Doctor of Laws degree in 1664. Then he went to
Moscow in the suite of a Dutch embassy. He met all kinds of people, even
the patriarch Nikon, and began collecting the information on Russia and

Asia that made him probably the greatest authority on these subjects in western Europe. In 1693 he was to publish a great folio volume, *North and East Tartary*, full of information and maps. When Tsar Peter visited Holland, he was astonished by the depth of Witsen's knowledge of his empire.

Witsen made the usual rich young man's visits to Paris and Rome, studied briefly at Oxford, and in 1670 settled down to a long career in the service of his native city. In 1671 he published a major book, *Ancient and Modern Shipbuilding*, in which his descriptions of ancient shipping showed considerable erudition in Greek and Latin sources. He skipped the Middle Ages almost entirely and then gave a comprehensive survey of the shipbuilding techniques of his own time. His political career moved rapidly after the upheaval of 1672, and in 1674 he was named for the first time to the Delegated Councillors. In 1676 he served, on the recommendation of William III, as a delegate of the States General with the army. Already he seems to have been part of the slow and tentative reconciliation between William and the great city. He built a splendid house on the Heerengracht, one of the main canals. In 1682 he was named for the first time one of the four *burgemeesters*. He sympathized with William's desire to strengthen the army and oppose Louis's slow aggression from the south, but he feared the risks as long as England was so unstable, with a possibility that it might ally with Louis. William saw his point but took the threat of French aggression more seriously. The positions of the many other towns were as usual complicated and ambiguous. Witsen also was organizing efforts to aid the Huguenot refugees who were flooding into Holland, reinforcing a widespread sense of the menace of French tyranny to Protestant Europe.

Witsen's letters are not easy reading. The style is formal, full of polite phrases. There are many references to conversations too sensitive to summarize on paper, to more and less appropriate ways to communicate with a dignitary without loss of face for anyone concerned. They are masterpieces of indirection, of avoidance of confrontation, of incremental movement toward difficult decisions. Just keep writing, he seems to say to himself, just keep everyone in touch, and something will work out. We're all in this together. William III could not have asked for a better counterpart in the delicate reconciliation between the stadholder and Amsterdam in the 1680s.

In 1688 Witsen was engaged in mundane discussions with an envoy from the tsars in Moscow, helped supervise major improvements in the fortifications and water control system around the town of Naarden, was involved in efforts to secure the ransom of some Dutch prisoners in Algiers, and was concluding a term as Amsterdam's representative on the Delegated Councillors in The Hague but was having to delay his move back to Amsterdam because his wife was in poor health. At the same time he was deeply involved with the delicate communication and decision making leading up to Amsterdam's commitment to the invasion of England.

October 27, 1688, was a day of fasting and prayer throughout the United Provinces for the success of Prince William's great venture to England. In Haarlem prayers were said in the Reformed, French Calvinist, Remonstrant, Lutheran, and Mennonite churches. In Amsterdam there was a special prayer to the God of Israel in the magnificent Portuguese Synagogue: ". . . bless, guard, favor, support, save, exalt, enhance, and raise to the most glittering peak of success the Noble and Mighty States of Holland and West-Friesland, the High and Mighty States General of the United Provinces, and His Highness the Prince of Orange, Stadholder and Captain-General by sea and land of these provinces, with all their allies, and the noble and illustrious burgomasters and magistracy of this city of Amsterdam."

The Sephardic Jews of Amsterdam had every reason to support William and his cause. Although hard-line Calvinists deplored tolerating them, the House of Orange favored them because of their major contributions as international traders and financers of military campaigns and their singular usefulness as back door communicators with Spain and Portugal. In Amsterdam they had a vigorous community life, with many schools and clubs, some of which were the places to go for stock market deals after hours. They produced a sophisticated literature largely in Spanish, the language of their most systematic and principled persecutors, with fondness for baroque conceits and formalisms not that different from Sor Juana's. An outstanding example of this literature, published in 1688, was Joseph Penso de la Vega's *Confusion of Confusions*, which seems to be the first book ever published on the art of stock market speculation. It takes the form of a dialogue among a philosopher, a merchant, and a stockbroker. The stockbroker does most of the explaining. There are three ways to profit from the market, he says: like a prince, holding your stock and living off the dividends; like a merchant, trying to gauge trends, buy, sell, buy options, and so on; or as a "player," making deals for others and earning commissions. The best example of stockowning, the stockbroker says, is the Dutch East India Company; a share is worth six times its original value in 1602 and has paid dividends totaling 1,482⅓ percent on the original price. But still there are many who think there is something unnatural about the stock market. To be sure, sometimes it seems like the Leaning Tower of Pisa; no matter from which side you look at it, it seems about to collapse in that direction. But he goes on to show how it is possible to invest sensibly for various purposes and how the market actually works.

It is oddly appropriate that a baroque style and sensibility should be brought to bear in this pioneer analysis of the intricacies of early modern capitalism. As in the pamphlet wars over political regulation of economic behavior in seventeenth-century England, a moral assessment of an economic practice often focused on its selfishness and inequity, while a more pragmatic view pointed to its hidden benefits. Capitalism always breeds these debates, right down to recent arguments about the pros and cons of derivatives, hedge funds, and dot.com IPOs. No one loves a speculator. So who better to make the case for the usefulness of speculation than an outsider writing elegantly and intricately in the language of the persecutors of his people? It also is noteworthy that *Confusion of Confusions* was published in August or September 1688, just as the Amsterdam stock market took a nosedive on the first rumors of William's risky enterprise against England. The book urges investing in the great East India and West India stocks, not panicking, and holding for the long term.

How was it that all the delicate web of influences and decisions of the United Provinces came together in support of William's assault on England? The Dutch state had been able to project its power beyond its frontiers in a few important naval engagements, notably in the Baltic. It had created an enormously successful military and commercial power halfway around the earth in the East India Company, and it had fought Spain's finest to a standstill on its land frontiers. But it had never mounted anything like this combined sea-land invasion, one of the riskiest forms of military action in any age. Here again, we find that the overreaching of Louis XIV plays a key part in the story. French concessions on tariffs had helped lure the rulers of Amsterdam and the other trading towns into the peace of 1678. Dutch merchants were selling more in French ports and also were carrying larger shares of France's exports. In 1687 Louis first banned imports of Dutch herring except for those that had been preserved with French salt. Then he revoked the 1678 tariff concessions. In 1688 several towns called for retaliatory measures against French trade and were more and more inclined to go along with William's moves toward an invasion. William was negotiating to hire large numbers of foreign troops, fourteen thousand Germans and six thousand Swedes, to man the frontiers of the United Provinces while their own best regiments invaded England. The agreements had to be ratified by the provinces. Most of Amsterdam's rulers continued to hope that Louis would back down and a confrontation could be avoided. But in 1688 the Sun King was not backing down in large matters or small. Incensed by Dutch threats, he had Dutch ships seized in French ports. On September 29 the States of Holland passed a secret resolution giving full support to the assault on England.

In November, as William's fleet made its way down the Channel on its way to its astonishing victories, the Church Consistory in Amsterdam petitioned the *burgemeesters* for more vigorous suppression of prostitution, closing of taverns on Sunday, and suppression of dance halls, "since Fatherland and Church are threatened with very dark clouds." Those particular clouds lifted, but the situation of the United Provinces did not improve. Heavily taxed, they made major contributions to the long war against France. William as stadholder-king, now resident in London and preoccupied with consolidating his position there, managed to keep control of Dutch politics until his death in 1702. Thereafter the anti-Orange rulers of the towns and provinces regained influence, and Holland decided not to appoint a new stadholder. The United Provinces in the eighteenth century often were neutral in European wars. Their cloth and other industries declined, and their business enterprise shifted toward financial services and transit trade. By the time of the French Revolution Holland seemed to be in deep economic and political decline. It was as if now that the floodwaters were not so threatening, the people had stopped pumping.

PART V

WORLDS OF WORDS

STYLES AND THOUGHT
IN EUROPE

The Europe of 1688 differed from that of all previous centuries and from all its contemporary "great others" in the commerce and culture of thought. Gazettes of daily news circulated widely in London, Paris, and Amsterdam. Monthly journals presented reviews of books, reports of scientific findings, and contributions to current debates to an audience of intellectuals all over central and western Europe. One of the most remarkable of the latter was the *Acta Eruditorum*, published in Leipzig. Through it we can see the European intellectual world facing back to its classical and Christian heritages and forward into an open, uncertain world of science and state politics. A rough-and-ready tabulation of the 171 books reviewed in the *Acta* during 1688 shows 72 of them dealing with theology (including a small amount of what we would call philosophy), church history, and other aspects of the Christian heritage; 44 dealing with science and medicine, some of it still deeply engaged with texts and ideas from Greek and Latin antiquity, but much of it experimental and mathematical; 10 on contemporary political problems; only 7 on language and literature; 19 on topics in European history; and 19 reporting on some part of the world outside Christian Europe. Among the books reviewed were a work on the medicinal benefits of coffee, tea, and chocolate; the *Confucius Sinarum Philosophus*; and Newton's *Principia*, published in 1687, which was hailed for "rescuing natural phenomena from the shadow of occult qualities and bringing them back into the light and law of mathematics."

Of the 171 books, 111 were in Latin, 42 in French, 5 in Italian, 7 in English, and 6 in German. The reviews were all in Latin, still the learned language of the German-speaking world. (Note the small number of German books reviewed in a journal published in a German-speaking city.) A sample of learned reading in England or France would reveal somewhat different proportions, but still a great deal of serious writing in Latin. French was everywhere the dominant modern intellectual language, and French prose style set a standard for apt, elegant, humane expression of all kinds of opinions, skeptical and pious, snobbish and disrespectful. English certainly had come into its own as a medium of poetry, drama, and prose by this time, but the *Acta* sample should remind us that it was not nearly as widely known on the Continent as French. Italian was in decline except in the form of words to be sung. Dutch had never really managed to spread outside its homeland, and many would say that by this time it was losing its literary vitality there.

The *Acta* sample is biased toward the world of abstract thought and authoritative tradition. It tells us little about what people read to amuse themselves or what plays or spectacles they watched. If we read more widely in the world of words of 1688, we find challenges to old authorities in these amusements as powerful as those of the men of learning. A woman draws on her own experiences and grievances to write a vivid fictional attack on the enslavement of Africans in the Americas. In the Europe of cities and trade, books were bought and sold in sufficient quantities to make it possible, as it was for Saikaku, for a person to make a living writing in a highly individual fashion. In the world of abstract thought, theological preoccupations still were powerful, but there emerged landmarks of a secular science and philosophy: Locke's philosophies of knowledge and of political right and the awesome achievement of Newton. There still was one great intellectual who hoped to reconcile old and new and to encompass all human knowledge within his system of thought. There is no better place to end these notes on the world of European writing than in the projects and frustrations, the works completed and left undone, of the great Leibniz.

CHAPTER 18

IN THE REPUBLIC OF LETTERS

In his great history *The Age of Louis XIV*, Voltaire wrote that in the long decades of that reign "one saw established imperceptibly in Europe a literary republic . . . despite the wars and despite different religions. All the sciences, all the arts, thus received mutual assistance in this way; the academies formed this republic. . . . True scholars in each field drew closer the bonds of this great society of minds, spread everywhere and everywhere independent. This correspondence still remains; it is one of the consolations for the evils that ambition and politics spread across the earth."

Since the 1400s learned Europeans occasionally had used the phrase "republic of letters" to refer to the social network of men (and rarely women) interested in literature and learning who kept in touch with one another by correspondence—thus in English and French a republic of letters in two senses—and who gained standing in the eyes of other participants by the quality of their learning and writing, not by their birth. This was an unthreatening "republic" in a world where that word made many princes and courtiers uneasy. All that suddenly changed, with the publication from 1684 to 1687 of a series of monthly reviews in compact duodecimo format entitled *Nouvelles de la République des Lettres*. A successful commercial printing venture, reaching an international audience through the rapidly developing postal systems of western Europe, the *Nouvelles* differed from the *Acta Eruditorum* and other earlier learned periodicals in its appeal to the tastes of readers who had some leisure and interest in ideas but were not professional scholars. Its reports on the latest works of philosophical and theological controversy—not as heavy going for the seventeenth-century reader, who could scarcely avoid constant exposure to these issues, as for the often baffled modern reader—frequently were lightened by asides and even modest jokes from the reviewer. The author did not hesitate to point out the weaknesses of the arguments he was reviewing or to make a plea for the principle of religious toleration and freedom of worship for all Christians in all Christian states. These views were being disseminated not by private letters but by the latest methods of production and distribution. The Republic of Letters was becoming much more political, much more of a challenge to intolerant princes.

The site of this remarkable project was Rotterdam, in Holland, Europe's center of religious freedom and free enterprise. Its editor–main writer was a French Protestant exile named Pierre Bayle. Voltaire and the other shapers of the French Enlightenment looked back on Bayle as one of their heroic predecessors, not only one of the founders of their now deeply subversive Republic of Letters but a key source of knowledge and argument for their assaults on absolutism and traditional Christianity. Bayle was a most unlikely forefather for these assaults. Despite his anguished and furious attacks on the persecution of French Protestantism, he believed deeply in the duty of obedience to princes. A tenaciously held Scripture-based Calvinism fed his earnest moralism, and his dissections of the spurious arguments he found in almost all the philosophy and theology of his time.

Bayle was born in 1647, the son of a Protestant pastor. Poverty, Calvinism, and the mentality of a besieged religious minority were the ground notes of his youth. There can have been little doubt that he was destined for the ministry. Then in 1669 and 1670 he embraced Catholicism, studied philosophy at the Jesuit college in Toulouse, and seventeen months later returned to his home and the church of his fathers. It seems that, having grown up with the view that the pope was Antichrist, he had been overimpressed by his first exposure to rational expositions of Catholic theology, but once in a Catholic milieu he had been repelled by the images and the rituals. In his mature thought he referred to Catholicism and the paganism of ancient Greece and Rome as perverted, externalized religions that lead man away not only from the true faith but even from the ideas and moral maxims that could be derived solely from human reason. Already obsessively textual and starved for news of the world of ideas, he read and took notes indefatigably all his life, as if he never again would risk leaping to a conclusion from insufficient evidence. He finally found his vocation in making the results of his reading and thinking available to people in situations as modest and provincial as his own origins.

His apostasy from Protestantism had deeply wounded his father; his renunciation of Catholicism made his life much more dangerous. The laws of France tolerated those born Protestant but not apostates from the True Faith. In 1675 he became professor of philosophy at a Protestant academy in Sedan. But he seems to have had a more realistic sense of the mounting dangers to French Protestantism than many of his colleagues and was on the lookout for a refuge abroad. In 1681 he accepted a position at a new French-language academy of Protestant studies in Rotterdam. As signs of official hostility mounted, more and more French Protestants followed him. For some of them, the mounting menace was apocalyptic, the coming of the Antichrist. The appearance of a comet late in 1680 was to them another sign of the coming Judgment, and in the Last Days disobedience to or rebellion against earthly authorities might be called for. Bayle was more prudent and inclined to value order. Although not himself much given either to mathematics or to systematic observation, he was more persuaded by evidence than moved by religious enthusiasm. He rejected apocalyptic interpretations of the comet and continued to move in the opposite direction from the would-be prophets. He sought naturalistic explanations of natural phenomena and thought that sovereigns ought to tolerate diversity of Christian belief among their subjects *and* that subjects ought to obey their sovereigns. His *Letter on the Comet*, later retitled *Various Thoughts on the Comet*, drafted before he arrived in Rotterdam and published and republished in 1682–84, was widely circulated inside and outside France and marked his real breakthrough to effective writing for wide audiences.

From March 1684 to February 1687 Bayle published thirty-six numbers of the *Nouvelles de la République des Lettres*, each about one hundred small pages. He seems to have done most of the reading and writing himself, a considerable task for which he received a modest income. In his preface to the first number he claimed that he wished to concentrate on what unites men, not what divides them. "This is the characteristic of the illustrious man in the Republic of Letters." The books he reported on included many editions of the Latin classics and the Church Fathers, contributions to current controversies, and a bit of everything from sine tables to sympathetic assessments of the moral qualities of Molière's comedies to reports from Istanbul and China.

In Rotterdam Bayle was ideally placed for such a pan-European publishing venture. The craft of printing and networks of distribution were highly developed. The Dutch authorities tolerated a very wide range of published opinions. Bayle never would have been permitted to publish the *Nouvelles* in the France of Louis XIV. He had declared that Roman Catholics would find nothing objectionable in his work, but its evenhandedness, insistence on evidence, and the Protestant allegiance of the editor aroused misgivings. The *Nouvelles* found many readers in France, but sometimes it had to reach them by devious channels; many booksellers would have nothing to do with it. In 1685, when the Edict of Nantes was revoked, the *Nouvelles* was formally banned. Bayle's brother in France was arrested for questioning and died in jail. (His father died the same year, before either the revocation or official hostility to his son's works could cause him any new grief.) Grieving for his people and his father, blaming himself for his brother's death, Bayle grew bolder, arguing for toleration of all opinions, even those that denied Christian fundamentals. The horrible news from France propelled him in 1686 and 1687 to write and publish a *Philosophical Commentary on the Words of Jesus Christ "Compel Them to Come In," in Which It Is Proved by Demonstrative Reasoning That There Is Nothing More Abominable Than to Make Conversions by Force.* Here he achieved his most coherent integration of his powers of reasoning with his moral and religious passions. Saint Augustine had used these words, which Jesus spoke at the wedding in Cana, to justify the use of force in presenting the Gospel to the heathen; despite his own profound Augustinianism, Bayle rejected this whole line of argument. He saw that Christianity by having recourse to compulsion lost the inwardness and individuality that made it different from pagan practices in which one simply followed the rites of the society in which one grew up. Those who sought to force conversions were the real blasphemers. The power of early learning, of customs, was such that there always would be variety in what men believed and practiced. Our tenacity in holding to our religious convictions in the face of persecution "can only come from what remains of the good in our nature after the sin of Adam." Religious truth is nothing until it becomes a matter of inner conviction. "In the condition in which man finds himself, God is content to demand of him that he seek the truth with as great care as he can, and that, believing he has found it, that he love it and regulate his life by it. . . . It suffices for each that he consult sincerely and in good faith the light that God gives him and that, following it, he give allegiance to the idea that seems to him most reasonable and most in accord with the Will of God." Founded in far deeper personal commitment to Christianity than Locke's somewhat similar ideas, approaching in a moving way the inwardness of Madame de Guyon and the Quaker doctrine of the Inner Light, Bayle here also seems to leave the way open toward Enlightenment reliance on human reason and even the profound moral and spiritual perfectionism of Immanuel Kant.

As a result of stress, intense intellectual concentration, and sheer work, Bayle's health collapsed early in 1687; he took to bed with fevers and terrible headaches. The February number of the *Nouvelles* was published in incomplete form, and others continued it thereafter. Bayle gave up his lectures and private pupils. Early in 1688 he was able to resume a few lectures but still was in poor health. He probably met John Locke, also a resident of Rotterdam, but there is no evidence of any influence in either direction between these two great theorists of tolerance.

Bayle never returned to the high-pressure work of publishing a monthly journal. He seems to have made good use of his months of illness and relative idleness from 1687 to 1689 to conceive an even grander project to serve the Republic of Letters by providing reliable information in usable form. By the end of 1690 he was firmly embarked on his great project to compile a *Historical and Critical Dictionary*, which occupied him for the rest of his life. His goal was to provide completely reliable information on ancient and modern authors and texts, "the touch-stone for other books, . . . the insurance agency for the Republic of Letters." As in the *Nouvelles*, he also slipped in, frequently in the articles on the most obscure authors and subjects, a host of sharp criticisms of the dogmatisms, superstitions, and intolerance of past and present. The *Dictionary* was a key resource for all the thinkers of the Enlightenment and the model for the great *Encyclopedia*. Voltaire and many others acknowledged an immense debt to this obsessive reader and writer, who had been so determined that no one after him should be as starved for reliable and up-to-date knowledge as he had been in his father's parsonage.

Bayle was in exile, but he was writing in French, and although he had readers in many countries, surely the audience that mattered most to him was in his now-hostile and inaccessible homeland. There 1688 may have been *the* year when everyone who was anyone in the cultural elite had to take sides in the quarrel of the ancients and the moderns. Many literary and artistic forms were enlisted in the struggle. In his *Poetical History of the War Newly Declared between the Ancients and the Moderns*, published in 1688, François de Callières included an elaborate engraving in the style of an order of battle map, showing the army of Greek poets, with Homer as its commander, that of Latin poets, and that of ancient orators drawn up on one side of a river, confronting the armies of French poets, of Italian and Spanish poets, and of modern orators.

In 1688 Charles Perrault published the first parts of his famous *Parallel of the Ancients and the Moderns*. Here he escapes the regularities and pompous sonorities—the effects of bad Latin—that afflicted even moderns when they wrote poetry in the 1680s. He contributed to the development of the deft, relaxed, conversational prose that is one of the most striking features of the French Enlightenment. It is no accident that the *Parallels* and several other breakthrough works of this style are in dialogue form, which keeps constant pressure on the writer to preserve the flavor of ordinary speech. It also is no accident that the protagonists are portrayed carrying on their debate as they stroll through the magnificent gardens of the Palace of Versailles, seen by many as a demonstration of the superiority of the moderns and of the French monarchy.

The three protagonists of the *Parallels* are a president of a judicial body, who is a dogmatic champion of antiquity; a cavalier, who is good company and a man of swift wit; and an abbot, Perrault's alter ego, who champions the moderns and has all the best lines and the longest and most thoughtful speeches. When the cavalier brings up the analogy of the history of the world with the course of a human life, the world now being in its aged decline, the abbot replies that by the same analogy we can argue that mankind has been continually accumulating experience. The modern age, he says, continually brings forth new mechanical devices, like the frame for the mechanical knitting of silk stockings, which had been invented recently. The abbot does not find it equally easy to argue for the superiority of the moderns in every art; it's hard in sculpture but much easier in painting, where the moderns continue to discover new techniques and to achieve new wonders of verisimilitude. Architects have continued to improve on the classical rules of proportion, so that there is more beauty in the facade of the Louvre than in any ancient building.

At the end of the *Parallels* Perrault published in 1688 (more followed later), all three friends, even the president, exclaim over the beauties of the sculptures and fountains of Versailles, the abbot saving special praise for the Three Fountains area, with its water, grass, and trees, so skillfully arranged that the artifice disappears and the beauty seems natural. The argument for the superior polish and regularity of the modern seems to give way to an anticipation of the eighteenth-century revolt against regularity and order.

Some would say that by 1688 Perrault's championing of the moderns was no longer anything like an uphill battle, that most articulate opinion in the French elite was moving his way. Perrault's personal circumstances suggest the contexts in which such a shift was taking place. His father was a prosperous lawyer, the kind of man who contributed to and benefited most from the royal centralization under Louis XIV. No expense was spared in the education of the Perrault brothers. They learned their classics well but also wrote verse burlesques of the *Aeneid* and other classics, their writing sessions sometimes dissolving into unstoppable fits of laughter. One brother became a lawyer, another an expert in government finance, yet another a vehemently anti-Jesuit Jansenist theologian, while Claude, fifteen years older than Charles, was a physician, architect, and biologist. After the rapid rise and disgrace of the financier, it was Claude's work as a supervisor of building projects for the great minister Colbert that assured the family's fortunes and shaped his own conviction that no past age could match the splendor and sophistication of the Age of Louis the Great.

Charles and Claude both were founding members of the Academy of Sciences, another of Colbert's image-building projects that also aimed to mobilize new forms of knowledge in the service of the monarchy. Claude, much more interested in dissection and experiment than most physicians of his time, was placed in charge of the academy's efforts to broaden biological knowledge by dissecting various animals, both domestic and exotic. The dissections were the work, Claude Perrault wrote, of "a company, composed of people who have eyes for such things more than most of the rest of the world, as well as hands to search for them with more dexterity and success; who see what is, and whom it would be hard to persuade to see what is not; who are not so eager to find new things as to examine well what one claims to have found; and to whom the assurance of having been mistaken in some observation gives no less satisfaction than a curious and important discovery; so much does the love of certainty prevail over everything else in their spirits." It would be hard to find a more elegant expression of the ideal of the advancement of knowledge through public, collective, falsifiable inquiry.

The dissections were not for the faint of stomach; the dissection of a bear that had died of diseased lungs and intestines released such a stench that pints of brandy were poured over the carcass. Between 1668 and 1676 specimens of over thirty species were dissected. Observations of a live chameleon and later dissections corrected many mistakes in the descriptions found in Pliny and other classical authors. In 1671 and 1676 Claude Perrault published the results of these investigations in two splendid volumes of *Memoirs for a Natural History of the Animals*, with remarkable engravings of the external appearances of the animals and key aspects of their dissected viscera and limb structures. This work continued into the 1680s, and in 1688 preparations were well advanced for a supplementary volume.

At the same time that Claude Perrault was supervising the early stages of this ambitious project in scientific observation, he was engaged in another project for Colbert, a translation of Vitruvius, the greatest Latin text on architecture. His medical education had required substantial learning in Greek and Latin, enabling him to deal smoothly with Vitruvius's odd vocabulary and many digressions. The translation contains plates illustrating Vitruvius's ideas and classifications that are as detailed and as clear in delineation of structure as those of dissected animals in the *Memoirs*. He went on to publish an *Abridgment* of Vitruvius, in which he managed some first statements of his own way of thinking about architecture. Architectural beauty, he wrote, is in some respects natural or "positive," inherent in the work itself, but it is mainly the result of arbitrary creation. What we admire is the clarity and coherence of the architect's inventions. Our admiration for the ancients is directed at that in which we can and do surpass them: their inventiveness, their clear and systematic development of their ideas, and even their links to the age of a great ruler. By the time Claude Perrault published these ideas in their fullest form, in his *Order of Five Types of Columns according to the Method of the Ancients* (1683), he had had some excellent opportunities to put them into practice. Although the details are controversial, it is clear that he made substantial contributions to the great east facade of the Louvre as it went through many changes between 1670 and 1680. His passions for science and architecture, royal glory and the work of the academy came together wonderfully in his designs for the Paris Observatory, completed in 1683 and still standing.

Claude Perrault's plans for a triumphal arch for the Faubourg St. Antoine were approved, and first stages of construction were under way when Colbert, the brothers' patron, died in 1683. Construction stopped and never resumed. Claude continued his dissections and preparations for a supplementary volume of the *Memoirs*. In the fall of 1688 he contracted an infection during the dissection of a camel and died on October 9. The anatomical plates that already had been prepared were not published until 1733.

Charles Perrault went on to publish his most famous work, the *Tales of Mother Goose*, in 1697. It was as if he had continued to stroll away from classical rigor into a lovely woodland where the voices of the simple and unlettered could be heard.

The Republic of Letters was a creation of Europe, with centers not just in Paris, London, and the Dutch cities but also in Venice, where Coronelli's map projects were under way, and in Leipzig, where the *Acta Eruditorum* was published. Some of its occasional participants wrote from incredible distances: Ambon, Batavia, Beijing. But to men of that time, and perhaps to us today, one of the more surprising of the men of learning was the lord of a fine little castle on the south slope of the Sava River valley, roughly halfway between Venice and Vienna.

Janez Vajkard Valvasor, baron of Bogenšperk,* spent 1688 working hard on the plates and the proofreading of his magnum opus, four huge volumes entitled *The Honor of the Duchy of Carniola* (*Die Ehre des Herzogtums Krain*). In that year he also published a Latin *Topography of the Archduchy of Carinthia*. At the end of the previous year he had known that he was about to be elected a member of the Royal Society of London, one of the most influential centers of the scientific province of the Republic of Letters. He had sent off to that society a detailed report on the famous and mysterious Cerknica Lake in his homeland. At the end of 1688, however, he still had no word that he had actually been elected, nor did he know that a summary of his report on the lake had appeared in the *Philosophical Transactions*. The physical distance from the Sava Valley to London was not enormous, but communications were by no means always reliable.

---

*Johann Weichard Valvasor, baron of Wagensberg, in German. I use Slovenian forms rather than German as far as possible, except for the English/Latin Carniola for Krain or Kranjska.

Carniola had been ruled by the Hapsburgs for centuries. German and Latin were the languages used by Valvasor and the rest of its elite in formal communication; the common people mostly spoke Slovenian, and almost certainly it was Valvasor's first language. The capital of the county, the urban center of Valvasor's world, was Ljubljana, Laibach in German; today it is the capital of independent Slovenia. The Sava has its origin in a waterfall above a mountain lake in the Julian Alps; it joins the Danube at Belgrade. Later in this book we shall meet a young Turk who spent some miserable months in 1688 as a prisoner somewhere along the Sava. Valvasor wrote of his Bogenšperk castle as a landowner's dream, with sloping but fertile fields, fine cherry orchards, springs inside and outside the castle, and views across the valley and toward the snowy peaks of the Alps to the north. It was perhaps a day's ride from Ljubljana, but he had all he needed at Bogenšperk: chemical apparatus for his experiments, several thousand books, a workshop for copper engraving.

Carniola is a lovely and varied country. There is good land for farms and roads, especially in the river valleys; but between them there are low, forested mountains, and in early modern times travel was especially difficult in the winter snows. Moreover, much of the bedrock is limestone. Water seeps through horizontal and vertical fissures in limestone and dissolves away caves and underground rivers. The roofs of such chambers may fall in to produce odd cliffs, spires, closed-off sinkholes and valleys; geologists call this karst topography, after a region in Carniola. Isolated pockets of farm settlement in such broken-up country are especially apt to produce distinctive local customs, beliefs and dialects that change every few miles. Rivers disappearing into sinkholes or gushing suddenly from mountainsides, caves full of stalactites and stalagmites reinforce local beliefs in uncanny subterranean forces.

Valvasor was the grandson of an immigrant from Italy in the sixteenth century, one of many who brought their skills in mining, crafts, and commerce to the region in those times. His grandfather had been bequeathed a small castle by a distant relative or employer of the same surname. Born in 1641, Valvasor enjoyed all the advantages of a provincial elite: a good Jesuit education in Ljubljana, military experience in a campaign against the Turks, and more than eight years of travel in western Europe and even to North Africa. Then in 1672 he married and bought Bogenšperk and other properties. In his travels he had seen quite a few books that collected information on the history, great families, buildings, and natural wonders of particular areas; such works were particularly common as expressions of local pride in the German lands. He had found that no one had heard of Carniola. (Present-day Slovenians have the same problem.)

Stopping at home often enough to keep his young wife pregnant (they had nine children in fifteen years of marriage), he spent much of his time traveling through Carniola and neighboring areas, sketching castles and cloisters, collecting information on towns and noble families, puzzling out some of the strange features of the landscape. He collected antiquities and strange objects and experimented with chemistry and alchemy. His first publication was a Latin *Topography* of the archduchy of Carinthia, with 223 copper plates. Finding no copper engraving shop in Ljubljana, he set up his own at Bogenšperk, the first in the archduchy. He published other topographical works, a rather oddly illustrated edition of the *Metamorphoses* of Ovid, and a *Theater of Human Death*, describing and illustrating various grisly forms of death suffered by sinners.

But Valvasor's real life's work was to make his beloved homeland known and to make a full record of its history, people, and natural wonders. Already in 1680 he had printed a notice asking people to send him information about their localities, their families, their castles. People were especially unwilling to give a stranger full descriptions of their castles, but as he traveled around, he accumulated more and more. He employed a number of artists and engravers. By 1687 he was able to start preparing *The Honor of the Duchy of Carniola* for publication. He asked the scholar Erasmus Franciscus in Nuremberg to go over his text and make his German regular and correct. By 1688 printed sheets were arriving at Bogenšperk, while more manuscript and illustrations made their way to Nuremberg. When completed and bound in 1689, it was a work of four splendid folio volumes, totaling 3,532 pages with 528 illustrations. It gave encyclopedic coverage to the history of the area since ancient times, including its various peoples and languages, its conversion to Christianity, and the long and victorious struggle of Catholicism against Protestantism; all its noble families, including their coats of arms; all its towns, cloisters, and castles, with illustrations; and the many rivers, springs, and caves.

In his great work and in other letters and records from 1687 and 1688, we find Valvasor reflecting an old Europe of witchcraft, pacts with the devil, and subterranean forces, at the same time that he was communicating with one of the centers of a new Europe, the Royal Society of London, where such themes were much less visible. He devoted one short section of his huge volumes to the superstitions and witchcraft beliefs of the people of Carniola, commenting that "it would be easier to find a land where there are no snakes than one that is entirely lacking in superstitious people." He particularly deplored the number and persistence of superstitious customs around the Christian festivals of Christmas and Easter. Carniolan peasants always put big logs on their hearth fires on Christmas Eve and placed on them a piece or spoonful of every item in their feasts, bidding the fire to eat along with them, clearly a survival, Valvasor said, of pagan sacrifices to the household god.

In this and in other scattered discussions on witchcraft and the works of the devil, Valvasor sought explanations through historical survivals or natural causes of apparently magical phenomena. Erasmus Franciscus of Nuremberg, who was editing Valvasor's work and making occasional additions to it, was much less inclined to explain away people's stories and fears of the devil and his works. In Book XI of the great work, ostensibly devoted to the cities, markets, and castles of Carniola, the editor began to include whole paragraphs in which he disputed the accounts of these matters given by "the honorable principal author"; the result is over fifty big folio pages of written debate on the theory of witchcraft and the works of the devil. These pages, in Volume III, probably were completed and in Valvasor's hands early in 1688, but there is one late addition recording an experience of his in that year.

Valvasor and Erasmus Franciscus agreed that there were many types of implicit and explicit pacts with the devil. Valvasor found the concept of the implicit pact troubling. What if a child stepped on a bewitched stone or innocently copied the words or gestures of a witch? Was the innocent child thus caught in an implicit pact with the devil and damned? Erasmus Franciscus replied that an implicit pact cannot have effect without the awareness of the person making it. In another connection Valvasor asserted that the devil has no power over the virtuous. The devil might give someone an invention that is effective for natural reasons, like a silk-finishing process he had heard about at Lyons; those who make use of it without awareness of its origins will be in no way caught in an implicit pact. And so this extended debate on ancient Christian fears and even older beliefs in dark supernatural powers turned toward questions of subjective belief and intention much like those we also see in the different religious worlds of Locke, Bayle, and William Penn.

Not to say that Valvasor did not believe in the devil and his works: On

March 8, 1688, as he was reading over some of the material he had previously prepared on this subject, there was a huge crash above him, and then another. He feared the roof was falling in but also seems to have sensed that he was playing with eternal fire. The danger went away after he recited several prayers and formulas, the last ending "you have no power to harm a hair of my head."

The Cerknica Lake in Carniola had been commented on by travelers and students of nature since the time of the classical geographer Strabo. At times it was simply a wide, grassy plain. Then water would rise out of openings in the plain, bringing abundant supplies of fish with it. Months later the water would drain away completely. Valvasor spent quite a bit of time exploring the lake and the area around it by boat and on foot. He was by no means the first to see that it must be fed and drained by the underground streams that were so common in the karst country. It was his awareness of an account of it by the English traveler Edward Brown that prompted him to send his first letter to the Royal Society in London in December 1685. Several letters were exchanged in 1686, and Valvasor sent in an extended report on a new process he had developed for the casting of large bronze statues. This was received with general approbation, and in 1687 Valvasor knew that he was about to be nominated for membership in the august society. In December 1687 he sent in an elaborate report on the Cerknica Lake. He believed that there must be an underground reservoir higher up in the mountains that filled up with runoff from the melting snows and drained by underground passages into a reservoir below the bottom of the lake, from which there was only one outlet channel of limited volume. At the peak runoff this reservoir filled up, and water gushed through channels in its roof into the bed of the lake. As the flow slackened, the reservoir beneath the lake drained to the point where the lake waters could drain back into it. On December 14, 1687, the first part of Valvasor's paper on Cerknica Lake was read to the Royal Society by Edmond Halley, who had built out of basins and tubing an elaborate model of Valvasor's mental model; apparently it worked. Valvasor's report was published in the *Philosophical Transactions* of the society and later in the *Acta Eruditorum*. At the same December 1687 meeting Valvasor was formally elected to membership in the society. Late in 1688 Valvasor was writing to the society to inquire if his report sent the year before had reached London. There is no evidence that he ever knew that his report on the lake had been so well received or that he had been formally elected. *The Honor of the Duchy of*

Carniola was published in 1689. But Valvasor was broken in finances and probably in health. In 1690 he sold his books and prints, and in 1692 he had to part with his beloved Bogenšperk estate. He died in 1693.

Valvasor's work on the Cerknica Lake was accompanied by an elaborate bird's-eye view and an intricate chart of the underground channels as he conceived them. But naturalistic explanation of the powers below the earth had not triumphed entirely; in the upper left of the bird's-eye view is a nearby mountain, with witches flying above it. Elsewhere in his great book Valvasor describes a few occasions on which he ventured into caves. He was acutely aware of the dangers of dropoffs in the dark into huge sinkholes. An illustration makes his fears and ambivalences stunningly clear. The general pattern of stalactites and stalagmites will look familiar to anyone who has visited such a cave, but in Valvasor's print they all are turning into devilish masks, monsters, and body parts. One of the two human figures in the foreground, pointing to the shapes, probably is Valvasor, observing a subterranean world that he would like to view naturalistically but that still awakens fear and loathing.

Valvasor in a cave

CHAPTER 19

APHRA BEHN

In 1688 Aphra Behn published a poem:

To the Fair Clarinda, Who Made Love to Me,
Imagined More than Woman

Fair lovely maid, or if that title be
Too weak, too feminine for nobler thee,
Permit a name that more approaches truth,
And let me call thee, lovely charming youth.
This last will justify my soft complaint,
While that may serve to lessen my constraint;
And without blushes I the youth pursue,
When so much beauteous woman is in view.
With thy deluding form thou giv'st us pain,
While the bright nymph betrays us to the swain.
In pity to our sex sure thou wert sent,
That we might love and yet be innocent:
For sure no crime with thee we can commit;
Or if we should—thy form excuses it.
For who, that gathers fairest flowers believes
A snake lies hid beneath the fragrant leaves.

Thou beauteous wonder of a different kind,
Soft Cloris with the dear Alexis joined;
When e'er the manly part of thee, would plead
Thou tempts us with the image of the maid,
While we the noblest passions do extend
The love to Hermes, Aphrodite the friend.

The language is simple but the style baroque. Behn's play with Hermes and Aphrodite, her intimation that she can pursue a boyish young woman with less embarrassment or risk than a young man, and that the erotic charge is no less real for being appropriate only toward a man, takes us about as far into the maze of human sexuality as any text of 1688. (Saikaku is more frank but much more crude; Sor Juana deeply hidden and allusive.)

Other baroque minglings of the licit and illicit, the hidden and the theatrically public are to be found, along with interesting shifts in style, in two major stories Behn published in 1688. Both stories begin by asserting in plain language a determination to tell only the verifiable facts but later shift to long and dramatic stories told by others to the narrator. Their melodramatic shifts of plot and expressions of the most violent emotions cry out for transformation into the scenes and arias of a baroque opera. The central figure in *The Fair Jilt* is a monster of feminine wiles and greed who throws herself at a handsome young priest and cries rape when he resists her, so that he almost goes to the gallows. She tempts a young servant with promises of her love until he tries to poison her younger sister so that she can gain her sister's share of their inheritance; she then persuades her husband to try to kill the sister. But Behn begins her account of this figure out of a misogynist's nightmares by describing her as a young woman "naturally amorous but extremely inconstant," loving the strongest quality of each man she met, wary of marriage because "she knew the strength of her own heart, and that it could not suffer to be confined to one man. . . ." In writing *The Fair Jilt*, one suspects, Behn was drawing not only on stories she heard during an early sojourn in Antwerp as a singularly unsuccessful spy but also on her own passions, frustrations, and resentments of society's hypocrisies and confinements.

By the 1680s Aphra Behn had survived for more than twenty years as a widow without fixed means of support in London's colorful and dissolute theatrical world. The men she fell in love with were married or unsatisfactory, and she probably did not want to settle down and put herself under the authority of one man, no matter how much comfort he could offer her. So she wrote for a living. She was good at it and added a distinctive woman's voice to the raucous chorus of Restoration melodrama, meta- phor, and bawdy. Her poem "The Disappointment," written before 1680, was an adaptation of a theme of impotence or premature ejaculation that can be traced all the way to Ovid. Her version takes the woman's part, describing her confusion, blushes, disdain, and shame as she flees her now- useless lover.

Behn's *Oroonoko: Or, The Royal Slave*, also published in 1688, is framed as an autobiographical account of events seen far across the seas, a popular genre in 1688. It draws on Behn's experiences on a brief stay in Surinam, on the north coast of South America, when she was young, but much in it almost certainly is fictional. The author is determined that her story "shall come simply into the world, recommended by its own proper merits, and natural intrigues; there being enough of reality to support it, and to render it diverting, without the addition of invention." It tells the story of the cap- ture and brutal punishment of the leaders of a group of African slaves that seek to flee the Surinam plantations. The scenes in Surinam are plain in style and often concrete in detail of places, plants, animals, and people. But the cruelty of the whites and the nobility of the slave leaders are presented in the most lurid colors possible.

The melodrama is even more dense in the first part of her little book, where Behn claims to relate her hero's story of how he came to be enslaved and transported to the Americas. Oroonoko is a prince and a great general of his people, very black, with a Roman nose, thin lips, and austere Stoic virtues. His beautiful fiancée, Imoinda, is summoned to the harem of the aged king, and there is no refusing such a summons. Her despair, Oroonoko's rage, and the turns of plot by which they finally consummate their love but then are betrayed and sold into slavery are the purest baroque theater. His speech rings out like a defiant hero's aria: "Whoever ye are that have the boldness to attempt to approach this apartment thus rudely, know that I, Prince Oroonoko, will revenge it with certain death of him that first enters. Therefore stand back, and know that this place is sacred to love, and me this night; tomorrow 'tis the king's."

In a final baroque twist, Oroonoko and Imoinda, transported across the ocean separately, are reunited and married on a plantation in Surinam. The other slaves and some of the whites recognize Oroonoko's natural nobility. The whites call him Caesar and give him many special privileges. Despite his comfortable situation and Imoinda's pregnancy, Caesar, as the author now calls him, leads a great escape of the slaves, who would head for the coast and defend themselves until they can find a ship and return to Africa. (As we have seen in Brazil and Jamaica, and as was true later, if not at this time, in Surinam, escaping slaves usually headed inland, organizing and defending themselves in remote areas.) Caesar's speech is ready to be set to music: "And why, my dear friends and fellow sufferers, should we be slaves to an unknown people? Have they vanquished us nobly in fight? Have they won us in honorable battle? And are we, by the chance of war, become their slaves? That would not anger a noble heart, this would not animate a soldier's soul. No, but we are bought and sold like apes, or monkeys, to be the sport of women, fools, and cowards, and the support of rogues, rene-gades, that have abandoned their own countries, for raping, murders, thefts, and villainies. . . .Will you, I say, suffer the lash from such hands?" The slaves all reply, "No, no, no; Caesar has spoken like a great captain, like a great king."

When the ragtag "militia" of the colony catches up with the fleeing slaves, the Africans are thrown into confusion not by superior weaponry but by the disorder of the whites and by their use of their whips to lash the slaves across the eyes. Finally only one gallant friend stands by Caesar, and Imoinda, late in her pregnancy but wielding a bow and wounding several whites. Caesar, tricked into surrender, urges the whites to kill him quickly, for he will not rest until he has killed the man who has whipped him. Still, his friends shelter him after he has been condemned to hang, and his rage for revenge grows, "pleasing his great heart with the fancied slaughter he should make all over the face of the plantation." But he and Imoinda both are determined that she should die first so that she will not be left prey to the vengeance of the whites. He will kill her himself.

All that love could say in such cases, being ended, and all the intermit-ting irresolutions being adjusted, the lovely, young, and adored victim lays herself down, before the sacrificer, while he, with a hand resolved, and a heart breaking within, gave the fatal stroke, first, cutting her throat, and then severing her, yet smiling, face from that delicate body, pregnant as it was with the fruit of tenderest love. As soon as he had done, he laid the body decently on leaves and flowers, of which he made a bed, and concealed it under the same coverlid of Nature, only her face he left yet bare to look on. But when he found she was dead, and past all retrieve, never more to bless him with her eyes, and soft language, his grief swelled up to rage; he tore, he raved, he roared, like some monster of the wood, calling on the loved name of Imoinda. A thousand times he turned the fatal knife that did the deed, toward his own heart, with a resolution to go immediately after her, but dire revenge, which now was a thousand times more fierce in his soul than before, prevents him. . . .

Caesar lies in mourning and rage near Imoinda's woodland bier for eight days. Weakened as he is, he still manages to kill one of the Englishmen who come to seize him. He is defiant to the end.

He had learned to take tobacco, and when he was assured that he should die, he desired that they would give him a pipe in his mouth, ready lighted, which they did, and the executioner came, and first cut off his members, and threw them in the fire. After that, with an ill-favored knife, they cut his ears, and his nose, and burned them; he still smoked on, as if nothing had touched him. Then they hacked off one of his arms, and still he bore up, and held his pipe. But at the cutting off the other arm, his head sunk, and his pipe dropped, and he gave up the ghost, without a groan, or a reproach. . . . Thus died this great man, worthy of a better fate, and a more sublime wit than mine to write his praise. Yet, I hope, the reputation of my pen is considerable enough to make his glorious name to survive to all ages, with that of the brave, the beautiful, and the constant Imoinda.

In 1688 Aphra Behn probably was in her late forties and not in good health. Although she was not conventionally religious, her political and aesthetic sympathies were with James II and his Catholic court. She died in 1689. In 1695 Thomas Southerne adapted *Oroonoko* for the stage, and Henry Purcell wrote incidental music for it. Her story was important for many who turned against the slave trade in the eighteenth century and for others who sought the liberation of women from convention and male domination in our own. Virginia Woolf wrote: "All women together ought to let flowers fall upon the tomb of Aphra Behn, for it was she who earned them the right to speak their minds."

CHAPTER 20

NEWTON, LOCKE, AND LEIBNIZ

To the eighteenth-century adherents of the new age of science and reason, descendants of the moderns we have discussed, the greatest hero of this new age was Isaac Newton. They saw in his work the triumph of the long struggle waged by Copernicus, Galileo, and so many others to establish a view of the cosmos founded on observation and reasoning rather than dogma and superstition. Modern students paint a more complicated picture of the very lively world of science that nurtured Newton's achievements in optics, mechanics, astronomy, and mathematics. We must still stand in awe, though, of the powers of mind and concentration that finally led to formulations—for which Newton himself had invented much of the mathematics—that remain basic to our understanding of nature. His most dramatic achievement was his synthesis of the universal law of gravitation. Here he followed his mathematical reasoning away from commonsense observations that things affect one another through direct contact toward a concept of action at a distance with which he remained uneasy and for which he could give no intuitive, commonsense explanation. After decades of vehement controversy the whole world of science eventually followed him.

The year 1688 was an extraordinary time in Newton's life. After decades of projects started and stopped, and near-paranoid reactions to mild criticisms, in 1687 he had pushed a major work through to publication. Not just major but one of the few books that have really changed how we all see the world, *Philosophiae Naturalis Principia Mathematica* (*Mathematical Principles of Natural Philosophy*). Its epochal importance was immediately proclaimed in reviews. At the same time the English political crisis had begun to bring him out of his apolitical solitude. He was on his way to being a public man for the rest of his life.

Newton was born in 1642 to a prosperous but unlettered family in a Lincolnshire village. His father died before he was born, and when he was three, his mother remarried. The boy was left with his mother's parents until the stepfather died seven years later; it is probable that this wrenching separation from his mother was one of the prime sources of his later mental instability. His mother's family, especially her clergyman brother, urged that the very bright and very strange boy get a solid education, especially after he proved to be an absentminded disaster on the farm. He made many sundials; all his life he had an accurate and attentive sense of the movements of the sun and of shadows wherever he was. In 1661 he entered Cambridge University. Little science or mathematics was taught, and he learned less from his formal studies than from the books he bought. In 1669 he was circulating essays in manuscript containing the basics of his invention of the calculus and was named Lucasian professor of mathematics at Cambridge. By 1672 he had been elected to the Royal Society and had published a paper in its *Philosophical Transactions* showing that white light was composed of many different colors, which could be differentially refracted by a prism. But his furious reaction to mild criticism by the pathbreaking physicist Robert Hooke led to his virtual withdrawal from interaction with other scientists into the study of alchemy.

For the next several years Newton copied and annotated alchemical treatises. He assumed that various old and new intellectual traditions might contribute to uncovering hidden truths, and he tended to follow one tradition at a time with monomaniacal concentration. Newton was interested in alchemy not as a quest for transmutation of "base metals" into gold but as a path to hidden truths about the principles of attraction among things. Alchemical symbols of light and the sun encouraged his speculations about an original and pure form of worship, in the Temple of Solomon and the ancient temples of Egypt and Greece, in which a flame at the center of the holy space represented the sun, "an emblem of the system of the world."

These speculations kept Newton on the trail of hidden realities that could be analyzed quantitatively. He had developed his basic quantitative explanation of planetary orbits a decade before; Hooke now mentioned his own vague hunch in that direction. Later, when Newton followed it up with mathematical rigor, Hooke accused him of plagiarism, and the old antagonism briefly threatened to derail publication of his great book. Then in 1684 Newton had a fruitful encounter with a generous colleague. Edmond Halley, hard at work on an effort to explain the orbit of a comet that had appeared in 1682, which we still call Halley's comet, came to see him. Newton said he had worked out the derivation of an elliptical orbit from his basic mathematics of orbits. Halley was astonished; this was just what he needed. He encouraged Newton to write up his calculations and in three months received a short tract, "On Motion." Newton went on expanding and refining his results, wholly absorbed, often forgetting to eat his meals. He found the full development of his ideas was "a thing of far greater difficulty than I was aware of." He formalized his three basic laws: inertia, the proportional relation between changes in motion and the force exerted and the equal and opposite reaction to every action. He had had several pieces of the law of universal gravitation for a long time, but it was only now that he brought them together in a rigorous way. Moreover, he even made his orbital calculations work for comets.

In 1686 Halley had enough manuscript in hand to propose to the Royal Society that it undertake the printing of the work. The society agreed but later insisted that Halley, who was not a rich man, be responsible for paying the printers. When Hooke claimed that Newton had plagiarized his work, Newton threatened to withdraw a key part of the work, but Halley managed to calm him down. Newton had a completed work, a publisher, and a most loyal friend; nothing could stop him now. Halley pushed on, working long hours on the details of the formidable diagrams and on the proofreading. Finally on July 5, 1687, he reported to Newton that the book was done and sent him twenty copies. As Newton walked down a street in Cambridge, a student was heard to say, "There goes the man that writt a book that neither he nor any body else understands."

The reviewers understood. Halley wrote the review for the *Philosophical Transactions*: "This incomparable author . . . has in this Treatise given a most notable instance of the extent of the powers of the Mind; and has at once shewn what are the Principles of Natural Philosophy, and so far derived from them their consequences, that he seems to have exhausted his Argument, and left little to be done by those that shall succeed him." Early in 1688 the *Acta Eruditorum* published a long and admiring summary, and the *Journal des Sçavans* called it "the most perfect mechanics one can imagine" but argued strenuously against the basic concept of action at a distance.

By then Isaac Newton was deeply embroiled in the crisis of relations between his university and James II. In 1687 the king had ordered the university to admit as Master of Arts a Benedictine monk who clearly planned to participate in university affairs. There was some resistance, and in March Newton, virtually done with his work on the *Principia*, emerged as one of its leaders. In April he played a major role in drafting the statements of eight delegates who appeared before a formidable Ecclesiastical Commission, presented the university's argument against giving the Benedictine an M.A., and surprisingly got off with nothing more than a lecture. We have almost no evidence about his life in 1688. He was suing his tenants for failure to maintain the farm he had inherited, the same farm on which he had been such a disaster early in life. In January 1688 he wrote a detailed letter about the conditions he found on the farm on a brief visit in March and April 1687. On the whole he probably was lying low, hoping the political storm would blow over, and reading his reviews.

In 1689 Newton was one of two delegates from the university to the Convention Parliament. He met Locke and many other important people. In 1690 he was named warden of the Royal Mint. He took the post seriously and helped send several counterfeiters to the gallows. He finally published his work on optics done long before, was elected president of the Royal Society, worked on improvements on the *Principia*, and got into a furious controversy with Leibniz over priority in inventing the calculus.

John Locke spent all of 1688 in Holland, most of it lodging in the house of his good friend Benjamin Furly on the Shipwrights' Harbor in Rotterdam. Furly was a prosperous Quaker merchant who had lived in Rotterdam since about 1660, when the Restoration had made England uncomfortable and often unsafe for people of his convictions. In 1688 Furly was spending some time petitioning Prince William on behalf of an Anabaptist preacher who had been hounded out of his native province by the Calvinist preachers and now was being threatened with expulsion from a town near Haarlem. For Locke, who had fled England in 1683, the Furly house was a refuge among people who shared his love of liberty and some degree of his love of books and curiosity about the world. Most important, the aging bachelor scholar found in the Furlys something like a family. Locke's letters to Furly when he was away are informal and chatty and never fail to send greetings to Mrs. Furly and to their youngest son, Arent, born in 1685. The boy's name was Dutch, and although Locke almost never wrote in the language, he used fragments of it in his greetings to the little boy: "Tell Toetje [Arent] I send this message that if he continue to be stout [Dutch for naughty] I will bring him nothing and that when I come Jantje [Jan, an older brother] shall be my friend and he no more."

Locke saved every piece of writing that came into his hands; the modern edition of his correspondence contains 105 letters from the year 1688, from Locke, to him, and a few others from and to close friends and annotated in his hand. Many of them contained praise for either the manuscript copies of his *Essay concerning Human Understanding* that were circulating among a few patrons and special friends or the printed copies of a French synopsis of the *Essay* that had just been published. Locke and his friends recognized that this long, complex book would make his reputation. They could not have suspected that it would shape Western thought for hundreds of years to come. Building on Descartes's questions about the nature and reliability of our ideas and Hobbes's first steps toward a causal account of human knowledge, Locke laid out the fundamentals of an empiricism, a unified account of the origins of our experience, that we still find plausible even when we know how to criticize it. Locke investigates perception and introspection as sources of knowledge and argues against any theory of innate ideas. He shows sensitivity to the ways our reasoning is led astray by language and an interest in how we acquire our ideas. This interest leads him to observation of infants and children and consideration of the physiology of perception. He argues against reifying concepts like "substance" that can't be readily explicated in empirical terms. In this the *Essay* was, and was rightly understood to be, a major attack on the foundations of earlier religious orthodoxies and some proofs of the existence of God. In years to come Locke, despite his own deep conviction of the moral necessity of religious belief and the possibility of demonstrating the existence of God, was drawn into vehement controversy with the guardians of orthodoxy.

In his Dutch exile in 1688 Locke's thoughts turned regularly to another work that had not yet been published and that he hoped no one was reading. In writing to the trusted relative who was hiding it for him he referred to it by the code name *De Morbo Gallico*, a nice joke. "The French disease" was a euphemism for syphilis, and Locke as a medical man might be expected to have a book about it; Locke and many others thought of royal absolutism as a French disease. The manuscript was Locke's explosive justification for resistance and rebellion against tyrants that was to be published in 1689 as *Two Treatises on Government*. Most of it had been written about 1680, and Locke made a few additions to fit the 1689 situation. It began with an extended attack on the prevailing theories of royal absolutism and went on to develop the famous theory of the state of natural equality and autonomy of men and how men "by their own consents . . . make themselves members of some politic society." Either the state of nature or that of society might turn into a state of war when one man attacks another or seeks to get him under his absolute power. "He that in the state of nature would take away the freedom that belongs to anyone in that state, must necessarily be supposed to have a design to take away everything else, that freedom being the foundation of all the rest; as he that in the state of society would take away the freedom belonging to those of that society or commonwealth, must be supposed to design to take away from them everything else, and so to be looked on as in a state of war." In a state of society private property is justified because individuals add labor to land or materials and have a right to the products of their labor. The protection of property is one of the chief goals of civil society. It is those who violate the constitutions and laws of a society who are the true rebels and must be dealt with as such. Developed to justify resistance against the absolutist policies of Charles II, updated to justify after the fact the rebellion against James II, far more radical in its implications than the moderate commitments and cautious temperament of its author, this famous work became a foundation of revolutionary thought in America and of much modern democratic thought. It was published anonymously in 1689, and although knowledge of Locke's authorship soon was fairly widespread, he acknowledged it only in his will.

Other sides of Locke appear in his correspondence with an English country squire named Edward Clarke, whose wife, Mary, was Locke's cousin. Landless, a bachelor, living in exile, Locke projected onto the Clarkes his frustrated domestic and landholding impulses, sending them saplings for their house, where some of the resulting trees survived past 1900. Early in 1688 he sent Clarke some fine Friesian sheep to improve his herd. Since 1686 Locke had been writing long letters to Clarke about the education of the latter's son. These thoughtful letters, eventually published as a book, *Some Thoughts concerning Education*, make Locke one of the founders of educational psychology as well as modern empiricism and liberalism.

On February 6, 1688, Locke wrote to Clarke, "The thing, then, that I am going to say to you is, that I would have your son learn a trade, a handicrafts trade. Will you not think now, that I have either forgot that he is your eldest son and heir, and have formerly written to you concerning his education, which all had a tendency to a gentleman's calling, with which a trade seems wholly inconsistent. I confess that so, and have not forgot either his birth or estate, or what breeding I thought suitable to it. . . ." Should the boy take up painting? No, for it will be of no benefit if he has no talent for it; "ill painting is one of the worst things in the world." Gardening and working in wood would be better, particularly since both are of immediate use to a country gentleman, in doing things for himself and in supervising his servants. "The skill should be so to employ their time of recreation that it may relax and refresh that part which has been exercised and is tired, and yet do something, which, besides the present delight and ease, may produce something which will afterwards be profitable." Finally he decides that the best trade for the boy to learn would be that of a jeweler. By working with a jeweler in Holland or another foreign country for a year or two, the boy would learn an exacting craft that can yield a good livelihood and brings the craftsman in contact with "persons of quality" and would have the experience of living abroad without the usual frivolous and dependent touring. Whatever the trade, the point is, in this and in the rest of the young man's education and life, to give him variety of activity, for "children hate to be idle. All the care then is, that their busy humor should be constantly employed in something of use to them."

In another correspondence Locke's lonely humanity takes on deeper colors. Damaris Cudworth, Lady Masham, wrote to Locke from Oates, her country house in Essex, on April 7, 1688, to comment on the French summary of the *Essay concerning Human Understanding*. She particularly took issue with Locke's opposition to any version of the theory of innate ideas. She thought Locke had exaggerated the differences between his own views and those he attacked. Proponents of innate ideas did not claim that they were "legibly writ there like the astronomical characters in an almanac; but only an active sagacity in the soul whereby something being hinted to her she runs out into a more clear and large conception; her condition being that of a sleeping musician who does not so much as dream of, or have any representation of anything musical in him, until being waked and desired to sing, somebody repeating two or three words of a song to him, he sings it all presently."

The musical metaphor, the use of the feminine for the soul, the assertion of a form of the doctrine of innate ideas all are signs of someone schooled in the tradition that called itself Platonic. Damaris Cudworth was the daughter of the Cambridge Platonist Ralph Cudworth and apparently received most of her education from her father. When she and John Locke met in 1682, she was twenty-four and he was fifty. She fell in love with him, but at first he could offer no more than friendship. By the time his ever-cautious feelings warmed, she was too disappointed and hurt to respond. They probably still had not entirely sorted out their feelings when Locke fled the country in the summer of 1683. Their letters continued in a mixture of deep and wary affection and wide-ranging intellectual discussion. But in an age when every woman was expected to marry at a fairly young age she could not be expected to wait for him forever. In 1685 she married Sir Francis Masham, a widower with nine children. In subsequent letters she had a great deal to say about the busyness and dullness of her life in the country. Near the beginning of her April 1688 letter she wrote, "You are indeed in the right to believe that I do not practice all the rules of the neighborhood, and that my kitchen and dairy do not engross all my time."

Locke returned to England in January 1689, to a pleasant degree of fame and influence as the intellectual godfather of the Glorious Revolution. The smoke and fog of London were not good for his lungs, and soon he began to take refuge at the house of Damaris and her husband in Essex. From 1691 on it was his principal residence. Damaris was with him when he died in 1704.

Gottfried Wilhelm Leibniz, philosopher, mathematician, legal scholar, historian, zealous proponent of the reunion of the Christian churches, expert on mines, coinage, and taxation, state councillor of the duke of Brunswick-Lüneburg, spent all of 1688 away from Hannover, the capital of his master. Traveling in his own coach, followed by his own baggage wagon (about half full of books, one suspects), he was pursuing information on the genealogy of the House of Brunswick-Lüneburg, information that was to lead in 1692 to its elevation to the status of electoral princes of the Holy Roman Empire. Seeking old records in cathedrals, monasteries, princely libraries, and private collections, he was able to indulge all his other interests, viewing collections of natural curiosities, discussing mining and coinage with experts, continuing his conversations and correspondences with Catholic, Lutheran, and Calvinist intellectuals sympathetic to his tireless efforts to overcome Europe's confessional schisms. In rural Bavaria the Lutheran scholar was fascinated by the alien spectacle of the scourging of a man bearing a cross in a Holy Week procession.

Reaching Vienna in May, Leibniz soon obtained access to the Imperial Library and found more important documents for his work. He renewed a cordial friendship with Cristóbal de Rojas y Spinola, Roman Catholic bishop of Vienna-Neustadt, as zealous for church reunion as he was. He also advised the Brunswick-Lüneburg envoy to the imperial court and wrote several policy proposals which he hoped to present to the emperor. He was exploring the possibility of obtaining a position there, as a court councillor, court historian and archivist, and director of an Imperial Institute of History for which he and his scholarly friends already had detailed plans. Finally late in October he was received in audience by the holy Roman emperor Leopold: "I now have experienced the day that I have wished for for many years, when I could offer my most humble devotion to Your Majesty in person."

The most unusual of Leibniz's proposals to the imperial court would have literally brought light to the capital. Leibniz's friend Johann Daniel Crafft already had obtained a concession from the court to assemble materials for the lighting of the streets of Vienna with oil lamps, but it was not clear where the oil could be found without spending a great deal of money or creating shortages for other consumers. But there were newly conquered lands in Hungary that were at the disposal of the emperor. If some of them were assigned to Crafft and his associates, rapeseed could be grown on them for oil, affording them a privileged market in the Viennese streetlighting enterprise. The land also could yield samples of other little-known vegetables and useful crops.

Leibniz is best known as the elaborator of an original metaphysical system of harmonious spiritual substances and as one of the inventors of the calculus. In the mid-1680s he made breakthroughs in both those areas, publishing articles on the basics of the calculus and writing in 1686 a "Discourse on Metaphysics" that is the first important statement of his mature philosophy. Leibniz now saw philosophy as a venture in the interpretation of human meanings that could take religious, moral, and political heritages and convictions as seriously as the rigors of mathematics, physics, and astronomy. Leibniz's metaphysics of autonomy and harmony reflected constant exchanges of opinions with learned men, his political duties, projects for economic improvement, and above all his great cause of the reunification of Christendom. For him substances had to be spiritual as well as material, capable of free will. He found in each substance some limited reflection of the autonomy and willing power of God, the immortal souls of human beings having the most of this power, inanimate objects the least. In a letter of 1686 he summarized better than at any one point in the "Discourse" the state of his thinking at this time: "I believe that every individual substance expresses the whole universe in its manner and that its following state is a consequence (though often free) of its previous state, as if there were only God and it in the world; but since all substances are a continual production of the sovereign Being, and express the same universe and the same phenomena, they agree with each other entirely, and that makes us say that the one acts on the other, because the one expresses more distinctly that the other the cause or reason of the changes, rather in the way we attribute motion to the vessel rather than to the whole of the sea." Leibniz had inherited puzzles of rationalist metaphysics and Christian theology, but in his emphasis on the autonomy of each substance, its continuity through time, and above all on the way it mirrors and *expresses* every other one, he had come to a distinctive vision. It was deeply consonant with his own fascinated affirmation of human variety and his conviction, clear in his philosophical correspondence and his efforts to reunify Christendom, that all individualities were mirrors of one another and of the one Truth.

In 1688 Leibniz was preparing for, but had not yet made, a last amazing leap in conviction that all people can understand one another. He had been drawn to the knowledge of China that was reaching Europe through the writings of missionaries since the early 1670s. Much of his early information had been filtered through learned Germans who had never been to China and whose understanding of it had at least as much to do with their search for a universal linguistic/logical key (an enthusiasm that the young Leibniz shared) as with Chinese realities. In December 1687 Leibniz had seen at Zunner's bookstore in Frankfurt a copy of the newly published *Confucius Sinarum Philosophus*, just published that year. It is not clear if he bought it; perhaps it was in that baggage wagon as he continued his travels. He noted that the earliest dates reported in the traditional Chinese chronologies seemed disturbingly close to the date of the biblical Deluge, and he remarked upon the moral and literary quality of Confucius's teachings: "He ordinarily makes use of similes. For example, he says that it is only in the winter that one learns which trees keep their greenery; and similarly all people seem the same in times of calm and happiness, but it is among dangers and disorders that one recognizes that man of merit and worth." He sought out Jesuit veterans of the China mission, corresponded with missionaries in China, and dreamed of a great "interchange of illuminations" with the Chinese.

Catholicism, Protestantism, skepticism, dogma, now even Confucianism all became in the eyes of this great man facets of reason, reflections of God. Properly understood, all could contribute, along with reformed coinage, streetlamps, taxes that did not burden the poor, even history, to harmony and prosperity under enlightened rulers. The basic values he sensed in 1687 on his first reading of Confucian texts in translation already were at the core of his own values in his "Philosophical Confession" of 1675: "It belongs then to him who loves God to be satisfied with the past and to exert himself to make the future the best possible; only he who is disposed in this direction arrives at the tranquility of spirit sought by the ascetic philosophers, at the resignation of all to God sought by the mystic theologians."

I think Leibniz would have been pleased if someone had pointed out to him how much his life in 1688 was like the life of Confucius himself: traveling, seeking the favor of princes, planning for the welfare of the common people, engaging in earnest conversation with good friends, studying history, remaining respectful of religion but a little distant from it. I think he would also have been pleased by the place he occupies in this book, reflecting, like one of his substances, so many facets of the world whose traces we are following: its Manchu and Ottoman empires, its scientific breakthroughs and largely traditional technology, its rootedness in the past and earnestness for conciliation and secular improvement, the dependence and insecurity of many of its finest thinkers, the long continuities and sudden upheavals of European dynastic politics, the individualities of voice and idiosyncrasies of life we still can trace three hundred years later.

PART VI

ISLAM AND ITS
OTHERS

"Haya 'alas Salat. . . . Haya 'alal-Falah. Allahu Akbar. La ilaha illa Allah. . . . Come to prayer. . . . Come to prayer. . . . God is Great. . . . There is no God but Allah." At first predawn light the call was heard from the minaret of the mosque, summoning the Muslim faithful to the first of five daily prayers. It was heard first in the Spice Islands and on Mindanao, then moved west with the light across Java, Sumatra, and the Malay Peninsula to the Indian subcontinent, while far to the north another sequence began in Beijing. Thence it flowed to Xi'an, to Turfan, and on through the oases of the Silk Road to join the southern stream in Persia. In Baghdad, Damascus, Cairo, Istanbul, the chants from the many mosques came from all sides, forming in the thin light an uncanny human sound that is as characteristic of Islam as the sound of bells is of Christendom. North of the Mediterranean it stopped abruptly where the Ottoman camps along the Danube faced the Christians; south of the Mediterranean it flowed on to Morocco and also south of the Sahara to the great mosques and schools of Timbuktu and the trading centers that reached down to the Atlantic along the Senegal River.

Everywhere the faithful turned toward Mecca in prayer. Everywhere they acknowledged one Prophet, one Holy Quran. Everywhere the faithful hoped to go once in their lives on the Hajj, the pilgrimage to Mecca. Islam is deeply rooted in events that took place in a particular place, in revelations made to a particular man. Those revelations were for all men, and while much of the first expansion of Islam had been warlike, its later extensions to China, Southeast Asia, and south of the Sahara had been the work not of warriors but of merchant communities settling and spreading their faith among the local people by example and teaching. In 1688 the world of Islam was politically dominated by what have been called the gunpowder empires: the Ottoman centered in Anatolia and reaching from Algeria to Bosnia to Yemen; the Safavid in Persia; and the Mughal in India. The Ottomans were locked in a long conflict with Christian Europe, in which they were losing ground, and in a stalemated struggle with Persia. The Mughals had neared the end of their advance into southern India and were grappling with the cultural and political problems of ruling the vast Hindu majority. The Hindus were not the only non-Muslims they had to worry about; the European presence in the Indian Ocean made more complications.

In the communications of their rulers, the travels of their merchants and pilgrims, and the rich mix of people in Istanbul or even more in Mecca at the time of the Hajj, the Muslims formed a vast network throughout the Old World, one of the most important connecting links of the world of 1688 and of 2000 as well.

CHAPTER 21

THE WORLD OF
THE GREAT SULTAN

"Oh Thou God Almighty! Thou Creator of Heaven and Earth! Thou who commandest all! Impenetrable is Thy Judgment! Why must Thou condemn Thy servant to die here so unexpectedly, before being able to taste fully his young life? At the very least do not deprive me of Thy Grace and Mercy in granting forgiveness for my sins, and allow me to end my life without being deprived of the True Faith." So prayed silently the seventeen-year-old Osman Agha, hands tied behind his back, facing the bared sword of a Hungarian pirate, kneeling beside the pirate's ship on the shore of the Danube on a summer day in 1688. Then aloud: "I testify: There is no god but Allah, the One and Incomparable! I testify: Muhammed is His Servant and His Prophet!"

Osman Agha's *Gavurlarin Esiri* (*Prisoner of the Unbelievers*) is one of the few autobiographies that have come down to us from the Ottoman world. The author, writing in middle life about his youthful adventures, had a vivid, almost cinematic way of recalling his experiences, what people said, the look of the roads he walked, the buildings he stayed in. We have no way of checking the details of his story, but the broad outlines fit known historical events. With him we walk the hot Hungarian plains and the forests of Croatia and sense in the anarchic violence around him a shift of power as momentous as any in the late seventeenth century.

Osman Agha was born about 1671, the son of a commander in the garrison of Temesvár, now Timişoara in western Romania. At that time it was near the northern frontier of the Ottoman Empire, which dominated all the coasts of the Black Sea, ruled all of Anatolia and Greece and all of the Fertile Crescent, and reached to Yemen, the edge of the Ethiopian highlands, Algiers, and Crete, taken from the Venetians as recently as 1669. The Ottoman Empire's golden age of military vigor and intelligent central administration had been more than a century earlier, but it still was one of the great powers of the world of 1688. Over the previous century the rising power of the Hapsburg Holy Roman Empire, much better organized than earlier Christian powers in southeastern Europe and drawing on Europe's steady stream of technical and tactical advances in the arts of war, had posed a new kind of threat that worried Turkish statesmen. In Osman Agha's childhood the Ottoman Empire still was holding its own and defending its frontiers. The Christian peasants worked their fields in peace and paid their taxes to their Turkish overlords, and his world seemed secure. Then in 1683 the Ottoman rulers thought they saw an opening in Hungarian opposition to the Hapsburgs and mounted a great campaign that threatened to take Vienna itself but then was driven off by a ramshackle coalition to which King Jan III Sobieski of Poland made one of the most important contributions. Ottoman losses, disorderly retreat, and the pursuit of Christian enemies plunged the Danube borderlands into chaos, opening the way for Christian conquests of Buda (modern Budapest) in 1685 and Belgrade in 1688, with much looting and massacre. Mounted bands of freebooters, already sometimes used by the Ottomans to supplement their regular cavalry, now found greater employment by both sides and more chances to pillage on their own in the vacuum of power. Young Osman Agha was able to buy a horse and join in some raids and fights around his hometown in these "bad times" and then managed to get, by the recommendation of a friend of his father, a commission as a junior cavalry officer at the age of fourteen or fifteen.

In June 1688 Osman Agha and his squadron were ordered to convey the pay for the garrison to the neighboring town of Lipova. They did this without incident, then decided to stay in Lipova an extra day because a fresh crop of cherries was in the markets. They still were there when Hapsburg forces besieged the town, set fire to it with artillery and mortars, and took it after four days of fierce resistance and heavy losses on the Turkish side. Osman Agha was allotted as a prisoner of war to a lieutenant, who demanded money from him. When he said he had none, the lieutenant stripped him naked and even checked his genitals to see if any was hidden there. The lieutenant then agreed to ransom him for sixty ducats; he was to go back to Temesvár to get the money as well as ransom money for one of his men who was to stay with the Austrians as a hostage.

True to his word, he stayed at home only four days, then set out with four other prisoners who had made similar deals to find their Austrian masters and pay their ransoms. Reaching the Danube, they saw a ship and sent Osman Agha to it to try to buy food. But the people on the ship were pirates, and when they learned that he was a prisoner carrying ransom money, they decided to kill him. They took him ashore so that they would not get blood all over their ship. At this point Osman Agha said his prayers, but instead of killing him the pirates took him along while they tried to catch his companions. He managed to get away and jump in a stream; his captors concluded that he had drowned and went away. Lost, naked, and hungry on a deserted plain, he again resorted to prayers, and they were answered: He found his companions again, found his master, spotted the pirate ship tied up at shore, and informed the Austrians, who with his help captured several of the pirates. Osman Agha got his money back.

Ever honest, ever credulous, he paid his ransom and allowed himself to be persuaded to accompany his master farther south into Croatia, where the master promised to give him a safe-conduct pass to cross the Sava River into Ottoman territory. But even there, with Ottoman troops right across the river, Osman Agha was talked out of leaving. He now found himself treated as a real prisoner, locked in a barn while the Austrians went off on campaign, and discovered that his master had sold him to a slave buyer from Venice. With the help of a sympathetic priest he managed to escape being sent to the Venetian galleys but still was not released. Accompanying the troops on a march to winter quarters, he pitied the sick soldiers who had diarrhea and had to get down from their wagons to relieve themselves and then hurry to catch up again. In winter Osman Agha found that bread from the commissary ovens was in desperately short supply. Since he was the only person who knew how to make unleavened bread and bake it in the ashes, he soon was able to improve his own position by making bread for the rest of the captives and their guards. But when he fell ill and lay unconscious with a high fever, his guards decided he was done for. They threw him out in the bitter cold; but the warmth from a nearby manure pile kept him alive until his fever broke, and he began to recover. He crawled to a nearby house, where several Croatian peasant families took pity on him. For three days he stayed in their communal kitchen. The

women gave him spoonfuls of the heavy bean soup that was their main sus-
tenance. He began to recover his strength. Still unable to return to
Ottoman territory, for the next eight or nine years he was employed in
Graz, at a castle, and finally in Vienna. In his memoirs he describes the
cities, the tavern brawls, the servant's life in a Vienna mansion, a journey to
Bavaria and Italy with his master, and how he avoided temptation with
Bosnian peasant girls, a chambermaid, and a young smith who had heard
about the peculiar practices of the Turks. The countess whom he served
promised him an excellent situation if he would convert to Christianity,
but he steadfastly refused. Not until the Peace of Carlowitz in 1699 did he
set out for home. He went back to his old post at Temesvár. Eventually his
long years of experience with the Austrians, his knowledge of German, and
his considerable perceptiveness and intelligence led to his employment as
an interpreter in sensitive border diplomacy and then at Istanbul, where he
served the Hapsburg ambassador. In the years of his service the Ottoman
forces did not lose all the battles, but step by step they lost territory, in a
turning of the tide he had seen at its beginning, in the raids and counter-
raids after 1683 and in the anarchy and devastation along the Danube that
he had so improbably survived in the hot summer of 1688.

The Christian traveler arriving at Istanbul by sea in the spring of 1688 was
likely to experience a jumble of contradictory impressions and emotions.
Wherever he came from around the Mediterranean he had heard stories
about the cruelty and fanaticism of the Turks and the Moors, and on his
voyage the crew had kept a sharp watch for the sails of Muslim pirates. He
might have heard a Christian preacher calling for another Crusade to liberate the Holy Places from the Muslim yoke. And here he was approaching
the capital of the Grand Turk, the most feared and powerful enemy of the
Christian faith.

It was beautiful almost beyond belief. As his ship turned into the deep,
sheltered bay called the Golden Horn, more experienced travelers pointed
out to him the walls of the magnificent Topkapi Palace, partly hidden in
groves of trees atop the southern headland. There were the domes of the
great mosques, of Süleyman, of Mehmet the Conqueror, and dozens more,
and close to the Topkapi the dome of the Aya Sofia Mosque, the former
Byzantine Hagia Sophia, its mosaics long since plastered over and replaced
by intricately inscribed passages from the Quran. Many houses were of

wood or of earth with wooden framing, gaily painted in pink, yellow, light
blue. The city had few wide avenues but was not uniformly crowded, and
there were many trees, gardens, places for a pleasant walk or ride. It also
was huge, the biggest city in Europe, with perhaps seven hundred thousand
people.

Landing on the northern, or Galata, side of the Golden Horn, across
from Istanbul proper, our visitor would feel right at home. This was the
quarter of the Latin Christians. There were several Catholic churches, one
rebuilt after a fire in 1686 but only after the French ambassador had intervened with the authorities, and many taverns. The visitor might spot an
occasional Turk, going on a business or official errand or just slumming,
noting the drunks in the gutter so characteristic of non-Muslim immoral-
ity. In Galata or anywhere in the great city our visitor, with a European's
eye for variation in skin color and facial type, would notice much variety in
the crowd and would hear of more variations that were not often seen in
the bazaars. Blond hair and blue eyes were to be seen, in slaves from the
Caucasus and the Russian frontier and in descendants of boys brought into
Ottoman society in slave levies, largely abandoned earlier in the century.
There was talk about the influential African eunuchs in the palaces. If our
visitor was French and shared his king's views on political order, he would
have found it hard to understand how Istanbul could be at all peaceful and
orderly, with all those different peoples and religions: Latin Christians,
Greeks, Armenians, Jews, and a Muslim majority that was far from uniform
in theology and practice. But it did work, for reasons deeply rooted both in
Islam and in long-established practices of Asian centers of sea or land trade.
An official hierarchy of judges enforced Islamic law for the Muslim majority, but it was normal to allow each people to practice its own religion and
to allow the headmen of each community to govern it largely by their own
laws and customs. In Istanbul the Jews, the Greeks, the Armenians, and the
Latin Christians had their own councils and their own quarters, although
residential segregation was not rigidly enforced. The Latin and Orthodox
Christians had their bishops and patriarchs, the Jews their own Grand
Rabbi. Islam accepted the Jewish prophets and Jesus as prophets, simply
insisting that Muhammad was God's last prophet and the Quran His last
Word but enjoining special respect for Jews and Christians as People of the
Book.

Taking a boat rowed by one of fifteen thousand boatmen across the
Golden Horn and making his way up into the center of the city, the visitor

would notice that the areas around the great mosques were full of special public buildings: schools with lodgings for their students, hospitals, lodgings for travelers. If he had a local guide, he would be impressed to learn that although there was no single corporate "church" structure of great wealth, many of these charitable activities, and many of the city's aqueducts and fountains, were supported by the income from perpetual endowments, derived from donations by pious individuals fulfilling one of their most basic duties as good Muslims. Most people walked, and well-to-do Turks rode horseback; they used carriages only to send their women to the baths. Away from Galata he would see no open taverns and little public drunkenness, but many coffeehouses where men gathered to socialize. These had been features of Muslim urban life for more than two hundred years, although only in recent decades had the people of London, Paris, and Amsterdam started drinking coffee. The public baths in every quarter were another distinctive and civilized feature unknown in Latin Christian cities; our visitor would have had to be a bit brave or have had good local connections to expose his uncircumcised self in order to experience one.

Shops and peddlers were everywhere. The vast central bazaars, carefully divided into zones for different kinds of goods, showed an amazing abundance and variety. Good order was maintained, and there were official prices and standards for each trade. Those who sold cooked sheep's heads must be sure they were fresh, well done, and free of wool. Slave sellers must not take the clothes off a slave and keep them as soon as the slave was sold. Watchmen patrolling the bazaars, members of various guilds, soldiers, and others all could be identified by differences in their dress and turbans. If he planned to be out after dark, our visitor would be sure to carry a lantern; if he did not, he might be arrested by the night watchmen. A frequent punishment for being out at night without a lantern was to be put to work until dawn prayers, carrying firewood for one of the public baths; it left one unkempt and dirty, an object of general derision. These night watchmen and others especially chosen in each district kept watch for fires, a major danger in a city mostly built of wood. Every house was supposed to keep a ladder and a barrel of water. There had been major fires in 1685 and 1687, and there were more, deliberately set, in the troubles of late 1687 and early 1688.

The sultan's court in Topkapi Palace, with its many gates and guards, had an air of unapproachability, but in fact the political structure was rather simple and visible. The chief administrative officer of the empire, the grand vizier, inspected the bazaars every Wednesday and approved the lists of fair prices to be charged for each kind of good. He and the other high officials then held their weekly council, *divan*. On Friday, the Muslim Sabbath, the sultan and his court and the high officials went in magnificent procession to prayers at one of the great mosques. Through the headmen of guilds and communities, the judges of Islamic and customary law, and the high officials who were seen every week in public, there was a general sense, much valued in Islamic political culture, that the ordinary man could have access to someone with authority if he had a real grievance and, if he were dissatisfied with a legal decision, could appeal it all the way to the sultan. Of course every Muslim was equal to every other in his prayers and in his reading of the Quran and the other basic sources of teaching and could and should sort out for himself the different understandings of them available in the great city. Members of various orders of dervishes, committed to lives of prayer and teaching, were conspicuous in their plain brown cloaks and tall hats. The Mevlevi dervishes, noted for their inducing of religious ecstasy by whirling dances, had four big study houses and many smaller ones in the city. Other kinds of innovative and mystical teachings also had their adherents, especially among soldiers and merchants, but there were those too who vehemently defended traditional teaching and practice.

Outside the city and especially along the Bosporus strait, the Ottoman elite enjoyed the civilized pursuit of leisure in their fine country houses and gardens. In Üsküdar, right across the Bosporus from Istanbul, where all the trade routes from Anatolia and farther east converged, there were many mosques and schools and many caravanserais, lodgings for travelers and storehouses for their goods. The quantities of grain, cattle, and sheep that arrived every day to feed the huge city were mind-boggling. Most of the food supply came by sea, from Greece, Egypt, and the region around the Black Sea. Greeks, Jews, and Armenians all were important in these large-scale trades, with Armenians probably gaining influence in the late seventeenth century.

The Ottoman Turks had come out of Central Asia into Anatolia in the 1200s, drawing together nomadic and trading peoples fleeing from the disorders of the Mongol conquests, sometimes putting their military forces at the disposal of the Byzantine emperors. In the 1300s they already were powerful in the Balkans, and although the Serbs would never forget their defeat at Kosovo in 1389, they and the Bulgarians sometimes found it possible to preserve their own societies while acknowledging Ottoman supremacy. The Ottomans gradually closed in on their onetime suzerains in Constantinople and in 1453 took the city. (Thereafter they sometimes used forms of this name but more often shortened it to Istanbul.) The formidable order the Ottomans built in Istanbul drew on Byzantine and so ultimately on Roman precedents—from bureaucratization to baths—and retained many features of a Central Asian heritage, as well as the discipline and moral seriousness of Islam. High office could be held by the descendants of foreigners as well as Turks. Like many Central Asian conquerors, the Ottomans drew levies of slaves from their subject populations. These slaves not only did much of the hard work but provided precious skills and might rise to great power in their masters' service. The Köprülü dynasty of grand viziers who dominated much of the late seventeenth century were descendants of an Albanian slave boy, the product of the last days of this system. Native-born Turks were predictably hostile to the domination of the administration by former slaves of foreign origin and thus were highly motivated to advance some of their own capable men and to perform well once in office.

Ottoman political writers of the late seventeenth century, deploring the violence and confusion of their own times, looked back to a golden age under Sultan Süleyman the Magnificent, who reigned from 1520 to 1566. Then Ottoman conquests had reached all along the south side of the Mediterranean and down the Red Sea, far into southeastern Europe, and their forces had held their own against the formidable power of Persia. Then the sultan had set out every summer from the capital at the head of a magnificent, well-organized military expedition. Then there had been much building of mosques and schools in the capital and all over the empire. Then all the systems had worked right, and everyone had known his place and done his duty. But in retrospect we might wonder if there had been such a golden age or such an early decline, and if there was trouble in the seventeenth century, as there surely was, had it been avoidable when a state so deeply rooted in conquest and military organization now had to be content with stability and prosperity?

For the Ottomans and all other large empires of early modern times, the achievement of unity and peace had paradoxical consequences. Trade flourished; population grew; people moved to the cities; prices rose. Provincial officers who were supposed to live off their land grants, like

Osman Agha's father, found their incomes inadequate. The central authorities needed professional, paid "new soldiers," called janissaries by the Europeans, to defend and control Istanbul and other growing cities. Janissaries depended on continuous employment, and when mustered out or defeated in factional warfare in the capital, they might fan provincial revolts. Provincial magnates found new sources of revenue in the growing economy and resisted attempts to recapture them for the capital. Farmers, hard pressed by the pressure of population growth, new taxes, and "tax farmers," who contracted for fixed payments of revenue to the state and kept whatever additional sums they could collect, rose in desperate revolt. If janissaries did not cause trouble in the provinces, they might settle in the capital, open shops, deepen their experience in bullying the palace, and spend their time listening to innovative or dissident Muslim teachers. In 1687 the state counted 38,131 Janissaries in Istanbul.

Mehmet Köprülü, grand vizier from 1656 to 1671, labored to restore discipline and increase revenues. With some order reestablished and some effectiveness restored to the military forces, the Ottoman forces mounted a conquest of Crete from the Venetians in 1669. Mehmet Köprülü was succeeded by a son and then a son-in-law, Kara Mustafa, who, tempted by the prospect of cooperation with Hungarian opponents of the Hapsburgs, mounted a massive expedition that besieged Vienna in 1683 but ultimately was driven off. In the anarchy of the no-man's-land of the Danube plain, evident in the adventures of Osman Agha, the imperial authorities made frantic efforts to gain control. Soldiers drawing pay were not even showing up for musters. But when new muster rolls were compiled, they objected to being listed individually, "like slaves." New efforts to tax more of the wealth of rich Muslims in the capital fared no better.

The situation deteriorated. A grand vizier was deposed, but when his successor appeared in the Hungarian garrisons, he encountered so much hostility that he fled to Belgrade. The soldiers chose a leader to present their complaints, and the sultan, needing them to turn back Christian advances near Belgrade, gave way at once. Sensing weakness, the soldiers streamed toward the capital. The sultan continued to give way, executing first the grand vizier and then his deputy. Now the leaders of the revolt targeted the sultan himself, accusing him of ignoring the problems of ruling while wasting his time in hunting and enjoying his harem. On November 8, 1687, a meeting of high officials and religious leaders in the Aya Sofia Mosque declared that Sultan Mehmet no longer was performing his duties, deposed him, and confined him to a remote part of the palace. Süleyman IV, named in his place, was thought to be relatively warlike but was unknown and totally inexperienced. Huge gifts were distributed to the rebels, and their leaders were named to high positions. Istanbul descended into a nightmare of looting and pillage, in which more and more ordinary people joined. By February 1688 the anarchy was nearly complete. The janissaries of the capital, with their own professional and commercial stakes in law and order, had resisted the chaos, but when their leader stabbed the leader of the rebels, he in turn was torn apart on the spot. Women were carried away from their homes. Several women related to the Köprülü brothers were maimed, their hands and noses cut off, and were driven naked through the streets.

On March 1, 1688, Sultan Süleyman held a meeting of the high officials and religious leaders in one of the great mosques. He called on them to join him in restoring order and in marching to defend the Danube frontier against the Christians. The elite and the janissaries rallied to him and eventually restored order. But as late as March 15, when the French ambassador's courier left to carry dispatches to Versailles, there still were new fires breaking out. In 1689 yet another Köprülü was named grand vizier and continued his relatives' efforts to remove useless troops from the rolls and get finances and administration in hand. Some see the Ottoman Empire enjoying a few decades of late prosperity and order down to about 1730. If this is correct, it may be partly because so many had stared anarchy in the face in the first weeks of 1688 and realized that there were worse things than indolent sultans and grasping officials.

In 1688 no state faced a more daunting task of frontier defense than the Ottoman Empire. A century before, one of the most dangerous of these had been the eastern border with Shia Persia, where theological enmity added a charge to the confrontation of two centralized empires. In 1688 Persia still was a rich and sophisticated country, a major producer of silk for the world market, but it seemed little interested in confronting its western neighbor. The sixteenth-century Ottoman Empire had sought to counter the Portuguese thrust into the Indian Ocean by extending its own power to the mouth of the Red Sea and occasionally sending a fleet to India. As a by-product of that effort it had controlled most of the cities and trade routes of Yemen for some decades. But Yemen, with its tough mountaineers in their high, inaccessible villages, has resisted every would-be conqueror from the Roman Empire to Nasser's Egypt, and the Ottomans were no exception. By 1688 they held only a few beleaguered outposts. Then there were the plains stretching from Poland and Hungary along the north side of the Black Sea, where the Ottomans faced fractious Christian subjects and the perpetual hostility of the rulers of Poland and Russia; they, to the great relief of the Ottoman rulers, hated each other as much as they hated the Turks. The mountains south and west of the Danube were an impossible patchwork of people speaking almost the same language, some of them good Muslims, some Turk-hating Serbs and Croats.

The Ottomans, heirs of Central Asian traditions of cavalry warfare, knew or thought they knew how to marshal their power to maintain these borders. The annual summer campaign, often commanded by the sultan himself, was a central motif of their political order. The state-subsidized pilgrimage caravans to Mecca looked and behaved like military expeditions. But the conquest of Constantinople and the eastern shore of the Mediterranean also had made the Ottomans a sea power. Their success at sea had been remarkable. They had built fleets of ships and galleys commanded by great admirals and had joined their sea and land forces to conquer Egypt, the southern shore of the Mediterranean all the way to Algeria, and Greece. The famous defeat by Spanish and Hapsburg forces at Lepanto in 1571 was a major setback, but they had revived to conquer Crete in 1669. In the late seventeenth century their organized sea power did not often reach west of Crete, but their support of Muslim redoubts as far west as Algiers formed one side of a nasty, ongoing Christian-Muslim confrontation. No one, Christian or Muslim, sailed on the Mediterranean without keeping an eye on the horizon for the sail of a ship from the other side. Christians captured by Muslims became slaves, most notoriously in Algeria. Muslims captured by Christians might wind up on the Slaves' Quay not far from the Doges' Palace in Venice. People with rich relatives, political influence, or luck, might be ransomed from slavery; of the rest, many of the men would pull an oar in a galley. Fernand Braudel, the twentieth century's great historian of the Mediterranean, writes of this as a "perpetual brawl."

In 1688 the brawl had turned into full-scale warfare in the Peloponnese. After the Christian victory at Vienna, Venice sought to carry the war to the Turks by sea. It found few allies, and thrusts by land near the Adriatic coast and landings at various points down the coast accomplished little. In 1687

Francesco Morosini, who already had won fame in the unsuccessful defense of Crete against the Turks, was placed in command of a major expedition on a large fleet of galleys. Venice was able to hire German troops and to obtain the services of French and German noble adventurers and some capable commanders. Venice's efficiency of command and logistics, backed by the massive production of arms and galleys by the Arsenal of Venice, had been a daunting force in the eastern Mediterranean for hundreds of years, but now it seemed increasingly marginal as the Atlantic powers gained strength and as Amsterdam and London replaced Venice as Europe's emporiums for Asian goods.

The Venetian expedition arrived at Piraeus, the port of Athens, on September 21, 1687. The Ottoman garrison was dug in and prepared to defend itself on the Acropolis but did not contest the Venetian advance on the city. The Venetians were told that the Turks were using the Parthenon as a storehouse for powder and ammunition and also had some of their women and children in it, relying on the thick walls and roof for safety. Big mortars were brought up. On September 26 several mortar rounds hit the Parthenon, setting off massive explosions that shook the whole city. At least two hundred people died. The fires burned for days, forcing the Ottoman garrison to surrender. But what could the Venetians do with such a large city, several miles from the harbor? Some Ottoman reinforcements had fled when confronted, but the next ones might be better trained. Already there were worrisome raids along the road from Piraeus to the city and reports of plague in the Peloponnese. The Venetians settled down for a miserable winter in Athens. In the spring of 1688 they made plans to withdraw, taking the people of Athens with them so that any returning Turks would find a deserted city. It took months to find enough shipping, and it is not clear how fully this depopulation was ever carried out.

Most of the isolated Ottoman garrisons in the Peloponnese had surrendered quickly when the Venetian fleet appeared in 1687 on its way to Athens. The one at Mistra, in the vicinity of ancient Sparta, had not. When the Ottoman soldiers finally began to seek terms of surrender, the Venetians told them they had waited too long, and unless they could pay an impossibly big ransom, all the men would be sent to the galleys. But the Athens campaign intervened, absorbing all the Venetians' attention, and it was only in January 1688 that they insisted on settling the Mistra case. When it was found that the people under guard in the citadel had not turned in all their arms, Morosini felt justified in making the terms of surrender even harsher: All the children, women, and men over fifty would be brought to Athens to be exchanged for Christian prisoners in Ottoman hands. But no such exchange had been worked out when the Venetians withdrew. The children were distributed among the ships, and the women and old people were abandoned on the nearly deserted shore at Piraeus.

The doge, the elective prince of Venice, Marc Antonio Giustiniano, died early in 1688. Morosini was elected his successor. Putting on the cap and robe of his new office, he seated himself in a special chamber on his command galley and received the homage of his officers. But the expedition had accomplished nothing. It is remembered today only for the destruction of the Parthenon and for the cruelty shown to the people of Mistra, which horrified even many Venetians.

The Ottoman presence in Algeria had been established by Muslim corsairs in the early sixteenth century, even as the main forces of the empire were preoccupied on its eastern and northern land frontiers. An Ottoman provincial capital took form at Algiers, with an appointed governor and a large garrison of janissaries, mostly recruited in the Levant. Its main business was trade up and down the south side of the Mediterranean and on the caravan routes across the Sahara. It also launched raids on Christian shipping, which produced loot, slaves for households and for the galley oars, and ransoms. European powers made treaties exempting a particular power's ships from attack in return for payments to Algiers. This business was in the hands of great independent entrepreneurs who always kept some distance from the Ottoman governors and janissaries. In 1671, with Algiers in constant turmoil from janissary factions and uprisings, the entrepreneurs revolted, made the Ottoman governor a figurehead, and elected a respected retired corsair as *dey*, "elder hero."

In the 1680s France played a leading role among the Christian powers attempting to reduce the threat of the Algiers regime to their shipping. It had a treaty with Algiers but was not living up to many of its provisions. In particular it refused to return or exchange able-bodied Muslim captives, sending back only the sick and aged. In a bit of arrogance and overreaching typical of France in these years, it provoked a war, and French ships bombarded Algiers in 1682 and in 1683, killing hundreds of people and destroying hundreds of houses. A huge mortar with an explosive projectile was especially effective. A local leader known to the Europeans as Mezzo

Morto, "half dead" in Italian, was a hostage in French hands. Sent ashore to broker a deal, he overthrew the aged dey, killed the latter's powerful son-in-law, and had himself elected dey. He then told the French that Algiers had its own uses for big cannon; if the bombardment continued, the French consul, priests who sought to arrange prisoner exchanges, and other French residents would be shot from a great cannon one by one. The French, with no forces or supplies for a landing, sailed away, leaving Algiers alone for several years. Negotiations led nowhere, and in 1687 Algiers declared war again.

On June 13–16, 1688, a substantial French fleet appeared off Algiers. The French made it clear that they had not come to negotiate and a week later began their bombardment. The French consul and four other French-men were fired from the great cannon. The French killed three hostages and floated their bodies ashore on a raft. On the twenty-fifth five more Frenchmen were fired from the cannon; the next day three more Muslim corpses were floated ashore. Early in August, with the European political situation heating up, the French fleet was ordered home. Even the courtiers at Versailles noted that the Algerians were "as obstinate as ever." English-men and others who hoped for peaceful trade and sensible dealing with the ports of northern Africa thought their efforts had been set back by at least twenty years.

CHAPTER 22

MECCA

The peak days of the great pilgrimage in 1688 fell on October 5 to 7. The pilgrims came from all the places where the Islam had taken root. It was a portable religion, but one highly focused on a single place. Mecca, set among rocky, low mountains in the stunning heat and desolation of the Arabian Peninsula, did not seem to the nonbeliever an attractive or impressive place. But Muslims wept with joy as they arrived, fulfilling one of their prime religious obligations and the dream of a lifetime.

The Prophet Muhammad (570–632 C.E.) had been a merchant. Already in his time Mecca had been a trading city and a center of pilgrimage, its people, many of them Christians and Jews, aware of tensions and changes elsewhere. Muhammad's teaching was accepted by the faithful as the purest and most complete way of submission (Islam) to the God of the Jews and Christians. The deeds performed at Mecca by Abraham at God's command had made it a sacred site, but it became supremely significant for Muslims as the site of the final revelation, recorded in the Quran, of God's way for man. Nearby was the cave where the angel Gabriel had dictated the Quran to Muhammad. As it spread, Islam might adapt to other cultures, but always with an impulse toward a purity of belief and practice that had little use for non-Islamic sources of wisdom or knowledge. A prime source of this impulse toward purity and exclusivity was the Hajj, the great pilgrimage to Mecca, where the Muslim encountered his faith in all its purity and intensity and non-Muslims were unwelcome.

At the edge of the sacred zone surrounding Mecca the pilgrims put on special clothing, exactly alike for all, a white wrapper around the middle and another over one shoulder, leaving the head and some of the torso exposed to the ferocious sun. The dress of women pilgrims covered much more but was equally austere and uniform. This was a moving demonstration of the spiritual democracy of Islam: King, rich merchant, small farmer who had saved all his life for the event all were dressed alike. They all entered the state of *ihram*, or pilgrim purity, abstaining from sexual activity and many kinds of luxury. All now hired guides so that they would go to the proper places and perform the ceremonies correctly. As they entered Mecca, they stopped to wash. Then they came to the Gate of Peace and stopped on the edge of the central Haram, or mosque courtyard, facing the modest, nearly cubical Ka'aba, which many simply called Beit Allah, the House of God. Holding up their hands toward the Ka'aba, they wept. Abraham had built the Ka'aba. Ishmael had handed him the stones. The angel Gabriel had taught Abraham the form of worship in which they now followed their guide's instructions, walking around the Ka'aba seven times and prostrating themselves twice toward it.

It had not been easy getting there. Some brought boxes and bales of goods, which they hoped to sell after the pilgrimage ceremonies were completed to finance the return trip. Most had traveled with the great caravans, supervised and subsidized by the Ottoman state, that came from Cairo and from Damascus. For many of these the experience had begun to build in intensity as they celebrated Ramadan, July 1 to 30 in 1688, in the city from which the caravan would depart. Ramadan was the month in which Muhammad had withdrawn from Mecca to a cave where he received the Word of God, the Holy Quran, from the archangel Gabriel. In Ramadan Muslims fasted from sunrise to sunset, spending much of their time in devotion and religious reading, making more charitable gifts than usual, gathering with friends after sundown to break the fast. The fasting and the reversal of day and night activities left one a bit light-headed, but purified and renewed.

About fifteen to twenty days after the end of Ramadan the Damascus and Cairo caravans set out. Each was the organizational equivalent of a military expedition, with a commander appointed by the sultan—always a high official and sometimes the governor of Damascus or Cairo himself—an escort of several hundred soldiers, and even some cannons. The financial burden on the Ottoman state was substantial, including a subsidy for the authorities at Mecca, the pay of the troops, the hire of camels provided free of charge to high dignitaries, and the sums used along the way to enlist the local Bedouin as auxiliaries or at least to buy safe passage through their areas. But the state-backed pilgrimage also represented an annual reassertion of Ottoman control over the Holy Places. The commanders inspected the cities and the shrines, gave orders for their upkeep, and could even depose the sharif, the descendant of the Prophet with general authority over the Holy Places, and install another in his place. Each expedition brought, amid the best troops and a great deal of pomp and music, a fine camel bearing the *mahmal*, a splendid litter containing a beautiful copy of the Quran and a fine carpet that would be a new covering for the tomb of the Prophet at Medina. This too was understood to be an assertion of Ottoman sovereignty in Mecca.

The pilgrims who gathered at Damascus came not only from Syria but from Istanbul, all Anatolia, the cities and steppes of Central Asia, perhaps a few from China, Iraq, and, most uneasily, Shia Iran. The Ottoman authorities, wishing to minimize contact between the Iranians and their own Shia subjects around what we call the Persian Gulf, would not let the Iranians take a more direct route. Most travelers rented their camels from brokers at rates that gave pilgrims their first taste of the limits of Muslim charity in the management of the expedition. Travelers who tried to get around the high rental rates by using their own camels would be regularly harassed en route, their animals the last to be allowed to the water holes. The huge throng, numbering perhaps twenty thousand people, had every reason to stay in good order and within sight of one another. As the caravan moved out of cultivated areas into the deserts of present-day Jordan, everyone slept lightly, listening for thieves, and scanned the horizon while on the march for a cloud of dust raised by Bedouin marauders. The Ottoman state maintained a string of forts, each with a well or cistern within it, but the sorry little bands of soldiers serving in them on rotation from the Damascus garrisons were not so much protectors as intermediaries in buying off the Bedouin and selling food and supplies to the pilgrims at extortionate markups.

We know a bit more about the Cairo caravan than the Damascus, thanks to a number of eyewitness accounts by European travelers. One of these was Joseph Pitts, an Englishman captured in the Mediterranean, enslaved and converted in Algiers, who made the trip with his master in 1685 or 1686. Pilgrims gathering in Cairo and Alexandria had come by sea from the Maghreb—Tunis, Algiers, Morocco—and the Balkans to join the large numbers from Egypt; the total was at least as large as for the Damascus caravan. In addition to its *mahmal*, this caravan had the special honor each year of bringing eight large pieces of fine cloth, embroidered with passages from the Quran, that would form a new *kiswa*, the cloth covering over the stone Ka'aba. Outside Cairo the expedition stopped to water its camels at a great pool formed by the inundation of the Nile. Then it set out, traveling mostly at night to avoid the daytime heat. At Suez some pilgrims, including the official party accompanying the *mahmal* and the *kiswa*, continued by ship to Jidda, the port for Mecca. The winds were erratic, the waters full of coral reefs; the damp heat was stunning. The alternative, which quite a few preferred, was days of camel riding across the Sinai and on to the south.

There were other pilgrim routes, less important in numbers but adding much in variety. One came up the peninsula from the mountains of Yemen. Africans made their way along the southern edge of the Sahara, from the Niger basin or even from as far away as the Senegal, to Suakin on the Red Sea, then by ship to Jidda. Those who came from the Indian Ocean had been waiting for months; their ships had had to sail from the Indian ports by March in order to catch the monsoon winds. They may have stopped to trade in Yemen and had spent their months of waiting visiting the tomb of the Prophet in Medina and other holy places and selling the goods they had brought. As soon as the joyful days of the pilgrimage ceremonies were over, they would have to head back south quickly if they wanted to catch the winds home that year. The Muslim calendar consists of twelve lunar months, so that its festivals shift through the solar calendar; there were times when the Indian Ocean pilgrims could stay and profit from the sales of their cloths and spices in the great markets after the ceremonies and then sail home. In 1688 they must have disposed of their goods earlier to local middlemen, who would get most of the profit.

Excitement built as the caravans arrived and the peak days approached. Individuals and groups hired local guides who knew where to go and just what to do at every stop. As the pilgrims neared the gate to the Great Mosque, they stopped first in areas set aside for them to wash and then left their shoes with men who would watch over them all day. Then they were at the Gate of Peace, looking out at the Haram, the sacred enclosure of the Great Mosque. Each of the small structures in the big square was of enormous importance: the small dome of the Station of Abraham, the colonnade of the well of Zamzam, the two wells of al-Safa and al-Marwa. But their eyes were fixed on the nearly cubical building of the Ka'aba, with its splendid cloth cover. Everywhere there were crowds of pilgrims, praying, running between the two wells, washing and filling containers at the well of Zamzam, but above all hurrying around and around the Ka'aba, looking for a moment of thinning in the crowd surrounding one corner so that they might approach it and kiss the Black Stone, moving in on the door six feet up one side of it where some lucky people were scrambling up a little ladder to the inner chamber, prostrating themselves toward the Ka'aba in prayer. Bosnian peasant and Malay merchant prince, blond slave from the Caucasus, and black warrior from the Niger: All were dressed alike, most weeping, often running, caught up in a frenzy of movement that often suggested the urgency of man's search for God.

Some traditions said that Adam had built the first Ka'aba and that the Black Stone from his building had been miraculously preserved on a nearby mountain during the Great Flood. All accepted that it had been built or rebuilt by Abraham when he brought Hagar and her son, Ishmael, to live at Mecca to avoid the jealousy of Sarah and Isaac. Abraham and Muhammad were seen as parallel prophets, setting out to purify a world in which most people were "associators" who worshiped the True God but also "associated" other gods with Him. Each had preached a return to a pure monotheism: "There is no God but God." God had commanded Abraham to build or rebuild the Ka'aba, to worship there by walking around it, and to summon all the people of the world to come there. Under the dome of the Station of Abraham was a stone preserving his footprint. God's instructions to Muhammad on the ceremonies of the Hajj had taken them as already well known and simply in need of fuller definition and purification, which accounts for something of their fragmented and cryptic quality. The small and unassuming room inside the Ka'aba where so many waited long hours to scramble in and say a few prayers had something of the air of a shrine to any or many gods that had been radically purified, deprived of names and images.

Abraham had left Hagar and the young Ishmael in this forlorn desert. The little boy had cried out for water. His mother rushed back and forth between two places where she heard strange noises but found no water; the running between al-Safa and al-Marwa commemorated her desperation. Then the boy had scooped at the earth and found water; this was the sacred well of Zamzam. Pilgrims drank it, contemplated the expensive purchase of a burial shroud that had been soaked in it, and certainly hoped to take a bottle or two home with them. They washed in it but were careful to wash their lower torsos only after they had first washed them in ordinary water. Joseph Pitts reported that those who drank large quantities of it were "purged" by it and their faces broke out, "and they call this the purging of their spiritual corruptions." Thirst and its relief as a metaphor for longing for God and finding Him; washing as a representation of the cleansing of sins: These are familiar themes to all Jews and Christians and all readers of the Old and New Testaments, all the People of the Book.

Pilgrims might repeat the circumambulation of the Ka'aba and other ceremonies many times in these days. Pitts, moved by their devotion even in memory after his return to England, recalled that he had heard quite a few stories of men who had led lives of violence and debauchery but then had suddenly changed, much as a Spanish swashbuckler might turn Franciscan, to spend the rest of their lives in austere "dervish" dress, reading the Quran and praying. But Pitts had kept a certain detachment even when he was in Mecca; there were great flocks of "pigeons of the Prophet," and everyone told him they never flew over the Ka'aba; but he watched and saw that they often did so.

After the ceremonies in the Haram some pilgrims might briefly abandon the state of *ihram* (pilgrim purity), but then they would return to it for the climactic ceremonies outside Mecca. On the eighth of Dhu al-Hija, October 5 in 1688, their guides led them off to the north to the town of Mina. The next day they went on to the plain surrounding the Hill of Arafat. This was the real core of the Hajj. All the many thousands of pilgrims and their guides crowded into the holy area. This was the day when God showed his mercy to repentant sinners. The pilgrims prayed without ceasing until sundown, shedding many tears and seeking mercy for all their sins and shortcomings. Pitts remembered: "It was a sight, indeed, able to pierce one's heart to behold so many thousands, in their garments of humility and mortification, with their naked heads and cheeks watered with tears, and to hear their grievous sighs and sobs, begging earnestly for the remission of their sins and promising newness of life."

After dark the pilgrims left Arafat. They spent the next three days at Mina. Here was the stone that had been cleft when God turned aside Abraham's sword as he struck to sacrifice his son—in Muslim tradition, Ishmael, not Isaac. Each day each pilgrim threw seven stones at one of a number of small pillars, symbolizing their attacks on the devil and all his minions.

Each pilgrim sacrificed a sheep, cooking some of the meat to eat and giving the rest to charity. The pilgrims now were Hajjis, and would use this title of wonderful pride and distinction for the rest of their lives. The scene became festive, with fireworks and the shooting of guns. All the new Hajjis returned to Mecca to repeat their devotions there at least once. Mecca now became a great market center, as the new Hajjis disposed of the goods they had brought to finance their trips. A great deal of silver, most of it ultimately of American origin, changed hands as pilgrims from around the Mediterranean bought spices, coffee, and Indian fabrics.

As they left Mecca for the last time, the new Hajjis walked backward out of the Haram, not turning their backs on the Ka'aba, weeping and praying. There too was the Station of Abraham, where according to one tradition, Abraham had grown as high as the highest mountain and had summoned all the earth, putting his fingers in his ears and facing the four directions in turn, calling out, "Oh you people! The pilgrimage to the ancient House is written as an obligation for you, so answer your Lord!"

The Indian Ocean pilgrim ships already were late for their return voyages to India; we do not know how many of them made it, and I suspect that some pilgrims spent another six months in Jidda or in the Yemen ports. The caravans returned to Cairo and Damascus by about the end of the year, and the new Hajjis continued on their long voyages home, to Algiers, Isfahan, and Beijing.

CHAPTER 23

HINDUS AND MUSLIMS

The twelfth century has arrived and Aurangzeb is king;
We have seen the sign of the Day of Judgment.
The orthodox leaders explain that Aurangzeb's rule is just.
Outwardly there is benevolence but in hearts there is spite.
The regulations of Aurangzeb are with the officials themselves.
They give us envelopes and keep the letters themselves.
Low people and money-lenders have become courtiers,
And in the houses of nobles are only simple soldiers.
Under Aurangzeb's rule bribery is everywhere;
Mean people have become governors, and the Islamic Judge himself is
*   called a thief.*
Young Sons of Saints have lost their social standing and respect;
Pawns have leaped to become queens.
Those who used to be nobles now have to serve these mean people.
Khayasts, Khatris, and Brahmins of the army have gained much;
Wearers of the loin-cloth, by means of iron weapons, have become an
*   estranged retinue.*
North Indian Leather-workers, Tanners, and Untouchables,
Washermen, Oil-sellers, and Gardeners—all have become rulers.
May God damn the tyrant!
In this world he is an infidel; in the next he shall be in Hell.

The author was a Sufi, a Muslim ascetic and holy man, living in Bijapur in the interior of western India. The year 1100 after the Hegira began on December 25, 1688; this alone accounts for the fixability of the date when it was written. Hinduism and Islam have confronted each other in North India for a thousand years. At first sight the two would seem to have no basis whatever for rapprochement, with Islam's uncompromising single-centeredness and rejection of imagery confronting the exuberant polytheism and visual richness of Hinduism. The rapprochement eventually had to deal with basic principles, but it also happened in the religious organizations and practices of ordinary people.

One of the most powerful developments in the last millennium of Hinduism has been the emergence of bhakti, devotionalism. This impulse—social and religious—broke with the elaborately intellectual mysticism and the ritual practices that made Brahmins the only active participants in worship. The bhakti faith called the ordinary individual worshiper to a fervent devotion to some manifestation of the great god Vishnu or Shiva. The devotees exuberantly expressed their faith in dances and in hymns whose verses were not in Sanskrit but in the vernacular language of a particular area. Bhakti cults became especially important in the regional cultures of Bijapur and other areas of central and western India south of the great river valleys. The bhakti devotee's single-minded and emotional commitment to his deity was comparable to the Muslim's devotion to God, despite the radical difference in content.

From the Muslim side the rapprochement was the work of Sufism, the mystical tradition of Islam. Sufism insists that it is orthodox, that it alone carries to its logical conclusion the radical split between devotion to God and the way of this world. It relies heavily on certain passages in the Quran, especially the report of Muhammad's own mystical voyage to heaven, and on the finding of esoteric meaning in others. Focused on the individual mystic's quest for union with God, Sufism is somewhat disdainful of other Muslims' literal-minded concentration on daily devotions and the keeping of Islamic law. Sufi teachings were brought to western India from the fourteenth century on, just as Muslim settlers and warriors were beginning to move down out of the northern river valleys and establish centers of power in Bijapur. New lines of transmission of Sufi teaching emerged as masters studied in the Arab world or Persia and then returned and as Sufis found favor at the courts of Muslim rulers. They began to compose sermons, songs, poems in the local Dakhni vernacular to guide their followers along stages of the path toward God. They developed something much like a Muslim bhakti movement, and they began to attract many Hindu devotees, who might gradually absorb their teachings and eventually become real converts to Islam. When they asserted their own closeness to God, their own mediation between their disciples and God, and when many of their most devoted disciples were women, they moved to the very limits of Islamic orthodoxy or beyond. Their tombs became centers of veneration and pilgrimage; they transmitted their spiritual powers, their devotees, their grants of land from the rulers to their sons.

Popular devotion at the tombs of the Sufis of Bijapur persists even today, but they faced increasing difficulties and then near disaster in the seventeenth century. The rulers of Bijapur swung back toward Islamic orthodoxy, antagonizing their Hindu subjects and threatening deviant Muslims. The Marathas, a new Hindu political power reacting against the growing Islamic bias of the Mughal regime, became increasingly aggressive. From the 1670s on Bijapur was in a state of anarchy, with all kinds of local people taking power where they could. In 1686 the capital of Bijapur fell to the forces of the Mughal emperor Aurangzeb, a militantly orthodox Muslim. Then in 1688 famine and bubonic plague spread across western India. For our anonymous Sufi poet, and no doubt for many others, the round number of the year was a further stimulus to thoughts of the Last Judgment.

India is a world of diverse religions, cultures, ethnic stocks. Several times in its history, political orders of amazing strength and flexibility have made it possible for most of these peoples to live within one state, and frequently side by side, in peace. One of the most brilliant of such orders was that of the Mughal Empire, founded in the early sixteenth century by Muslim invaders from the northwest (modern Afghanistan). Their Muslim religion, their refined Persian court culture, even their tall statures and relatively pale complexions distinguished them sharply from most of their subjects. Still, Hindus or Muslims might give their allegiance to the Mughal emperor and eventually be rewarded by appointment to a high military command or civil office. But the tolerant, somewhat syncretistic court culture that expressed and supported this order was unraveling in the late seventeenth century. After the death of Shah Jahan in 1658, the new emperor,

Aurangzeb, was the victor in a savage civil war against three of his brothers. By conviction a much more orthodox Muslim than many of his family, he presented himself as an Islamic champion in waging war against one of his brothers, who had proclaimed that Islam and Hinduism were essentially identical. Once firmly in power, he set out to purify the court culture of non-Islamic elements, forbidding the use of alcohol and opium and even the celebration of the Persian New Year festival. From 1669 on he ordered the destruction of some great Hindu temples, revoked land grants held by Hindu officials, and began to levy the *jizya* poll tax on non-Muslims and other discriminatory taxes. These were not the whims of one bigoted despot but part of a general trend toward orthodoxy already apparent in the previous reign. Aurangzeb frequently had the enthusiastic cooperation of his Muslim soldiers in the harassment of non-Muslims and the desecration of their temples.

The resulting growth of resistance was visible from the beginning of Aurangzeb's reign. Clumsy efforts to force the raising of a Sikh or Rajput heir as a Muslim provoked revolts that did not spread but could not be conclusively crushed. Hindus crowded around the emperor to protest the new taxes as he rode to Friday prayers in Delhi. In the hills of South India the Maratha leader Shivaji was building up an autonomous Hindu power that also had had its origins in 1658–59. Shivaji's father had pieced together a modest sphere of local power in rough hill country, not radically different from the local power of Hindu nobles under earlier Muslim rulers. In 1659 Shivaji assassinated a Muslim general who had been desecrating Hindu sacred places. He was of low-caste origin, not of the military castes that could become Hindu rulers, but in 1674 he found an ingenious Brahmin who declared that he had warrior ancestry. The Brahmin then supervised elaborate ceremonies in which Shivaji was anointed with many sacred liquids and declared a true Hindu sovereign, carrying the bows and arrows and mounted on the chariot of the god Indra.

Shivaji and his successors continued to elaborate their appeal to Hindu feelings, to the defense of cow and country against Muslim repression. They also developed a mode of warfare very different from the Mughal, which the Mughals ultimately could not crush. A Mughal campaign, like the one that brought Aurangzeb to Hyderabad in 1687–88, was a huge, slow-moving, implacable marvel of organization, including long supply trains, excellent artillery, marvelously mounted and disciplined cavalry, all the equipment to besiege a fortress if necessary, and sometimes the splendid insignia and white tents of the emperor's camp. An expensive mode of campaign, it could pay for itself only by conquering new territory from which fresh revenue could be drawn and which could be granted to imperial generals and officials. The Marathas, on the other hand, had risen as raiders, sweeping as light cavalry out of their hill forts, looting or extracting contributions from terrified local officials, then moving on. In the eighteenth century they were to build up one of the state structures that were to fight over the corpse of the Mughal Empire, but they always retained something of an atmosphere of gallop, raid, and derring-do. They were immensely destructive to the areas they raided. Shivaji died in 1680; his son Sambhaji probably was not his equal as a leader, but Maratha power continued to increase. The Mughals won many victories against them, only to find them springing back to life in another area.

Aurangzeb spent the first days of 1688 in or near the city of Hyderabad, the capital of Golconda. Then on January 25 the huge procession of the imperial court and army set out to the west. Hyderabad was a splendid, orderly, foursquare Muslim city, with a multitude of fine mosques, schools, and charitable institutions. Many but by no means all of its most distinguished and powerful residents were Muslim, often of families that had started from as far away as Persia or Afghanistan and had joined early or late in the advance of Muslim power and culture toward southern India. But the surrounding countryside was a complex realm of Hindus speaking Telugu, a non-Indo-European language, tough fighters and hardworking farmers who had toiled patiently for centuries to overcome a landscape of thin soil, erratic water supplies, and much bare granite.

Aurangzeb's stay at Hyderabad marked the consummation of a long process of growing Muslim power over a Hindu society. When the immense fortress outside Hyderabad fell to Aurangzeb's armies on October 2, 1687, it had been garrisoned by Muslim forces for more than three hundred years. But shaky Muslim domination of the Hindu population had been converted into a stable political and social order only as Muslim rulers made far-reaching concessions to the society around them. To the conquerors, more at home in the North Indian plains where Indo-European languages were spoken and where Hindus and Muslims had centuries of experience in dealing with each other, the Hindus of Golconda, varied in skin color and facial type, speaking Telugu, were as alien and obdurate as the broken-up landscape, with its narrow river valleys and low granite mountains. The mountains provided easily defended locations for fortresses like Golconda and for compact walled villages. The granite was excellent material for the many temples and their immense variety of images, especially those of the great god Shiva, threatening destruction from his third eye, dancing the creation and destruction of the universe. Hindus and Muslims hardly ever saw the interiors of each other's places of worship, but the Muslim rulers, who recognized only one supreme and unrepresentable God and viewed all portrayals of human and animal forms as usurpations of the powers of the Creator, surely knew enough to shudder at the wild profusion of the Hindu imagination, with its gods and goddesses with many arms or animal heads. Also, in many Shiva temples the holy of holies was a great stone *lingam*, the erect phallus of the god, worshiped, anointed with water or melted butter, emblem of transformation and generative power, about as far removed from Muslim singularity of devotion and sexual puritanism as any religious expression could be.

The Muslim rulers of Golconda could not rule without the cooperation of the Hindu warriors. Far-reaching concessions might be required. The terms of appointment of a Hindu headman might concede to him a large part of the revenue theoretically due to the ruler. The poll tax on non-Muslims was not collected, and the rulers frequently donated lands for the building and upkeep of Hindu temples. In turn the Telugu warriors transferred their traditional bravery and loyalty to the service of the Muslim sovereigns. The whole system, of course, rested on the backs of the lower-caste cultivators who waded in the rice paddies under the tropical sun and spent the off-season cutting stone and repairing reservoirs and irrigation channels.

For decades before 1688 all this local concession and adjustment had failed to produce political stability for the kingdom of Golconda as a whole. In 1635 the Mughal armies briefly conquered it, then withdrew, leaving a resident to make sure that a large tribute was sent annually to the northern court. In 1656 the Mughals looted Hyderabad again but accepted a confirmation of the tribute relation. In the 1670s the court was dominated by an immensely powerful and wealthy Brahmin family, and the émigré Persian administrators lost influence. Under Brahmin influence Golconda aligned itself with and subsidized the Marathas. In 1686, as the Mughal army besieged the capital of Bijapur, a letter that revealed the Golconda-Maratha connection was intercepted. The furious Aurangzeb promptly sent an army toward Hyderabad. The ruler of Golconda and his Muslim ministers tried to placate the Mughals by murdering the two leading Hindu ministers and sending their heads to Aurangzeb. A general upheaval followed in which most Hindu financial officers lost their jobs and quite a few were killed. The Mughal armies kept coming. Aurangzeb would not forgive Golconda's support of the Marathas. In January 1687 Mughal forces occupied the city of Hyderabad; the Golconda rulers and his loyal ministers retreated to a huge fortress nearby. The walls were high and strong, and the storehouses were full. The besiegers endured much misery, especially in the monsoon rains. The whole region was suffering from famine and epidemic, and the Mughal army was not spared. When they tried to plant explosives under a key portion of walls, the charge misfired, killing many of the besiegers. Finally in September 1687 a traitor let them into the great fortress.

Now the Mughal rulers settled down to practice what was, along with siegecraft and military supply, another of their specialties: surveying the administration of a conquered province that already was ruled by Muslims according to institutions roughly similar to their own and forming a regime that was more equitable, thorough, and lucrative than what had preceded it. Most of the Muslim officials of the old Golconda regime were given posts in the Mughal administration. The new rulers relied on the religion, political culture, and languages they shared with the local Muslims, who, once thoroughly assimilated and tested as Mughal administrators, would be sent to serve in other parts of the empire. One eminent general, Shaikh Nizam, who had surrendered before the final fall of the fortress, already was given a responsible command in 1688. Almost all Hindu administrators who had survived the bloodbath of late 1686 now were dismissed; even the famous Hindu pilgrimage center at Kancheepuram got a Muslim administrator. The Mughal rulers opted for a total resurvey and reassessment of all tax obligations in their new realm. The resulting quotas were higher but seldom were completely collected. It is clear that despite the Mughal will to thoroughness and system, there were many compromises with local conditions and power holders. But the revenue collected, after years of war and famine, was roughly equal to what the rulers of Golconda had collected in good years, an impressive achievement. If Aurangzeb's newest province was not as thoroughly integrated into Mughal rule as the core provinces on the North Indian plain, still he got what he most wanted from it, a steady stream of revenue to support his continuing war against the Marathas.

Three great columns of Mughal forces moved out to the west from Hyderabad in January 1688. They were plagued by shortages of food and outbreaks of disease. But they pushed on, occupying what they could and laying waste towns and villages whose rulers refused to surrender. With their usual maddening mobility, the Marathas raided right up to Hyderabad in April. Still, the Mughal columns rumbled west into Maratha country. In January 1689 Shaikh Nizam, the former Golconda general, learned that Shivaji's son and heir, Sambhaji, was lying low not far away. A quick dash by a picked force caught him off guard. He was brought to Aurangzeb's camp, blinded, tied to a camel's back and sent swaying through the camp for all to mock, and killed slowly, his limbs hacked off and thrown to the dogs. But Rajaram, his nineteen-year-old heir, and the young man's mother kept the struggle going, and from 1691 to 1698 held out against a Mughal siege of the fortress of Jinji south of Madras.

The death of Aurangzeb in 1707 was followed by another vicious succession struggle, but neither the victor nor the structure he presided over had anything like the focus and power of Aurangzeb and the imperial machine of a half century before. From the 1720s on a new autonomous Muslim dynasty based at Hyderabad joined the regional powers, including the Marathas, contending for shares of the unraveling Mughal regime. And soon Frenchmen and Englishmen were learning how to play Indian power games, and the British in Bengal were emerging as formidable contenders.

The story of the stresses on the Mughal state in 1688 should not be told entirely in terms of the great conquests and movements of armies. Much depended on the details, on the ability of the Mughals to draw into their court culture and politics the indigenous power holders of their new subjects, as they had done so well in the sixteenth century. But the difficulties were very great. For example, with the collapse of the Muslim state of Bijapur in 1686, the small kingdom of the Bedar people on its southern flank was exposed to Mughal power. Dark-skinned, classed as an outcaste hunting group in Hindu society, speaking a non-Indo-European language, relying on their own formidable martial skills and on the cohesion of their tribal organization, the Bedars had been loyal supporters of Bijapur. When a Mughal army appeared before their capital town late in 1687, the ruler, Pam Nayak, surrendered. The Mughals immediately set up a mosque in the town, making it crystal-clear that this was a Muslim conquest. Pam Nayak was brought to the splendid camp of Aurangzeb. He was to be immediately given a high command with a substantial income. Court nobles, Hindu and Muslim, all fully at home in the refined court life, were jealous. To them, Pam Nayak was a strange creature, "pot-black," deformed, of a tribe of carrion eaters. "Night has gone into mourning at being taken for his emblem. . . . Bears and pigs would have felt deeply disgraced if likened to him. . . . Even the washer of the dead was disgusted at the sight of him."

The nobles mocked him, laughed at him when he appeared for his audience before the emperor. "After attending the Court for five or six days, he suddenly set off to visit Hell." It seems that he died sometime in January 1688. Possible causes include the order of Aurangzeb, his own reaction to his humiliation, and the plague that was raging in western India.

Pam Nayak's sons were given Mughal commands and apparently remained loyal, but a nephew fled from the Mughals, fortified a hill town, and sent out mounted raiders for many miles around until 1703 or later, spreading destruction, disrupting trade, demonstrating by his survival the hollowness of Mughal claims to rule.

CHAPTER 24

ENGLISHMEN, INDIANS, AND OTHERS

Throughout the year 1688 the English East India Company was in a state of formal, declared war with the Mughal Empire. One is tempted by metaphors of a demented mongoose nipping at the leg of a war elephant, and certainly the English did not distract the emperor and his court and army from the pursuit of Sambhaji and the imposition of Mughal rule on Golconda, but a few regional officials were seriously annoyed. The English had attacked ships carrying pilgrims from the Mughal realms to Mecca. Muslim sea warriors in the Mughal service had attacked the English at Bombay. Also, early in 1688, in the waterlogged delta of Bengal, a few hundred fever-ridden Englishmen who had withdrawn from untenable positions farther inland were hanging on and hoping the political storm would blow over.

Down to the 1680s the directors in London had consistently rejected proposals to build forts and increase the company's military and political presence in Asia. But in 1681–82 the company came under the control of forces led by Sir Josiah Child, who believed that "profit and power must go hand in hand." So the directors were ready to take a forceful line when the next occasion presented itself. But no one experienced in the Indian Ocean would have grasped at their casus belli or devised the plan they sent out in 1686. Bengal was rising in importance as a source of cloth imports to Europe. The English, holding nothing but an unfortified trading post, had many disputes with the Mughal governor concerning the interpretation of the trading privileges they had been granted. But any old Asia hand knew that such matters were personal, had their ups and downs, and that force should be used judiciously, as a last resort, and with local allies firmly in place. The directors had none of this in hand in January 1686, when they dispatched ten ships with six companies of infantry to sail directly to Bengal, occupy a port, ally with the king of Arakan (now part of Myanmar), declare war on the Mughal Empire, and march on its provincial capital. It was assumed that the Mughal governor would flee from this fearsome assault and then would be agreeable to a restoration of peace and all the privileges previously granted.

By the time this fleet reached Bengal, the endless local disputes over terms of trade had reached such a pitch that the company's merchants there had been forced to withdraw from the big cities. Their leader, Job Charnock, was the first of the great "old India hands" in the history of British power in India. He had been in India for more than thirty years. He had a Hindu wife; some people said he had saved her from her husband's funeral pyre. In 1687 his band of a few hundred sickly refugees had lodged near the mouth of the Ganges but then had managed to get a tolerated foothold farther upstream, at a place called Kalikata. There they clung to life through the hot season and the monsoon rains of 1688. In November of that year the captain of a company ship insisted that they board it and join in a misconceived expedition farther east. In separate theaters of these farcical hostilities, English threats to pilgrim ships bound for Mecca and the willingness of the company to pay a stiff indemnity led to peace with the Mughal Empire in 1690. Charnock returned to Kalikata with the permission of more friendly provincial authorities and began building up a trading center there. He died in 1693. He knew the advantages of Kalikata: a high bank, a wide patch of river, not too close to the centers of Mughal power in Bengal. The English spelled its name Calcutta. Tenacious old Job Charnock was buried in its churchyard and memorialized as the founder of the great colonial city.

The farce in Bengal had little effect on the English at their oldest settlement, Fort St. George at Madras on the Coromandel (southeast) Coast of India. There, on February 3, 1688, the English ship *Moulsford* arrived from Xiamen (Amoy) on the south coast of China. Among its passengers were three Chinese sent by "the General of Emoy [Amoy], to treat with us of a mutual trade to those parts." After some inconclusive discussions with the English, the Chinese expressed a desire to go inland to "Conjeveron . . . to see a pagoda built by their ancestors" and report on it to their "King and Master." The English, anxious to build up goodwill for their trade at Xiamen, did all they could to assist them. The Chinese probably went back to Xiamen on ships that went there from Madras late in 1688, but there is no further record of them. We already have met Shi Lang, the "general" of Xiamen who had sent them to Madras, kneeling in the court of the Kangxi emperor in August 1688, being honored for his commanding role in the conquest of Taiwan for the Qing Dynasty in 1683.

Those Chinese envoys who wanted to go to "Conjeveron" to see a "pagoda built by their ancestors" were following a lead in the writings of the most famous pilgrim-traveler in all Chinese history, the Buddhist monk Xuanzang, who made an epic overland journey from China to India between 629 and 645 and brought back many important Buddhist Scriptures. Xuanzang mentions a city named Jianzhibuluo located at the point farthest south of his travels in India. Although difficult to identify, we know that any stranger arriving at Madras in the 1600s and wanting to make a pilgrimage to something sounding a little like "Kanchipulo" would have been sent off inland toward the gate towers and riotous profusion of images of the temples of "Conjeveron"—that is, Kancheepuram, still a great Hindu pilgrimage center, about fifty miles from Madras. It is not too surprising that the envoys were following a lead in a text from the seventh century; Xuanzang's *Record of Western Regions* is a famous book, some Chinese seafarers were quite well read, and there was an important Buddhist monastery at Xiamen whose monks or lay devotees may have suggested the investigation.

The last of the improbably world-encircling connections of this little story involves the governor of Fort St. George in 1688 and one of the leading instigators of English efforts to trade with China in the 1680s, Elihu Yale. Governor Yale and his brother Thomas were growing rich on private trade, some of it permitted by the company and some of it not, all of it contributing to the rise of Madras as a commercial center. Born in Connecticut, taken to England when he was two years old, Yale had kept in touch with relatives in New England and had a certain sentimental attachment to his native land. He returned from India to England in 1699, with one of the first of those Anglo-Indian fortunes that made "nabob" part of the language. Beginning in 1713, he made several gifts to a new college in Connecticut. The total value of all his gifts was about £1,162 (perhaps $100,000 at prices in 2000), comparable to John Harvard's gift to the college in Massachusetts, but not much in relation to Yale's considerable fortune. In recognition of his generosity the college was named after him. Yale University is proud of its long-standing China connections and its great distinction in scholarship on China; not many Yale people know that the connection goes back to old Elihu himself.

In the midst of all these confusions Bengal and the Coromandel Coast were emerging in the 1680s as the greatest frontiers of opportunity and growth for Europeans trading in Asia. Parisians, Londoners, Amsterdammers, and some of their country cousins acquired a whole new vocabulary and set of tastes in cloth goods. English men and women, even some seamen and ordinary workers, wore undergarments of calico. Chintzes were especially in demand among wealthy ladies in the Netherlands. Merchants hoped to have new patterns in flowered silks available every year, "for English ladies and they say the French and other Europeans will give twice as much for a new thing not seen in Europe before, though worse, than they will give for a better silk [of] the same fashion worn the former years." Words like "chintz," "calico," "muslin," and a bewildering variety of others that have not remained current down to our own times came into the English language from India, along with the great variety of goods they named. Textiles were forming a larger and larger part of the English and Dutch companies' investments in Asian goods. The year 1688 was one of plague and famine in India, and the English war with the Mughal Empire temporarily stopped the trade in Bengal. The cloth exports from India of both companies dropped off sharply; the English in 1688 exported less than one-fourth of their 1687 quantity, less than one-tenth of the peak year of the Indian cloth boom in 1684. The companies' trade in Indian textiles did not fully recover until the late 1690s but then remained strong throughout the early 1700s.

The agents of the two great companies in their Indian forts and trading posts found that their demand for textiles was welcome but scarcely essential to the survival of a sophisticated world of production and trade that had been there long before them. The weavers of western India had big markets in Central Asia—Persia, Bokhara, Samarkand—and the countries around the Red Sea. The textile industry of the Coromandel Coast exported huge quantities to Southeast Asia; Dutch access to a share in these exports was vital to their trade in the spice-producing areas. Production was intricately specialized; different groups of people occupying different niches in local caste systems grew the cotton, spun it, wove it, and dyed it. At each point merchants were involved in the transmission of the goods from each stage to the next, and frequently had to advance money to the producers before they could plant, spin, weave, or dye. The surroundings might seem primitive—everywhere in southern India weavers worked outdoors, under trees—but the quality of the best products, like the famous "flowing water" transparent muslin, was far beyond the competence of European craftsmen. Highly detailed knowledge of production procedures for certain kinds of goods was passed down through particular groups of families tied to specific places. Procedures for the fixing of vegetable dyes through a complex series of chemical treatments were triumphs of folk technology. The southern Indian weaver family with its looms in the shade of a great tree and the dyer family washing its cloth in a river especially known for the qualities of its water, feeding their goods into a vast network of trade and passing their skills on to their children, were remarkably important and effective pieces of the world of 1688.

Europeans coming by way of the Cape of Good Hope were by no means the only outsiders trading in the Indian subcontinent. From the sixteenth-century Portuguese down to our own times, the Europeans had found Armenians spread out on the land and sea trade routes of Asia. One of them, Hovhannes Joughayetsi (John of Julfa), spent 1688 in Lhasa, the largest town in Tibet. He had set out in 1682 from New Julfa outside Isfahan in Persia, the most important Armenian center outside the homeland in those times, with goods provided to him by one of the leading Armenian merchant families, the Guerak. A branch of the Guerak family is known to have lived in Venice and to have used as its personal emblem a beehive with a swarm of bees heading straight for it, perhaps alluding to the wealth that accumulated in the family's storehouses as a result of the far-flung journeys of its agents. Hovhannes was to sell his masters' goods in India and remit to them three-fourths of the profit on the transaction. Educated in the careful commercial methods taught in the special school for merchants in New Julfa, he was obliged to keep a record of his movements and transactions for his masters. His willingness to undertake such a long and hazardous voyage on such terms becomes more comprehensible when we learn that his masters did not object to his buying and selling on his own account or entering other partnerships on his own and that in every major commercial center in India he found a little colony of Armenians and an Armenian church.

Hovhannes moved from Surat to Agra and back again, buying and selling textiles and indigo in partnership with other Armenian merchants. The Armenians, who knew the country and its trade better than the Dutch and the English, could avoid some of the Indian intermediaries and buy textiles 30 percent cheaper than the English East India Company. In 1686 Hovhannes went to Bengal, bought cloth to sell in Tibet, and made the arduous trek up through Nepal, over a 15,000-foot pass, and on to Lhasa, more than 12,000 feet above sea level. There he lived for almost five years. There too he found a little colony of Armenians, some of them settled and raising families there. He traded directly with the Tibetans or with the other Armenians, some of whom regularly made an appalling journey of more than 900 miles through largely uninhabited mountain country, almost entirely above 13,000 feet, down to Xining in the Qinghai basin on the far northwest frontier of China. He entrusted to his fellow countrymen amber to be sold to the Chinese and silver to be exchanged for Chinese gold, since the price of gold in terms of silver was much lower in China than in India. Disputes among the Armenian residents of Lhasa were settled as far as possible in meetings of the little community, without recourse to the Tibetan authorities. Hovhannes mourned when they died and gave small presents on festive occasions. When another employee of the Gueraks died on February 10, 1688, he had to take charge of the dead man's goods and personal effects. On his way down through Nepal in 1693 he noted at one point, "The entire track is obliterated by flood waters; it is the road to Hell; you have to cross a hair's bridge."

Tibetan culture was steeped in "Lamaist" Buddhism, in which the basic Buddhist beliefs in reincarnation and in the spiritual powers that result from meditation became extraordinarily highly developed; the various great lamas of the monasteries were believed to be reincarnations of their predecessors, and there were endless reports, right down to our own times, of demonstrations of precognition, out-of-body travel, and other manifestations of spiritual power. In the 1680s the prestige of the Dalai Lamas, based in Lhasa, had just been brought to a high point by the "Great Fifth" Dalai Lama, supported by the military power of the Khosot Mongols and the distant approval of the Qing emperors in Beijing. The fifth Dalai Lama had died in 1682, and real power was in the hands of a regent nominally subordinate to the Khosots. The regent was keeping the death secret, claiming that the "Great Fifth" was in meditative seclusion and could not be disturbed. Not until 1696 was the secret revealed and the Sixth Dalai Lama enthroned. The huge fortress-monastery-palace of the Potala, shining with red and white plaster and ornamented with gold leaf, was nearing completion, glittering in the thin air above the town where the caravans came and went and Hovhannes visited, argued, and made deals with his fellow countrymen.

PART VII

EXILE, HOPE, AND FAMILY

Early modern hopes were not often for betterment by some abstract standard. Usually they were linked to particular people, as most hopes still are, or to places—home, in some sense. These feelings might be especially intense for people who found themselves without homelands to which they could return or where if they did return, they would be subject to foreign rulers: the Armenians, African slaves in the New World, Ming Loyalists among the Chinese in Southeast Asia. For those whom Islam calls the People of the Book—Muslims, Christians, and Jews—Jerusalem was one of the cities of hope and pilgrimage. For the Jews, the longing for Jerusalem and the awareness that they could be there but only under a foreign ruler were near the core of their sense of themselves as a Chosen People in Exile. For seventeenth-century Christians, except for the few Catholics who still dreamed Crusader dreams, Jerusalem had become less a concrete place than a symbol of special destiny and hope. Jews in exile, Englishmen facing daunting uncertainties turned to the family, sang the same psalms in their celebrations of it, passed sleepless nights, and heard voices of loss and longing.

CHAPTER 25

NEXT YEAR IN JERUSALEM

In 1688, as in every year, there were two moments in the ritual year, at
the end of the service on Yom Kippur and at the end of the Passover
Seder, when Jews turned to one another and said, "*L'shanah haba-ah
b'yerushalayim*. . . . Next year may we be in Jerusalem." One was in public,
at the end of the deep self-searchings of the Day of Atonement; the other
was around the family table, questioning the children, teaching them to
remember.

There were Jews in Jerusalem and elsewhere in the homeland they
called the Land of Israel, but for most, this ceremonial phrase was the
expression of a deep longing that was not at all likely ever to be fulfilled. In
fact the paradoxes of exile and nonfulfillment were especially deep in
Jerusalem. There, on the solemn fast of the ninth of Ab (August 5 in 1688),
Jews gathered at the Western Wall of the Temple of Solomon to commem-
orate the destruction of the temple in 586 B.C.E. and the destruction of the
Second Temple by the Romans in 70 C.E.; both were supposed to have
taken place on this date. Jerusalem in 1688 was not rigidly divided into
ethnic or religious quarters, but the most important center of Jewish residence was a bit to the west of the Western Wall, and the Jews had to make
their way through a neighborhood crowded with North African Muslims
to get there. There also were quite a few Muslim schools and pious foundations in the area, but some of these may have been shifting to use as private residences by this time. Worst of all for the Jews, the site of the temple,

above the Western Wall, was occupied by the splendid Muslim shrines of the al-Aqsa Mosque and the Dome of the Rock; Jews might be chased away if they even tried to look through the gates. Thus, even though they were in Jerusalem, it was altogether appropriate that they should mourn the destructions of the temples with a fast as strict as that of Yom Kippur, that the morning service on this day should be the only worship in the year when men did not wear their prayer shawls and tefillin (small boxes containing scriptural passages), and that everyone wept and cried in distress.

In exile, as understood by main line rabbinic Judaism, there was little prospect of a breakthrough, a radical healing and returning, within one's lifetime. Careful adherence to tradition became, as it does for many other kinds of émigrés, a prime means of remembering, of keeping faith with one's origins. For all Jews, the community, its annual round of observances, its adherence to law remained fundamental to personal and cultural survival in exile. In addition, family values and observances were somewhere near the center of what it meant to be a Jew.

In the summer of 1688 Glikl bas Judah Leib* watched with deep pleasure as her son Mordecai stood beneath the wedding canopy with the daughter of Moses ben Nathan, an eminence in the Jewish community of Hamburg. Mordecai was a fine young man and, young as he was, already a great help to his father, Haim Leib, in his business; recently he had gone with his father to Leipzig and had nursed him devotedly when he fell ill. Haim had given the bride a dowry of one thousand Reichsthalers, and Moses ben Nathan had given her three thousand Reichsthalers in Danish currency. The two families had shared wedding expenses of more than three hundred Reichsthalers, and the groom's parents had agreed to give them free room and board for two years, as was often done, especially since many Jewish couples were married quite young. Glikl had been married at the age of fourteen and had celebrated the first wedding of a child when she was twenty-six or twenty-seven. Mordecai, aged nineteen or twenty, was the fourth to be married; there were eight to go.

Glikl was the daughter of Judah Joseph or Judah Leib, a prosperous Hamburg merchant, and Beila, daughter of Nathan Melrich of Altona. Her father's treating his widowed mother-in-law "with all the honor in the world" was an important lesson in the values that remained central to her

---

*In many works referred to by the German form, Glückel of Hameln.

life. Hamburg was a major port and commercial center, a good location for a diligent and intelligent merchant, but it was not always hospitable to Jews. The Lutheran clergy were hostile, and sailors and apprentices taunted the Jews in the streets and were always looking for an excuse to attack them and plunder their houses. Nearby Altona, in the lands of the king of Denmark, was less central but more tolerant. Glikl's family and many others moved back and forth a good deal. Haim traded in gold, silver, pearls, and jewels, traveling regularly to the fairs at Leipzig and Frankfurt am Main and using reliable Jewish agents for transactions elsewhere. Glikl was a full partner in all his business decisions.

With no secure place of their own in the world of war and statecraft, Jews depended on their good names to support their commercial credit. In addition to their troubles with Christian rulers and merchants, they could be ruthless in collecting debts from each other, especially when they feared that the debtor was not a person of good character and credit. Thus it is not surprising to find Glikl much concerned with *oysher un koved*, wealth and honor. The Yiddish that was her first language is a language rooted in German, written in the Hebrew alphabet and with an abundance of borrowings from Hebrew; the appearance of two Hebrew-rooted words here expresses her seriousness about these matters. Early and good marriages were important components of wealth and honor. Most of the Jewish communities in German-speaking lands were fairly small, and a wide search might be required to find a son-in-law or daughter-in-law of good character and lineage. A kinship network in several trading centers definitely had its uses.

Haim and Glikl had not started out with much; but they were intelligent and hardworking, and their wealth and credit grew steadily. Of the fourteen children Glikl bore, twelve lived to adulthood, a far better proportion than in most noble or royal families. Then in January 1689 Haim fell as he was going to a business appointment and aggravated an old abdominal hernia or other "rupture." The doctors could do nothing. Glikl had not yet gone to her cleansing bath at the end of her menstrual period. She offered to embrace him anyway. He replied, "God forbid, my child; it will not be long before you go to your bath." But he died before she could hold him again. The doctor, leaning close to his lips, heard him whisper, "Hear, O Israel, the Lord our God, the Lord is One."

Haim had left no executors or guardians for his family. "My wife knows everything. She will do as she has always done," he said. She simply carried on his business, occasionally traveling herself but more often using trusted agents. But she still had eight children to marry off. The sense of loss and uncertainty kept her awake at night. She began to write out her recollections of her life, for the future benefit of her children. She wrote in Yiddish, but a close reading of her memoirs makes it clear that she could read German and a bit of Hebrew, although it seems that more of her knowledge of Hebrew came from what she had heard from the women's gallery of the synagogue than from her own reading. It was far from rare for seventeenth-century Jews, men and women, to leave behind ethical testaments and life recollections for their children. Glikl had a real knack for storytelling; today she might have written mysteries. I suspect one of the first full expressions she gave to this talent, as she wrote in those sleepless nights, was an involved tale of how the murders of two Jews for their money had been uncovered in 1687 because a sleepless Jewish wife happened to look out her window in the middle of the night and saw a Christian couple sneaking away with a large, heavy chest. She began her telling of this story with a double-edged quotation of Scripture: "He watching over Israel slumbers not nor sleeps."

Glikl's account of her married life occasionally gave way to anguished exclamations of how soon and suddenly it would be over: "But I, foolish one, did not know how well things were with me when 'my children were like olive trees around my table.' " If God never slept in watching over His People, her loss must be explained by her sins, as the Exile was explained by the sins of the Jews. It was not easy to reconcile this with her well-founded sense of herself as a good wife and mother, rich in wealth and honor. Once she speculated that God "had already long ago decided on my doom and affliction to punish me for my sins in relying on people." She wrote this in describing her troubles after her husband's death, when a beloved daughter made an unsuitable marriage in Berlin and soon died, and a son turned out to be such a feckless businessman that she had to pay off his debts and make him her employee.

In her widowhood she turned down a number of attractive marriage offers, which she later regretted. One by one her children were married off. Hamburg had not gotten any more comfortable for its Jews. In 1699 she accepted a proposal from the rich Hirsch Levy of Metz, where a prosperous Jewish community sometimes was able to exploit its trading connections across the frontier between France and the Holy Roman Empire. In 1700 she left Hamburg, taking her last unmarried daughter with her. She was impressed by Hirsch Levy's lavish household, but in less than two years he went bankrupt. The couple had to be helped out of their debts by their married children. Hirsch died in 1712; Glikl lived on in Metz with a married daughter until her death in 1724.

On Friday, April 2, 1688, in the small city of Colorno near Parma in northern Italy, a marriage contract was signed between Samuel Hayyim, son of Yosef Fontanella, and Stella, daughter of Zechariah Fontanella. For the Jews of southern Europe in early modern times, the marriage contract (ketubbah) was not a legalistic preliminary to a marriage but a vital feature of its consecration, to be lovingly prepared and elaborately ornamented, a celebration of the Word and of the deepest sanctities of family and community. In the Fontanella ketubbah a central inscription in Aramaic spelled out the terms of the marriage agreement. All around it, on a sheet of parchment about sixty centimeters square, were elaborate and beautiful decorations. Near the top was a crown, below it a dove carrying an olive branch. Within the outer border were two framed passages, one from Jeremiah—"The Lord named you 'verdant olive tree,' fair, with choice fruit"—and the other from the Song of Songs: "Only one is my dove, my perfect one. The only one of her mother, the delight of her who bore her." Both this outer border and the space between it and the central inscription were filled with an elaborate pattern of vines, leaves, flowers, and fruit, painted in green with a great deal of gold overlay. The Italian wish "May they be fruitful and multiply, full of vigor. May it be granted to them to see their children's children" began in large letters flanking the crown and continued above the contract text. Interspersed among the vines were the words of Psalm 128: "Thy wife shall be as the fruitful vine upon the walls of thine house, thy children like the olive branches round about thy table. The Lord thy God from out of Zion shall so bless thee, that thou shalt see Jerusalem in prosperity all thy life long. Yea, thou shalt see thy children's children, and peace shall be upon Israel." Most remarkably, all the leaves and vines of the decoration were outlined with lines of micrographic Hebrew script, the letters about one millimeter high, repeating the entire texts of Esther and the Song of Songs.

The Jews of early modern Italy did not live entirely cut off from the surrounding Christian society, and many of their ketubbot used elements from that society or from the Mediterranean's common heritage of Greek

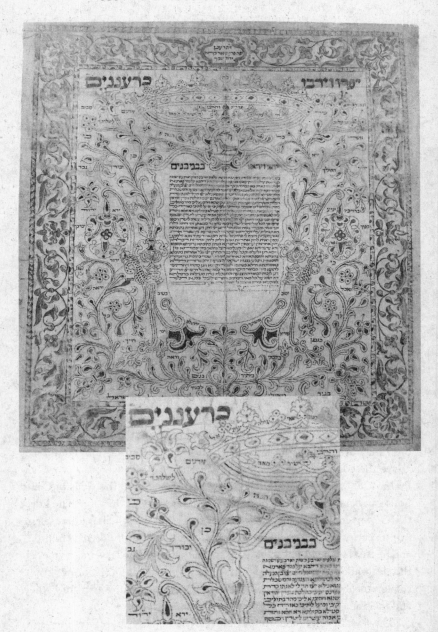

The marriage contract of Samuel Hayyim Fontanella
and Stella Fontanella, Colorno, 1688, with detail

and Roman themes. In the contract of Samuel Hayyim and Stella Fontanella, there are only a few such non-Jewish elements. The painstaking beauty of the micrographic script outlining the stems, leaves, and flowers is a distinctive Jewish art form. The tiny letters spell out a story of wifely commitment and steadfastness and a passionate love poem. Sacred text creates a fruitful world.

Who, then, were these two young people with the same last name? There were many Fontanellas in Colorno. Presumably the couple's cousin-hood was distant enough to avoid the prohibitions of Mosaic law. We know of them only because generations of descendants and collectors preserved their magnificent marriage contract, which today is in the collection of the Jewish Theological Seminary of America in New York. Only one of the couple left a personal trace in the historical record; by custom, the groom and a witness signed the marriage contract, but the bride did not sign. Another ketubbah from Colorno has been preserved, from the 1720s; the bride is Grazia, daughter of Samuel Hayyim Fontanella.

CHAPTER 26

O WELL IS THEE

Blessed are they that fear the Lord,
And walk in his ways.
For thou shalt eat the labor of thine hands;
Thy wife shall be as the fruitful vine
Upon the walls of thine house,
Thy children like the olive branches round about thy table.
The Lord thy God from out of Sion shall so bless thee,
That thou shalt see Jerusalem in prosperity all thy life long.
Yea, thou shalt see thy children's children,
And peace shall be upon Israel.

Henry Purcell, organist of Westminster Abbey and of the Chapel Royal, Composer in Ordinary to His Majesty, Keeper of the King's Wind Instruments, and harpsichordist in the King's Private Music, composed this new anthem on a text from Psalm 128 for a thanksgiving service held in the Chapel Royal on January 15, 1688. The noble text on fruitfulness and family joys was most apt for the occasion, which celebrated the queen's pregnancy. There may have been people present who feared the consequences of this pregnancy and would see a Roman Catholic prince of Wales as a threat to the peace of Israel/England. But few could have guessed that the king and queen and infant prince would have fled by the end of the year, never again in their lives to see the unattainable Jerusalem that London became for them.

The anthem opens with a noble instrumental triumph, followed by the words of the psalm, in which this public celebration of a private occasion is cast in the Mediterranean imagery that seemed completely natural to northern European Christians. The setting of "thy wife shall be as the fruit-ful vine" for the bass soloist is exceptionally moving; Purcell had in his chapel choir a fine bass named John Gostling and often outdid himself in writing for him. The anthem, less than ten minutes long, is full of minor harmonies and strange forebodings, especially in the phrase "O well is thee" for the two trebles, harmonizing on minor thirds, that separate the bass and alto passages:

Bass: Thy wife shall be as the fruitful vine upon the walls of thine house.
Trebles: O well is thee.
Alto: Thy children like the olive branches round about thy table.
Trebles: O well is thee.

At the beginning of 1688 Henry Purcell, not yet twenty-nine years old, was busy and (I suspect) worried. His wife had borne him three sons, none of whom had lived to his first birthday, and now she was pregnant again. His appointments were impressive; but James II had turned his patronage to his separate Roman Catholic chapel and its musicians, Purcell's pay as organist was a year in arrears, and "the organ at present is so out of repair that to cleanse, tune and put in good order will cost £40 and then to keep it so will cost £20 per annum at the least." This statement was part of a petition Purcell had submitted to the court in May or June 1687; he finally was paid in March 1688.

Purcell's large body of compositions exhibits an amazing range of inventiveness, technical skill, and expression. He wrote a great deal for the theater and could turn out a march or a dirge or a sailor's dance or a hero's shout of triumph. The man whose "Rejoice in the Lord Alway" seems to make "the peace of God that passeth all understanding" a simple fact also wrote jolly little rounds on the text "Kiss my arse." His theatrical music touched all the themes of his age, from the opera *Dido and Aeneas* to songs and incidental music for *The Marriage Hater Matched*, *Aureng Zebe* (Dry-den's play about the Mughal emperor Aurangzeb), Aphra Behn's *Abdelazer or the Moor's Revenge*, and Southerne's dramatization of Mrs. Behn's *Oroonoko*.

Mrs. Purcell gave birth in May 1688 to a daughter who lived to adulthood, married, and had a child of her own; two more children, one of whom lived to have children of his own, were born later. Purcell continued to compose furiously, especially for the theater, but also occasional pieces for the new monarchs just as he had for James. He died in 1695, aged only thirty-six.

Purcell, like every musician of his time, was treated as a craftsman and wrote a great deal to order for specific occasions. Genius of course frequently finds its way even when it is not treated as most of us think it should be. But for a long time I still was surprised and puzzled by the haunted melancholy that slips so naturally into the warm festivity of "Blessed are they that fear the Lord." Then I remembered the Purcells' three dead infants and one not yet born in January 1688, and listened again to the minor thirds of the young treble voices: "O well is thee."

SOURCES AND FURTHER READING

This lists the main primary sources and modern studies I have drawn on for each section. Readers also can use it as a guide to further reading on subjects they find especially intriguing.

Among general works that deal with many parts of the world of 1688, I owe a special debt to the immense and quirky erudition of Fernand Braudel's *Civilization and Capitalism: 15th–18th Century*, trans. Siân Reynolds, 3 vols. (New York, 1981). I have found exceptionally helpful two general works on European history in this period—John B. Wolf, *The Emergence of the Great Powers, 1685–1715* (New York, 1951), and John Stoye, *Europe Unfolding, 1648–1688* (London and New York, 1969)—and the theoretical approach developed in Jack A. Goldstone, *Revolution and Rebellion in the Early Modern World* (Berkeley, Los Angeles, and Oxford, 1991).

Part I. On Coronelli and his globe, see the scholarly modern edition of Vincenzo Coronelli, introduction by Helen Wallis, *Libro dei globi* (Amsterdam, 1969).

Chapter 1. The Empire of Silver. The basic account of the silver fleet system is based on C. H. Haring, *Trade and Navigation between Spain and the Indies in the Time of the Hapsburgs* (Cambridge, Mass., 1918). The most recent landmark in the large and sophisticated literature on the flows of New World silver and their effects is Michel Morineau, *Incroyables Gazettes et Fabuleux Métaux: Les Retours des Trésors Américains d'après les Gazettes Hollandaises (XVIe–XVIIIe siècles)* (Cambridge, U.K., and Paris, 1985). The tale of Doña Teresa in Potosí is from Bartolomé Arzáns de Orsúa y Vela, *História de la Villa Imperial de Potosí*, ed. Lewis Hanke and Gunnar Mendoza, 3 vols. (Providence, R.I., 1965), also included in Orsúa y Vela, *Tales of Potosí*, trans. Frances M. López-Morillas, ed. and intro. R. C. Padden (Providence, R.I., 1975). On Potosí institutions, see Jeffrey A. Cole, *The Potosi Mita, 1573–1700: Compulsory Indian Labor in the Andes* (Stanford, 1985). For the texts of poems by Sor Juana de la Cruz and a magnificent account of her life and work, see Octavio Paz, *Sor Juana* (Cambridge, U.K., 1988). On Kino, see Herbert Eugene Bolton, *Rim of Christendom: A Biography of Eusebio Francisco Kino, Pacific Coast Pioneer*, 2d ed. (Tucson, 1984), and Eusebio Francisco Kino, ed. and trans. Herbert Eugene Bolton, *Kino's Historical Memoir of Pimería Alta*, 2 vols. (Cleveland, 1919). For aspects of the Pima and the Sonora Desert setting, I draw on Donald Bahr, Juan Smith, William Smith Allison, and Julian Hayden, *The Short Swift Time of Gods on Earth: The Hohokam Chronicles* (Berkeley, Los Angeles, and London, 1994); Buford Pickens, Arthur Woodward, et al., *The Missions of Northern Sonora: A 1935 Field Documentation* (Tucson and London, 1993); and Charles W. Polzer et al., eds., *The Jesuit Missions of Northern Sonora* (New York and London, 1991). On Manila in 1688, see John E. Wills, Jr., "China's Farther Shores: Continuities and Changes in the Destination Ports of China's Foreign Trade, 1680–1690," in *Emporia, Commodities and Entrepreneurs in Asian Maritime Trade, c. 1400–1750*, ed. Roderick Ptak and Dietmar Rothermund (Stuttgart, 1992), pp. 53–77.

Chapter 2. Many Africas. For general West African background, see B. A. Ogot, ed., *UNESCO History of Africa*, vol. 5 (Berkeley, Oxford, and Paris, 1992); Richard Gray, ed., *Cambridge History of Africa*, vol. 4 (Cambridge, U.K., 1975); and John Thornton, *Africa and Africans in the Making of the Atlantic World* (Cambridge, U.K., and New York, 1992). The Western-language literature on the Portuguese and the kingdom of the Kongo is surprisingly rich. The best general account is John Thornton, *The Kingdom of Kongo: Civil War and Transition, 1641–1718* (Madison, Wis., 1983). For cultural interpretation, see Wyatt MacGaffey, *Religion and Society in Central Africa: The BaKongo of Lower Zaire* (Chicago, 1986). The documents and details on 1688 are from Levy Maria Jordão, Visconde de Paiva Manso, *História do Congo (Documentos)* (Lisbon, 1877). On Dahomey, see Robin Law, *The Slave Coast of West Africa* (Oxford and New York, 1991), and P. Roussier, ed., *L'Établissement d'Issiny, 1687–1702* (Paris, 1935). On the Senegambia, see the masterful work of Philip D. Curtin, *Economic Change in Precolonial Africa: Senegambia in the Era of the Slave Trade* (Madison, Wis., and London, 1975). For the 1680s eyewitnesses, see Chambonneau, "Relation du Sr. Chambonneau," *Bulletin de Géographie Historique et Descriptive*, vol. 2 (1898), pp. 308–21, and Thora G. Stone, "The Journey of Cornelius Hodges in Senegambia," *English Historical Review*, vol. 39 (1924), pp. 89–95.

Chapter 3. Slaves, Ships, and Frontiers. The fundamental collection of statistics on the slave trade is Philip D. Curtin, *The Atlantic Slave Trade: A Census* (Madison, Wis., and London, 1969). Controversies concerning Curtin's totals and interpretations do not affect the general points drawn from his work. A basic collection is Elizabeth Donnan, *Documents Illustrative of the History of the Slave Trade to America*, 4 vols. (Washington, D.C., 1930–35). On the Royal African Company, see Kenneth G. Davies, *The Royal African Company* (London, 1957). On the Coymans affair, see I. A. Wright, "The Coymans Asiento (1685–1689)," *Bijdragen voor Vaderlandsche Geschiedenis en Oudheidkunde*, vol. 6, part 1 (1924), pp. 23–62. For colonial Brazil, I have relied on C. R. Boxer, *The Golden Age of Brazil, 1695–1750* (Berkeley, Los Angeles, and London, 1962), and Bailey W. Diffie, with editorial assistance of Edwin J. Perkins, *A History of Colonial Brazil, 1500–1792* (Malabar,

Fla., 1987). On Palmares, see R. K. Kent, "Palmares: An African State in Brazil," *Journal of African History*, vol. 6, no. 2 (1965), pp. 161–75; and Edison Carneiro, O *Quilombo dos Palmares* (Rio de Janeiro, 1966). On Vieira, see Thomas M. Cohen, *The Fire of Tongues: Antonio Vieira and the Missionary Church in Brazil and Portugal* (Stanford, 1998), and Antonio Vieira, *Sermões*, ed. Gonçalo Alves, 15 vols. (Porto, 1945–48).

For background on the West Indies, see J. H. Parry and P. M. Sherlock, *A Short History of the West Indies*, 2d ed. (London and New York, 1968). On Worthy Park and its contexts, see Michael Craton and James Walvin, *A Jamaican Plantation: The History of Worthy Park, 1670–1970* (Toronto, 1970), and Carey Robinson, *The Fighting Maroons of Jamaica* (Kingston, Jamaica, 1969). On the Texas episode, see Robert S. Weddle, *Wilderness Manhunt: The Spanish Search for La Salle* (Austin and London, 1973), and Adolph F. A. Bandelier and Fanny R. Bandelier, comps., *Historical Documents Relating to New Mexico, Nueva Vizcaya, and Approaches Thereto, to 1773*, ed. Charles Wilson Hackett, 2 vols. (Washington, D.C., 1926). On the Caddo, see John R. Swanton, *Source Material on the History and Ethnology of the Caddo Indians* (Washington, D.C., 1942), and F. Todd Smith, *The Caddo Indians: Tribes at the Convergence of Empires, 1542–1854* (College Station, Texas, 1995).

Chapter 4. Dampier and the Aborigines. The basic text is William Dampier, *A New Voyage around the World*, intro. Sir Albert Gray and Percy G. Adams (New York, 1968). For close examination of the location of his landfall, see Leslie R. Marchant, *An Island unto Itself: William Dampier and New Holland* (Carlisle, Western Australia, 1988). On the Bardi, see the articles by Roland M. Berndt, Michael V. Robinson, and C. D. Metcalfe, in *Aborigines of the West: Their Past and Their Present*, ed. Ronald M. Berndt and Catherine H. Berndt (Perth, Australia, 1980).

Chapter 5. The Cape of Good Hope. On the Dutch and the Khoikhoi, see Richard Elphick, *Kraal and Castle: Khoikhoi and the Founding of White South Africa* (New Haven and London, 1977). On the general situation and the coming of the Huguenots, see Richard Elphick and Hermann Giliomee, eds., *The Shaping of South African Society, 1652–1820* (Cape Town, 1979) and Colin Graham Botha, *The French Refugees at the Cape* (Cape Town, 1919). The resolutions and proclamations are quoted from Suid-Afrikaanse Argiefstukke, ed., *Resolusies van de Politieke Raad*, 6 vols. (Cape Town and Johannesburg, 1957–68), vol. III.

Chapter 6. The World of Batavia. The foundation of this chapter is the 160 pages of annotated transcription of the letters of the governor-general and council in Batavia to the Gentlemen Seventeen in the Netherlands dated December 1687 to December 1688, published in W. Ph. Coolhaas, ed., *Generale Missiven van Gouverneurs-Generaal en Raden aan Heren XVII der Verenigde Oost-Indische Compagnie*, vol. 5 (The Hague, 1975). The section on Rumphius relies on G. E. Rumpf, *The Poison Tree: Selected Writings of Rumphius on the Natural History of the Indies*, ed. and trans. E. M. Beekman (Amherst, 1981), and Rumpf, *The Ambonese Curiosity Cabinet*, ed. and trans. E. M. Beekman (New Haven and London, 1999), especially Beekman's splendid short biography in the latter; that on Cornelia van

Nijenroode, on Leonard Blussé, *Strange Company: Chinese Settlers, Mestizo Women and the Dutch in VOC Batavia* (Leiden, 1988), chap. 8, and Blussé, *Bitters Bruid: Een Koloniaal Huwelijksdrama in de Gouden Eeuw* (Amsterdam, 1997). For context and additional detail on various areas, see M. C. Ricklefs, *A History of Modern Indonesia since c. 1300*, 2d ed. (Stanford, 1993); Leonard Y. Andaya, *The World of Maluku: Eastern Indonesia in the Early Modern Period* (Honolulu, 1993); and Barbara Watson Andaya, *To Live as Brothers: Southeast Sumatra in the Seventeenth and Eighteenth Centuries* (Honolulu, 1993).

Chapter 7. Phaulkon. E. W. Hutchinson, *Adventurers in Siam in the Seventeenth Century* (London, 1940), and Hutchinson, ed. and trans., *1688: Revolution in Siam: The Memoirs of Father de Bèze, S.J.* (Hong Kong, 1968). Some details also are drawn from manuscript reports of the Dutch at Ayutthaya and Melaka preserved in the Archives of the Dutch East India Company, Algemeen Rijksarchief, The Hague, VOC 1453, fol. 225v–232 and 428–436v.

Chapter 8. Tsar Peter's Russia. The basics on Moscow and Tsar Peter are drawn from Evgenii V. Anisimov, *The Reforms of Peter the Great: Progress through Coercion in Russia*, trans. and intro. John T. Alexander (Armonk, N.Y., and London, 1993), and Robert K. Massie, *Peter the Great: His Life and World* (New York, 1981). On relations with the Mongols and the Qing Empire, see Mark Mancall, *Russia and China: Their Diplomatic Relations to 1728* (Cambridge, Mass., 1971), and Morris Rossabi, *China and Inner Asia: From 1368 to the Present Day* (London and New York, 1975). On General Gordon, see Patrick Gordon, *Tagebuch des Generals Patrick Gordon*, ed. and trans. Prince M. A. Obolenski and M. C. Posselt (Moscow, 1849–51), and Gordon, *Passages from the Diary of General Patrick Gordon of Auchleuchries, A.D. 1635–1699* (Aberdeen, 1859). On the Old Believers, see Robert O. Crummey, *The Old Believers and the World of Antichrist: The Vyg Community and the Russian State, 1694–1855* (Madison, Wis., and London, 1970), and Ivan Stouchkine, *Le Suicide Collectif dans le Raskol Russe* (Paris, 1903).

Chapter 9. Survivors and Visionaries. For Wang Fuzhi, I have found especially helpful Ian McMorran, "Wang Fu-chih and the Neo-Confucian Tradition," in William Theodore de Bary et al., *The Unfolding of Neo-Confucianism* (New York, 1975), and Ian McMorran, "The Patriot and the Partisan: Wang Fu-chih's Involvement in the Politics of the Yung-li Court," in *From Ming to Ch'ing: Conquest, Region, and Continuity in Seventeenth-Century China*, ed. Jonathan D. Spence and John E. Wills, Jr. (New Haven, 1979). Passages from Wang's writings also are quoted from Wing-tsit Chan, ed. and trans., *A Source Book in Chinese Philosophy* (Princeton, 1963), and William Theodore de Bary, Wing-tsit Chan, and Burton Watson, eds., *Sources of Chinese Tradition* (New York, 1960). The 1688 poem is translated from Anon. ed., *Wang Chuanshan shiwen ji* (Beijing, 1962), p. 357. I am grateful to Mr. Sun Shaoyi for assistance with the translation. See also the chronology of Wang's life and works at the end of Anon. ed., *Wang Chuanshan xueshu taolun Ji* (Beijing, 1965). On Shitao, sometimes called Tao-chi or Daoji, there is an excellent collection of studies, including a historical introduction by Jonathan Spence and a study of the paintings by Richard Edwards, in an exhibit catalog, *The Painting of Tao-chi, 1641–ca. 1720*

(Ann Arbor, Mich., 1967). See also Ju-hsi Chou, *The Hua-yü-lu and Tao-chi's Theory of Painting* (Tempe, Ariz., 1977).

Chapter 10. At the Court of Kangxi. Basic documentation is from China First Historical Archives, ed., *Kangxi qijuzhu* (Beijing, 1985). Important insights on the life and politics of the Kangxi court can be found in Jonathan D. Spence, *Emperor of China: Self-Portrait of Kangxi* (New York, 1974), and Silas H. L. Wu, *Passage to Power: K'ang-hsi and His Heir Apparent, 1661–1722* (Cambridge, Mass., and London, 1979). Useful biographies of all the named individuals are in Arthur W. Hummel, ed., *Eminent Chinese of the Ch'ing Period* (Washington, D.C., 1944). Aspects of the water control dilemmas are discussed in Richard E. Strassberg, *The World of K'ung Shang-jen: A Man of Letters in Early Ch'ing China* (New York, 1983), pp. 117–21, 208–15.

Chapter 11. The Jesuits and China. The descriptions of the funeral of Verbiest and of Gerbillon's journey into Mongolia are based on contemporary accounts published in J. B. du Halde, S.J., *Déscription Géographique, Historique, Chronologique, et Physique de l'Empire de la Chine et de la Tartarie Chinoise,* 4 vols. (The Hague, 1736). Some details are drawn from John E. Wills, Jr.,"Some Dutch Sources on the Jesuit China Mission, 1662–1687," *Archivum Historicum Societatis Iesu,* vol. 54 (1985), pp. 267–93. On Verbiest, see John W. Witek, S.J., ed., *Ferdinand Verbiest, S.J. (1623–1688): Jesuit Missionary, Scientist, Engineer and Diplomat* (Nettetal, Germany, 1994). On the *Confucius Sinarum Philosophus,* see David E. Mungello, *Curious Land: Jesuit Accommodation and the Origins of Sinology* (Stuttgart, 1985), chap. 8. On Wu Li, see Jonathan Chaves, *Singing at the Source: Nature and God in the Poetry of the Chinese Painter Wu Li* (Honolulu, 1993).

Chapter 12. Kanazawa, Edo, Nagasaki. For excellent introductions to Tokugawa Japan, see John W. Hall, ed., James McClain, assist. ed., *The Cambridge History of Japan,* vol. 4, *Early Modern Japan* (Cambridge, U.K., and New York, 1991), and Conrad Totman, *Early Modern Japan* (Berkeley, Los Angeles, and London, 1993). On Kanazawa, see James L. McClain, *Kanazawa: A Seventeenth-Century Japanese Castle Town* (New Haven and London, 1982). For Edo, see James McClain, John M. Merriman, and Ugawa Kaoru, eds., *Edo and Paris: Urban Life and the State in Early Modern Times* (Ithaca and London, 1994). On *shunga* prints, see Richard Lane, *Images from the Floating World: The Japanese Print* (New York, 1978). Some details on *jôruri* are drawn from Donald Keene, *The Battles of Coxinga: Chikamatsu's Puppet Play, Its Background and Importance* (London, 1951). On Tokugawa Tsunayoshi, see Donald H. Shively, "Tokugawa Tsunayoshi, the Genroku Shogun," in *Personality in Japanese History,* ed. Albert M. Craig and Donald H. Shively (Berkeley, Los Angeles, and London, 1970); Harold Bolitho, "The Dog Shogun," in *Self and Biography: Essays on the Individual and Society in Asia,* ed. Wang Gungwu (Sydney, 1976); and Beatrice Bodart Bailey, "The Laws of Compassion," *Monumenta Nipponica,* vol. 40, no. 2 (Summer 1985), pp. 163–89. *Bakufu* documentation for 1688 was sampled from Kuroita Katsumi, ed., *Tokugawa jikki,* in *Shintei Zôho Kokushi Taikei* (Tokyo, 1919–35). On Nagasaki, see Wills, "China's Farther Shores," cited under chapter 1 above.

Chapter 13. *Saikaku and Bashô*. For excellent introductions to all facets of Tokugawa literature, see Donald Keene, *World within Walls: Japanese Literature of the Pre-Modern Era,
1600–1867* (New York, 1976), especially chap. 5 on Bashô and chap. 8 on Saikaku. Translations of sections from Saikaku's *The Japanese Family Storehouse* are from G. W. Sargent's
translation bearing that title (Cambridge, U.K., 1959), which also is excellent on background and interpretation. The account of Bashô and the translations rely on Bashô, *The
Narrow Road to the Deep North and Other Travel Sketches*, intro. and trans. Nobuyuki
Yuasa (Baltimore, 1966). See also the excellent chapter on Bashô in William R. LaFleur,
The Karma of Words: Buddhism and the Literary Arts in Medieval Japan (Berkeley, Los
Angeles, and London, 1983).

Chapter 14. *The Sun King and the Ladies*. My most important guides to a Versailles-centered
account of France have been Pierre Goubert, *Louis XIV and Twenty Million Frenchmen*,
trans. Anne Carter (New York, 1970), and John B. Wolf, *Louis XIV* (New York, 1968). I
also have learned from W. H. Lewis, *The Splendid Century: Life in the France of Louis XIV*
(Garden City, N.Y., 1957), and Robert Mandrou, *Louis XIV et Son Temps: 1661–1715*
(Paris, 1973). Nancy Mitford, *The Sun King: Louis XIV at Versailles* (New York, 1966), is
useful for anecdotes and illustrations. The published text of the diary of the marquis of
Dangeau is Philippe de Courcillon, marquis de Dangeau, *Journal du Marquis de Dangeau*,
ed. M. Feuillet de Conches, 19 vols. (Paris, 1854–60). See also Charlotte Haldane,
Madame de Maintenon: Uncrowned Queen of France (Indianapolis and New York, 1970);
Théophile Lavallée, *Madame de Maintenon et la Maison Royale de St.-Cyr (1686–1793)*
(Paris, 1862); Jeanne de Guyon, *La Vie de Madame Guyon Écrite par Elle-même*, ed. Ben-
jamin Sahler (Paris, 1983); Marie-Louise Gondal, *Madame Guyon (1648–1717): Un Nou-
veau Visage* (Paris, 1989); Marie-Louise Gondal, ed., *Madame Guyon: La Passion de Croire*
(Paris, 1990).

Chapter 15. *A Family Quarrel and a Glorious Revolution*. This chapter seeks to find an autodi-
dact's way through libraries of documentation and controversy. A particularly intelligent
and useful summary, including full citations of recent controversies, is Geoffrey Holmes,
The Making of a Great Power: Late Stuart and Early Georgian England, 1660–1722 (London and New York, 1993). I also have learned much from Mark Kikshlansky, *A Monarchy
Transformed: Britain 1603–1714* (London and New York, 1996), and Maurice Ashley,
James II (London, Toronto, and Melbourne, 1977). A very good summary on 1688 is John
Carswell, *The Descent on England: A Study of the English Revolution of 1688 and Its Euro-
pean Background* (New York, 1969). Of the many fine edited volumes produced around
1988, by far the most important for my purposes has been Jonathan I. Israel, ed., *The
Anglo-Dutch Moment: Essays on the Glorious Revolution and Its World Impact* (Cambridge,
U.K., and New York, 1991). The account of William's landing and march across southern
England also draws on Henri and Barbara van der Zee, *1688: Revolution in the Family: A
Royal Feud* (London, 1988). Information on Wilton House and its Van Dycks is from
tourist literature acquired on a 1994 visit. For the crisis in London, see especially Robert
Beddard, ed., *A Kingdom without a King: The Journal of the Provisional Government in the*

Revolution of 1688 (Oxford, 1988), and John Evelyn, *Diary*, ed. E. S. de Beer, 6 vols. (Oxford, 1955).

Chapter 16. Echoes across the Oceans. On Albemarle, see Estelle Frances Ward, *Christopher Monck, Duke of Albemarle* (London, 1915), and Hans Sloane, M.D., *A Voyage to the Islands Madera, Barbados, Nieves, S. Christopher, and Jamaica*, 2 vols. (London, 1707). On Increase Mather, see Robert Middlekauff, *The Mathers: Three Generations of Puritan Intellectuals, 1596–1728* (New York, 1971). I have profited from a number of biographies of William Penn, including Hans Fantel, *William Penn: Apostle of Dissent* (New York, 1974). Representative of the best current scholarship are Mary Maples Dunn, *William Penn: Politics and Conscience* (Philadelphia, 1967), and Richard S. Dunn and Mary Maples Dunn, eds., *The World of William Penn* (Philadelphia, 1986). For specifics on Penn in America, see Richard S. Dunn, Mary Maples Dunn, and Jean R. Soderlund, eds., *William Penn and the Founding of Pennsylvania, 1680–1684: A Documentary History* (Philadelphia, 1983); on relations with James II and other themes in 1688, see Vincent Buranelli, *The King and the Quaker: A Study of William Penn and James II* (Philadelphia, 1962); Joseph E. Illick, *William Penn the Politician: His Relations with the English Government* (Ithaca, 1965); and Richard S. Dunn and Mary Maples Dunn, chief eds., *The Papers of William Penn* (Philadelphia, 1986), vol. 3.

Chapter 17. A Hundred Years of Freedom. The new standard authority in English is Jonathan Israel, *The Dutch Republic: Its Rise, Greatness, and Fall, 1477–1806* (Oxford, 1995). Fascinating information and insight on Dutch culture are to be found in Simon Schama, *The Embarrassment of Riches: An Interpretation of Dutch Culture in the Golden Age* (Berkeley, Los Angeles, and London, 1988). For Joseph Penso de la Vega's book on the stock market, see M. F. J. Smith, ed., and G. J. Geers, trans., *Confusion de Confusiones de Josseph de la Vega* (The Hague, 1939), and the essay by Harm Den Boer and Jonathan I. Israel in *The Anglo-Dutch Moment*, ed. Israel. For Dutch politics in 1688 I have drawn heavily on Jonathan Israel, "The Dutch Role in the Glorious Revolution" in *The Anglo-Dutch Moment*, loc. cit. For Witsen, see J. F. Gebhard, Jr., *Het Leven van Mr. Nicolaas Cornelisz. Witsen (1641–1717)*, 2 vols. (Utrecht, 1881).

Chapter 18. In the Republic of Letters. On the idea of a Republic of Letters, see Dena Goodman, *The Republic of Letters: A Cultural History of the French Enlightenment* (Ithaca and London, 1994). The great work on Pierre Bayle is Elisabeth Labrousse, *Pierre Bayle* (The Hague, 1963–64). On the *Nouvelles*, see especially Louis-Paul Betz, *Pierre Bayle und die "Nouvelles de la République des Lettres" (Erste Populärwissenschaftliche Zeitschrift) (1684–1687)* (Zurich, 1896, repr. Geneva, 1970), and Hubert Bost, *Pierre Bayle et la Question Religieuse dans le "Nouvelles de la République des Lettres," 1684–1687* (Montpellier, 1991). On Claude Perrault, see Antoine Picon, *Claude Perrault, 1613–1688, ou, La Curiosité d'un Classique* (Paris, 1989). For the text of Charles Perrault's *Parallels*, I consulted Perrault, *Parallèles des Anciens et des Modernes*, ed. H. R. Jauss and M. Imdahl (Munich, 1964). On Valvasor, see P. von Radics, *Johann Weikhard Freiherr von Valvasor*

(Laibach [Ljubljana], 1910); Johann Weichard Valvasor, *Die Ehre des Herzogtums Krain* (Laibach [Ljubljana] and Nürnberg, 1689); facsimile edition with editorial matter by Branko Reisp (Munich, 1971); Branko Reisp, *Kranjski Polihistor Janez Vajkard Valvasor* (Ljubljana, 1983), English summary, pp. 385–417; Branko Reisp, ed., *Korespondenca Janeza Vajkarda Valvasorja Z Royal Society: The Correspondence of Janez Vajkard Valvasor with the Royal Society* (Ljubljana, 1987).

Chapter 19. *Aphra Behn*. See especially Angeline Goreau, *Reconstructing Aphra: A Social Biography of Aphra Behn* (New York, 1980), and Aphra Behn, *Oroonoko, The Rover, and Other Works*, ed. Janet Todd (London and New York, 1992).

Chapter 20. *Newton, Locke, and Leibniz*. For Newton, see Richard S. Westfall's magnificent *Never at Rest: A Biography of Isaac Newton* (Cambridge, U.K., and New York, 1980); Isaac Newton, *Sir Isaac Newton's Mathematical Principles of Natural Philosophy and His System of the World*, trans. Andrew Motte, trans. and annotated Florian Cajori (Berkeley, Los Angeles, and London, 1962); and H. W. Turnbull, ed., *The Correspondence of Isaac Newton*, 7 vols. (Cambridge, 1959–).

Students of Locke have been especially blessed with splendid editions of his letters and works. I have used especially E. S. De Beer, ed., *The Correspondence of John Locke* (Oxford, 1978), vol. 3; John Locke, *An Essay Concerning Human Understanding*, ed. Peter H. Nidditch (Oxford, 1975); and Locke, *Two Treatises of Government*, ed. Peter Laslett (Cambridge, U.K., 1960). By far the best biography is Maurice Cranston, *John Locke: A Biography* (New York, 1957). My understanding of Locke owes much to John Dunn, *Locke* (Oxford and New York, 1984), and to Laslett's introduction to the *Treatises* and takes a few points from John W. Yolton, *Locke: An Introduction* (Oxford and New York, 1985).

Coming to terms with Leibniz is intrinsically harder than for Newton or Locke, and the modern literature offers, in my experience, much less satisfactory guidance. I have found much help in R. W. Meyer, *Leibnitz and the Seventeenth-Century Revolution*, trans. J. P. Stern (Cambridge, U.K., 1952); Stuart Brown, *Leibniz* (Minneapolis, 1984); and the various essays in Centre International de Synthèse, ed., *Leibniz, 1646–1716: Aspects de l'Homme et l'Oeuvre* (Paris, 1968). For his interest in Chinese thought, see David E. Mungello, *Leibniz and Confucianism: The Search for Accord* (Honolulu, 1977), and Leibniz, *Discourse on the Natural Theology of the Chinese*, trans. Henry Rosemont and Daniel J. Cook (Honolulu, 1977). For specifics of experiences and interactions in 1688, see Leibniz, *Allgemeines Politischer und Historischer Briefwechsel*, ed. Kurt Müller and Erik Anburger, vol. 5 (Berlin, 1954).

Chapter 21. *The World of the Great Sultan*. For a very stimulating revision of our views of the seventeenth-century Muslim empires, see C. A. Bayly, *Imperial Meridian: The British Empire and the World, 1780–1830* (London and New York, 1989), chaps. 1 and 2. A roughly parallel line of revision on the Ottomans is pursued in Goldstone, *Revolution and Rebellion*, and in Rifa'at 'Ali Abou-El-Haj, *Formation of the Modern State: The Ottoman Empire, Sixteenth to Eighteenth Centuries* (Albany, N.Y., 1991). The basic authority in English is Stanford Shaw, *History of the Ottoman Empire and Modern Turkey*, vol. 1, *Empire of the Gazis: The Rise and Decline of the Ottoman Empire, 1280–1808* (Cambridge, U.K., and New York, 1976). On Osman Agha, see Osman Aga, *Der Gefangene der Giauren*, ed. and trans. Richard F. Kreutel and Otto Spies (Graz and Vienna, 1962). With the assistance of Ayse Rorlich I have checked a few points in Temesvari Osman Aga, *Gâvurlarin Esiri* (Istanbul, 1971). On Istanbul, see Robert Mantran, *Istanbul dans la Seconde Moitié du XVIIe Siècle: Essai d'Histoire Institutionelle, Économique, et Sociale* (Paris, 1962). On the crisis of 1687–88, I have drawn on Joseph von Hammer, *Geschichte des Osmanischen Reiches*, 10 vols. (Pest, 1827–35), and on synopses given me by Ayse Rorlich of Mehmed Aga Silahdar, *Silahdar Tarihi* (Istanbul, 1928). On the Venetians in Athens and the Peloponnese, see James Morton Paton, ed., *The Venetians in Athens, 1687–1688, from the Istoria of Cristoforo Ivanovich* (Cambridge, Mass., 1940); on Algiers, John B. Wolf, *The Barbary Coast: Algiers under the Turks, 1500 to 1830* (New York and London, 1979).

Chapter 22. Mecca. The best modern authority in English is F. E. Peters, *The Hajj: The Muslim Pilgrimage to Mecca and the Holy Places* (Princeton, 1994). For 1680s specifics, see Sir William Foster, ed., *The Red Sea and Adjacent Countries at the Close of the Seventeenth Century, as Described by Joseph Pitts, William Daniel, and Charles Jacques Poncet*, Works Issued by the Hakluyt Society, Second Series, No. C (Cambridge, U.K., 1949; reprint, Liechtenstein, 1967).

Chapter 23. Hindus and Muslims. Excellent recent summaries of political structures and changes are two volumes in *The New Cambridge History of India* (Cambridge, U.K., and New York, 1993): John F. Richards, *The Mughal Empire*, and Stewart Gordon, *The Marathas, 1600–1800*. For the Sufi of Bijapur, his poem, and his contexts, see Richard M. Eaton, *Sufis of Bijapur, 1300–1700: Social Roles of Sufis in Medieval India* (Princeton, 1978). On the Mughal conquest of Golconda, see J. F. Richards, *Mughal Administration in Golconda* (Oxford, 1975). For narrative detail, see also Jadunath Sarkar, *History of Aurangzib*, 2d ed., 5 vols. (Calcutta, 1930), and Niccolo Manucci, *Storia do Mogor, or Mogul India, 1653–1708*, trans. William Irvine, 4 vols. (New Delhi, 1981). On the Pam Nayak episode and its contexts, see J. F. Richards, "The Imperial Crisis in the Deccan," *Journal of Asian Studies*, vol. 35, no. 2 (February 1976), pp. 237–56, and the sources cited there.

Chapter 24. Englishmen, Indians, and Others. The best general accounts of the English East India Company are in Holden Furber, *Rival Empires of Trade in the Orient, 1600–1800* (Minneapolis, 1976), and K. N. Chaudhuri, *The Trading World of Asia and the English East India Company, 1660–1760* (Cambridge, U.K., and New York, 1978). On the conflict with the Mughals, see also William W. Hunter, *A History of British India* (reprint, New York, 1966). Basic documentation on Madras is from *Records of Fort St. George: Diary and Consultation Book*, 86 vols. (Madras, 1894). On Elihu Yale, see Hiram Bingham, *Elihu Yale* (New York, 1939). On textile production and trades, see especially K. N. Chaudhuri, and John E. Wills, Jr., "European Consumption and Asian Production in the Seventeenth and Eighteenth Centuries," in *Consumption and the World of Goods*, ed. John Brewer and Roy

Porter (London and New York, 1993), pp. 133–47. On Hovhannes Youghayetsi and the Armenians in Asia, see Philip D. Curtin, *Cross-Cultural Trade in World History* (Cambridge, U.K., and New York, 1984), chap. 9; Michel Aghassian and Kéram Kévonian, "Armenian Trade in the Indian Ocean in the Seventeenth and Eighteenth Centuries," in *Asian Merchants and Businessmen in the Indian Ocean and the China Sea*, ed. Denys Lombard and Jean Aubin (New Delhi, 2000); Lvon Khachikian, "The Ledger of the Merchant Hovhannes Joughayetsi," *Journal of the Asiatic Society* (Calcutta), vol. 8, no. 3 (1966); and Lvon Khachikian, "Le Registre d'un Marchand Arménien en Perse, en Inde, et au Tibet (1682–1693)," *Annales: Économies, Sociétés, Civilisations*, vol. 22, part 1 (January–June 1967). The text has been published: L. S. Khachikian and H. D. Papazian, eds., *Hovhannes Ter-Davtian Jughaietsu Hashvetumare* (Erevan, Armenia, 1984). Richard Hovanissian tells me it would be a dissertation-length project to translate and annotate this difficult text.

Chapter 25. Next Year in Jerusalem. For Jerusalem, see F. E. Peters, *Jerusalem: The Holy City in the Eyes of Chroniclers, Visitors, Pilgrims, and Prophets from the Days of Abraham to the Beginnings of Modern Times* (Princeton, 1985). On Glikl bas Judah Leib, see Natalie Zemon Davis, *Women on the Margins: Three Seventeenth-Century Lives* (Cambridge, Mass., and London, 1995). The best translation of her autobiography is by Beth-Zion Abrahams, *The Life of Glückel of Hameln, 1646–1724, Written by Herself* (London, 1962, and New York, 1963). For information on the Colorno ketubbah, I am indebted to Professor Shalom Sabar of the Hebrew University in Jerusalem, who is the major authority on this art form; see Shalom Sabar, *Ketubbah: Jewish Marriage Contracts in the Hebrew Union College Skirball Museum and Klau Library* (Philadelphia, 1990). I am deeply grateful to the Library of the Jewish Theological Seminary in New York for allowing me to see and reproduce this treasure.

Chapter 26. O Well Is Thee. For Purcell, I have drawn on J. A. Westrup, *Purcell* (London and New York, 1965); Westrup's article on Purcell in *The New Grove Dictionary of Music and Musicians*, 20 vols. (Washington, D.C., 1980); and Franklin B. Zimmerman, *Henry Purcell: An Analytical Catalogue of His Music* (London and New York, 1963). I am especially grateful to Joseph Styles for finding for me the magnificent recording of the anthem "Blessed Are They That Fear the Lord" by the Choir of King's College, Cambridge University, the Philip Jones Brass Ensemble, and the Academy of St. Martin-in-the-Fields, conducted by Philip Ledger, Angel S-37282.

CREDITS

Text:

for permission to reprint copyright materials:

Reprinted by permission of the publisher from *Sor Juana or, The Traps of Faith* by Octavio Paz, translated by Margaret Sayers Peden, Cambridge, Mass.: The Belknap Press of Harvard University Press. Copyright © 1988 by the President and Fellows of Harvard College.

From Bartolomé Arzáns de Orsúa y Vela, *Tales of Potosí*, Brown University Press, 1975. Reprinted with the consent of Brown University.

From William Dampier, *A New Voyage Round the World*, Dover Publications, 1968. Reprinted with the consent of Dover Publications.

From *Singing at the Source: Nature and God in the Poetry of the Chinese Painter Wu Li*, by Jonathan Chaves, University of Hawaii Press, 1993. Reprinted with the consent of the University of Hawaii Press.

From *The Narrow Road to the Deep North* by Matsuo Bashô, translated by Nobuyuki Yuasa (Penguin Books, 1966). Copyright © Nobuyuki Yuasa, 1966. By permission of Penguin Books, Ltd.

From Richard M. Eaton, *Sufis of Bijapur, 1300–1700*. Copyright © 1978 by Princeton University Press. Reprinted by permission of Princeton University Press.

Illustrations:

Unknown, Mexican, *Portrait of Sor Juana Inés de la Cruz*. By permission of the Philadelphia Museum of Art The Robert H. Lamborn Collection.

Illustration of durian from Rumphius, *Herbarium Amboinense*. By permission of The Bancroft Library, University of California, Berkeley.

Shitao, untitled landscape, before 1679. Courtesy of the Freer Gallery of Art, Smithsonian Institution, Washington, D.C., accession number F1982.23.

Print of *jôruri* theater, from *Seikyoku ruisan* by Saitô Gesshin. By permission of Harvard-Yenching Library, Harvard University.

Print of *ketubbah* from Colorno. By courtesy of the Library of the Jewish Theological Seminary of America, New York.

INDEX